Sheep, Shepherd & Land

STORIES OF SHEEP FARMERS REINVIGORATING CANADIAN WOOL

Anna Hunter

Photography by Christel Lanthier

PUBLICATIONS

Vancouver | Toronto

Text © 2023 Anna Hunter
Photographs © 2023 Christel Lanthier
All rights reserved.

NINE TEN PUBLICATIONS, Inc.
Vancouver | Toronto
ninetenpublications.ca

Printed and bound in Canada by Minuteman Press Kitsilano on Rolland Enviro® Text. This paper contains 100% recycled fibre, manufactured using renewable energy—biogas—and is processed chlorine-free. It is FSC® certified and designated Ancient Forest Friendly™.

ISBN (print) 978-1-7773870-2-0
ISBN (ebook) 978-1-7773870-3-7

Editing by Kim Werker
Copyediting by Michelle Woodvine
Proofreading by Lianne Johnsen
Indexing by Marnie Lamb
Design by Ninth and May Design Co.

Production of this book was made possible by the enthusiasm and financial support of readers and wool lovers who backed the project on Kickstarter. Without you, dearest backers, this book would not exist. Thank you!

Visit ninetenpublications.ca for more Canadian works about art, craft and creativity.

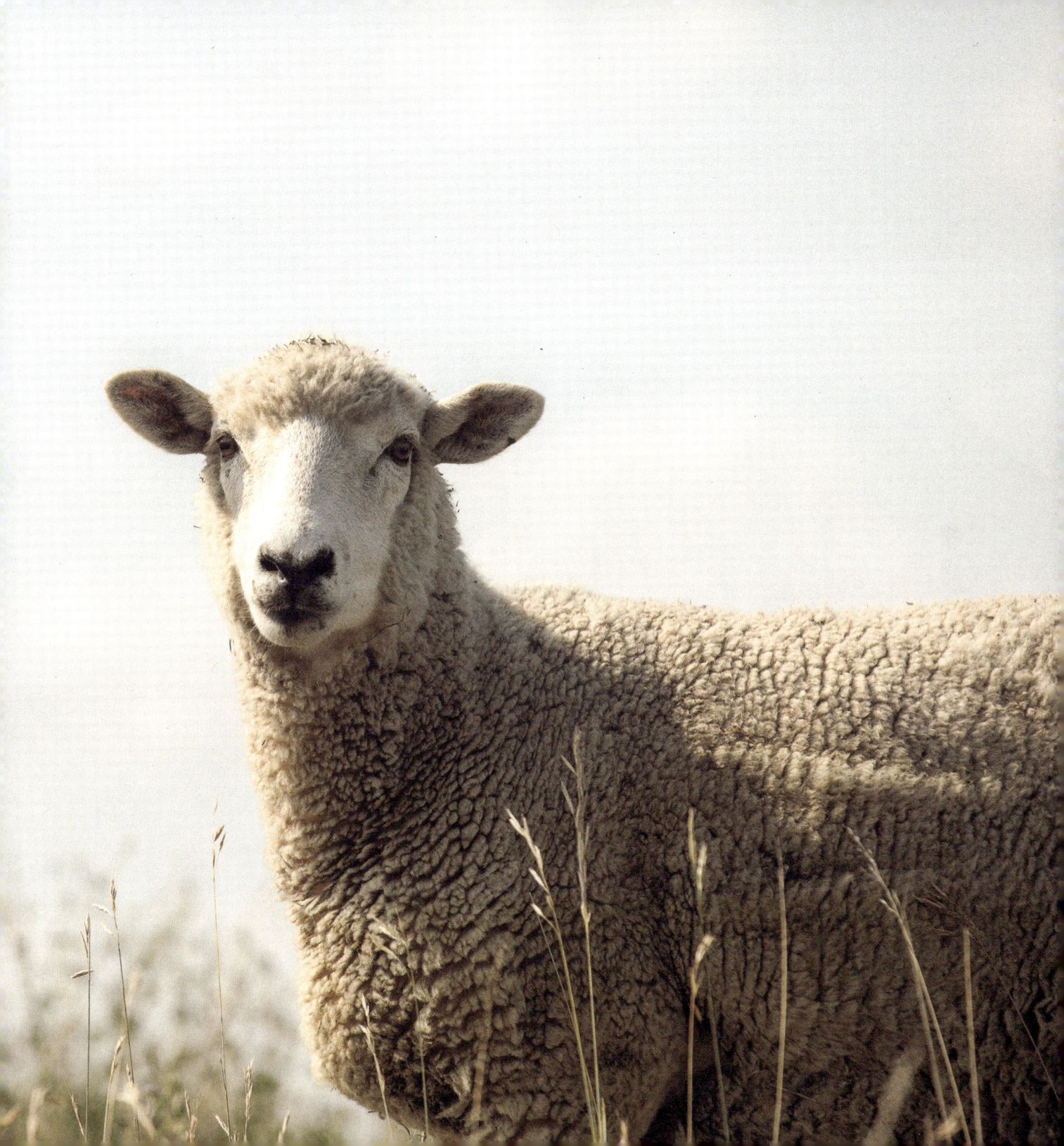

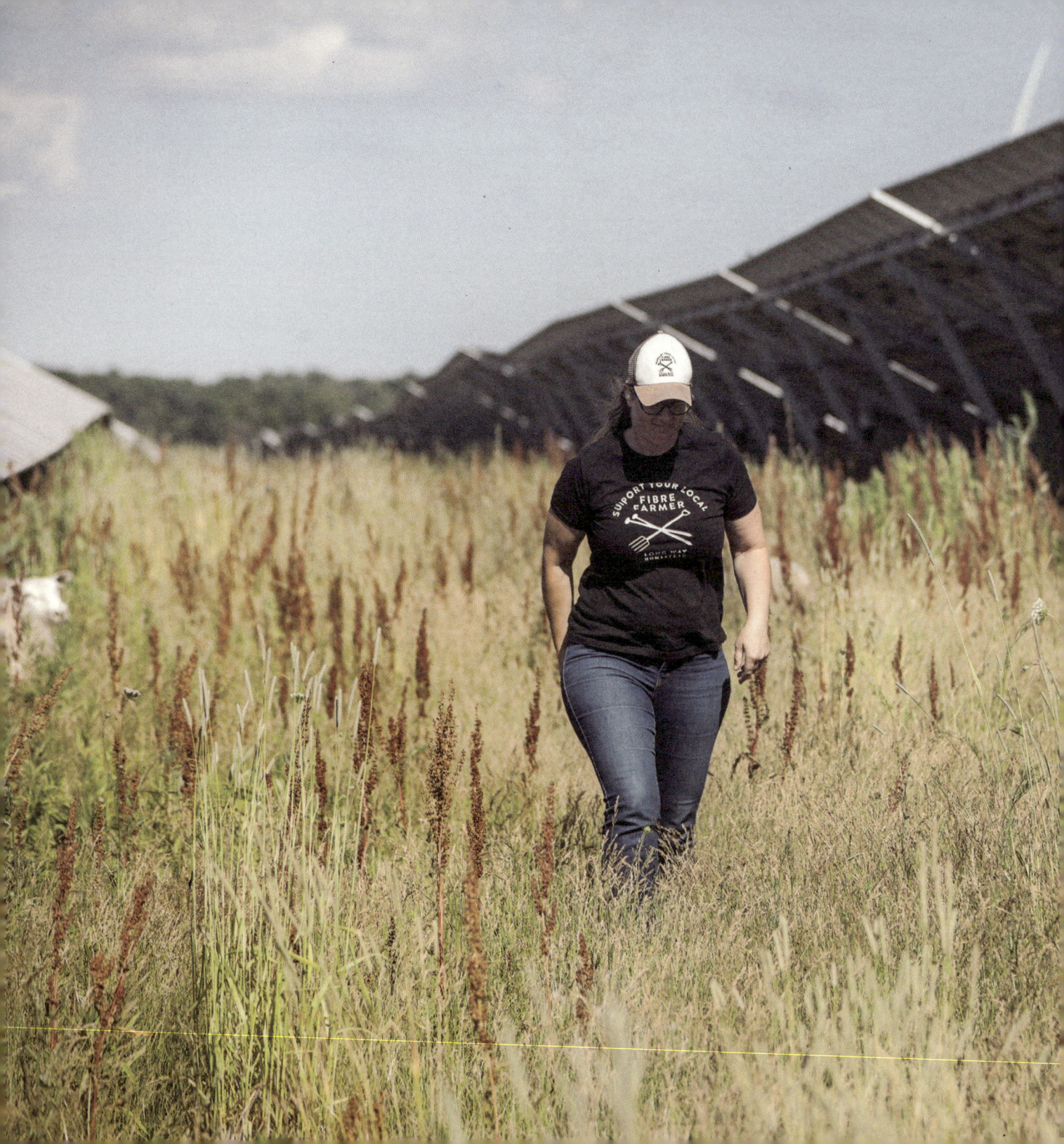

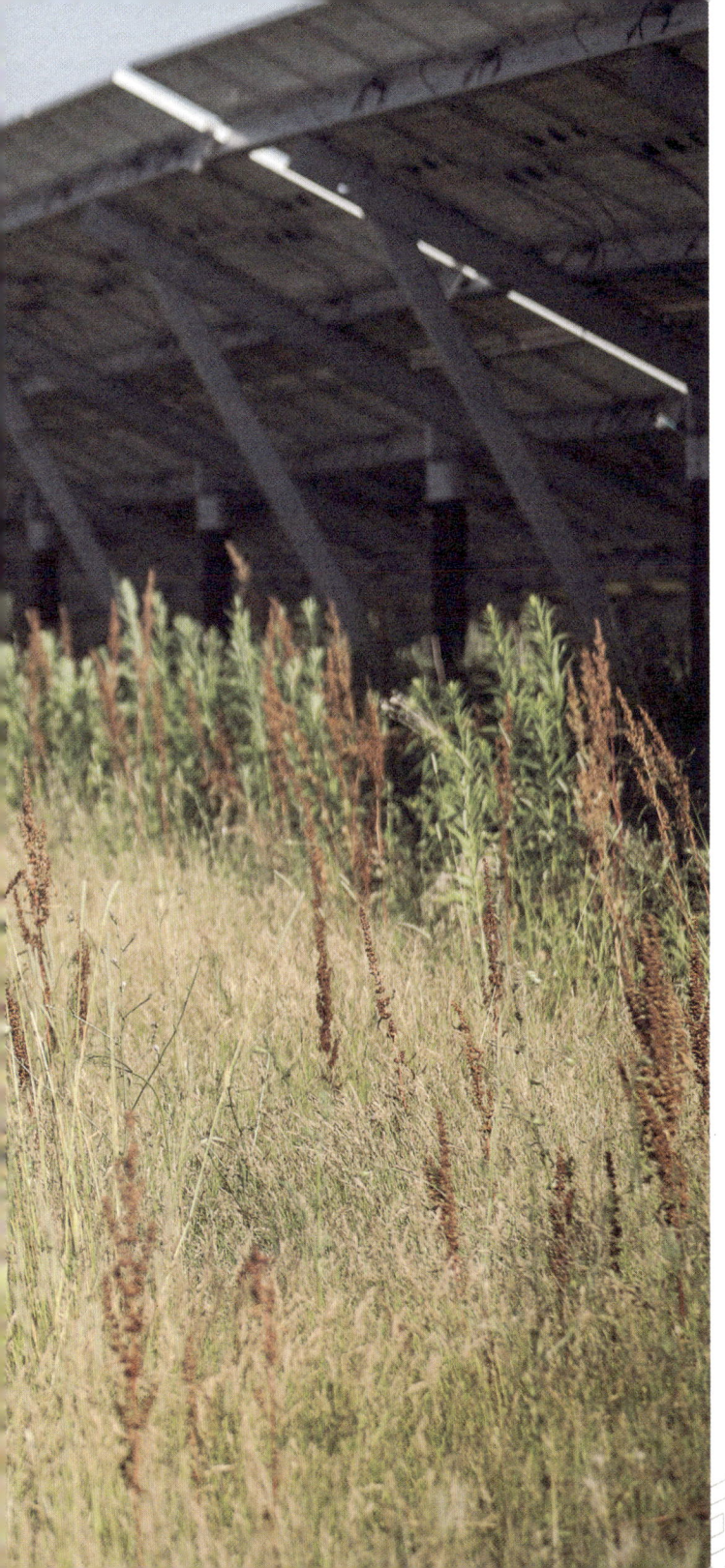

This book is dedicated to everyone who has been scared to death of doing something new or hard but decided to do it anyway.
—A. H.

Featured Farms

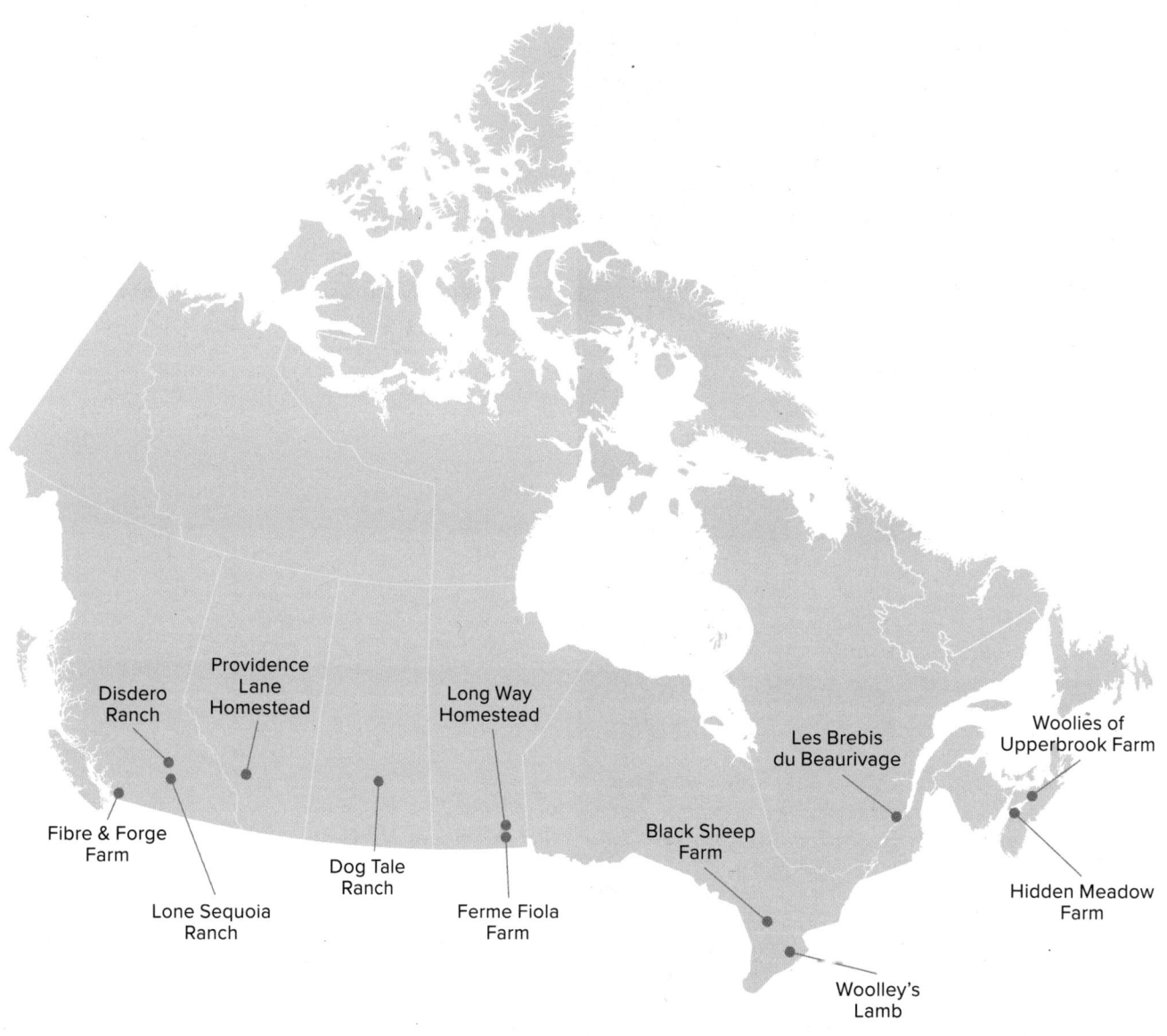

Contents

8	》	**Acknowledgements**
13	》	**A Journey in Wool**
25	》	**Sheep Breeds and Why They Matter**
43		*Sheep and Land*
41	》	**West Coast**
43		*British Columbia* Bluefaced Leicester and Fibre & Forge Farm
48		*British Columbia* Romney and Disdero Ranch
53		*British Columbia* Navajo Churro and Lone Sequoia Ranch
61	》	**The Prairies**
62		*Alberta* Border Leicester and Providence Lane Homestead
68		*Saskatchewan* Corriedale and Dog Tale Ranch
72		*Manitoba* Rideau Arcott and Ferme Fiola Farm
79	》	**Ontario & Québec**
80		*Ontario* Shetland and Black Sheep Farm
86		*Ontario* Coopworth and Woolley's Lamb
94		*Québec* East Friesian and Les Brebis du Beaurivage
101	》	**East Coast**
102		*Nova Scotia* North Country Cheviot and Woolies of Upperbrook Farm
109		*Nova Scotia* Lincoln Longwool and Hidden Meadow Farm
118	》	**Where do we go from here?**
122	》	**References & Resources**
124	》	**Index**

Acknowledgements

There are so many people that have been a huge part of making this book happen, and I'm so grateful to everyone in this fibre community who has supported and encouraged my journey. A huge thank-you to Luke—my love, my partner, the one that keeps everything going while I chase wild ideas—I wouldn't be here without you. Thank you to Christel Lanthier for saying yes, before I even finished asking if she would join me for this project; your friendship means the world to me. Thank you Lisa Friesen of Ninth and May Design Co. for the design and layout of this book, and for always capturing my vision and making it look beautiful! Thank you to Kim Werker and Kate Atherley of Nine Ten Publications, who took a chance on me, and have made this process so supportive and positive.

A huge thank-you to the all the farmers that hosted us, fed us, toured us around their farms and shared their stories with us. Thank you to the Kickstarter backers who blew me away with your belief in this project. You made this dream a reality.

Thank you to Nicole, our trusty sidekick who kept us on track and hydrated—we love you. Thanks to Nicky for driving me through rural roads and feeding me! Margaret, thanks for always pointing out my spelling mistakes and reminding me that I can do this. Thanks Mia for the classical music playlist that kept me company as I wrote most of these words.

Thank you to Ang, Francesca and Natalie, who delivered, mailed and gifted chocolate when I needed it most. Thank you Arianne for driving us all over Québec!

Thank you Emily, Alexa, Murielle and Gilles for providing us cozy accommodations across the country. Thank you Christina, Natalie, Kat, Pamela, Bethany, Ang, Caitlin, Alexa, Heather, Nicole, and Christel for being my sounding boards and keeping me grounded.

Finally—thank you, Mom and Dad, for teaching me from day one that I can do anything I put my mind to.

—Anna Hunter

I have endless gratitude…

Anna, for your belief in me and taking a chance in asking me to be a part of this amazing journey, I have endless gratitude for your friendship. I love our crazy ideas, and accomplishing them together is the best part. Joey, for supporting my artistic dreams while holding down the fort/farm at home, it means so much to me and I love you so much. To Kate and Kim, you didn't know me and have supported us beyond words throughout this process, I'm so grateful for you both. To Lisa, for making the images I captured look even better in layout—your work never ceases to amaze me! To all the kind warm welcomes throughout our journey: farms, and friends and family who opened up their spaces for us in a time of uncertainty. To all the farmers we interviewed, thank you for letting me have a glimpse at your lives and letting me capture the essence of it; thank you for your hospitality, the warm drinks, the meals in some cases! Thank you to Alexa, Emily, Mimi et Gilles, for your hospitality and allowing us to rest after long drives, and making us feel right at home. Merci Arianne, for offering your time off to drive off to Québec, et ton amitié, j'taime. Thank you to Nicole for keeping us on track, with good company and your stellar navigating skills; love you! To all the amazing folks who believed in this book and supported Anna and me, and supported us in the Kickstarter campaign: You blew us away and I was, and am still, speechless.

To Lise, Scott, Kara, for everything you did for my girls in my absence, thank you so very much; it means the world to me, love you guys.

À Oli, Anne et Lila, merci pour les beaux mots d'encouragement, et votre amour.

Maman, Charles, Papa: Je vous aimes tellement, merci pour votre support, votre amour, les appels, l'encouragement, l'aide avec les filles en mon absence, et votre amour continuel. Je vous aimes gros comme le ciel.

To all reading this book, who supported us in so many more ways: Thank you, merci, maarsii!

—Christel Lanthier

Land Acknowledgement

>>>>>>>>>>>>>>>>>>>>>>>>>>>>>>>>>>

Farming has historically been, and continues to be, used as a tool of colonization. Agriculture has played a key role in dispossessing Indigenous people from their homelands. As we look forward to the future of fibre and sheep farming, it must include a commitment to reconciliation and land repatriation.

We were honoured to interview people on the traditional territories of S'ólh Téméxw (Stó:lō), Semiahmoo, Kwantlen, Nuxwsa'7aq (Nooksack), Secwepemcúl'ecw (Secwépemc), Syilx (Okanagan), Ktunaxa ʔamakʔis, Niitsítpiis-stahkoii ᖹᒍᖷ ᑊᓬ (Blackfoot / Niitsítapi ᖹᒍᑐ), Tsuut'ina, Îyâĥé Nakón mąkóce (Stoney), Niitsítpiis-stahkoii ᖹᒍᖷ ᑊᓬ (Blackfoot / Niitsítapi ᖹᒍᑐ), Michif Piyii (Métis), Cree, Anishinabewaki ᐊᓂᔑᓈᐯᐧᐊᑭ, Očhéthi Šakówiŋ, Anishininiimowin (Oji-Cree), Odawa, Mississauga, Ho-de-no-sau-nee-ga (Haudenosaunee), Wabanaki (Dawnland Confederacy), N'dakina (Abenaki / Abénaquis), Wendake-Nionwentsïo, Mi'kma'ki.

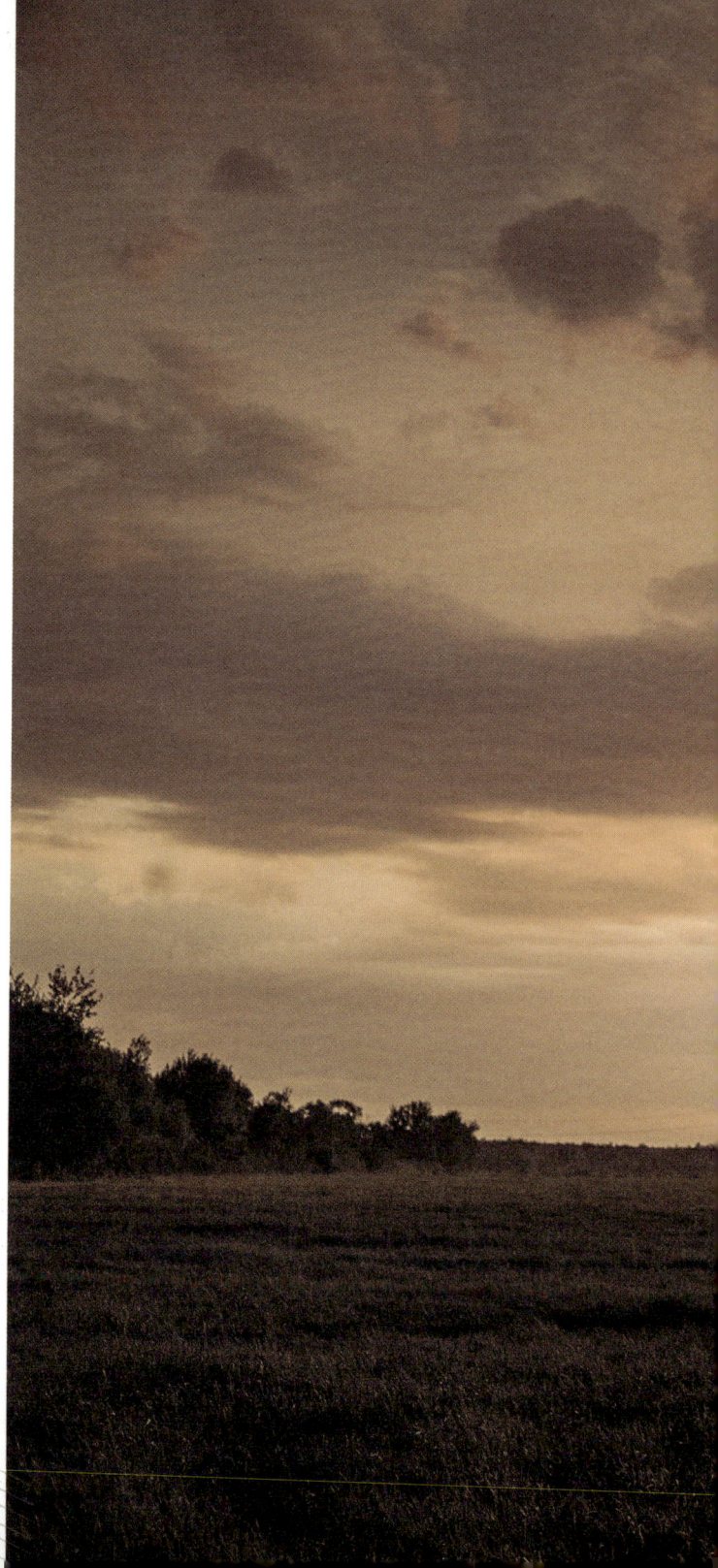

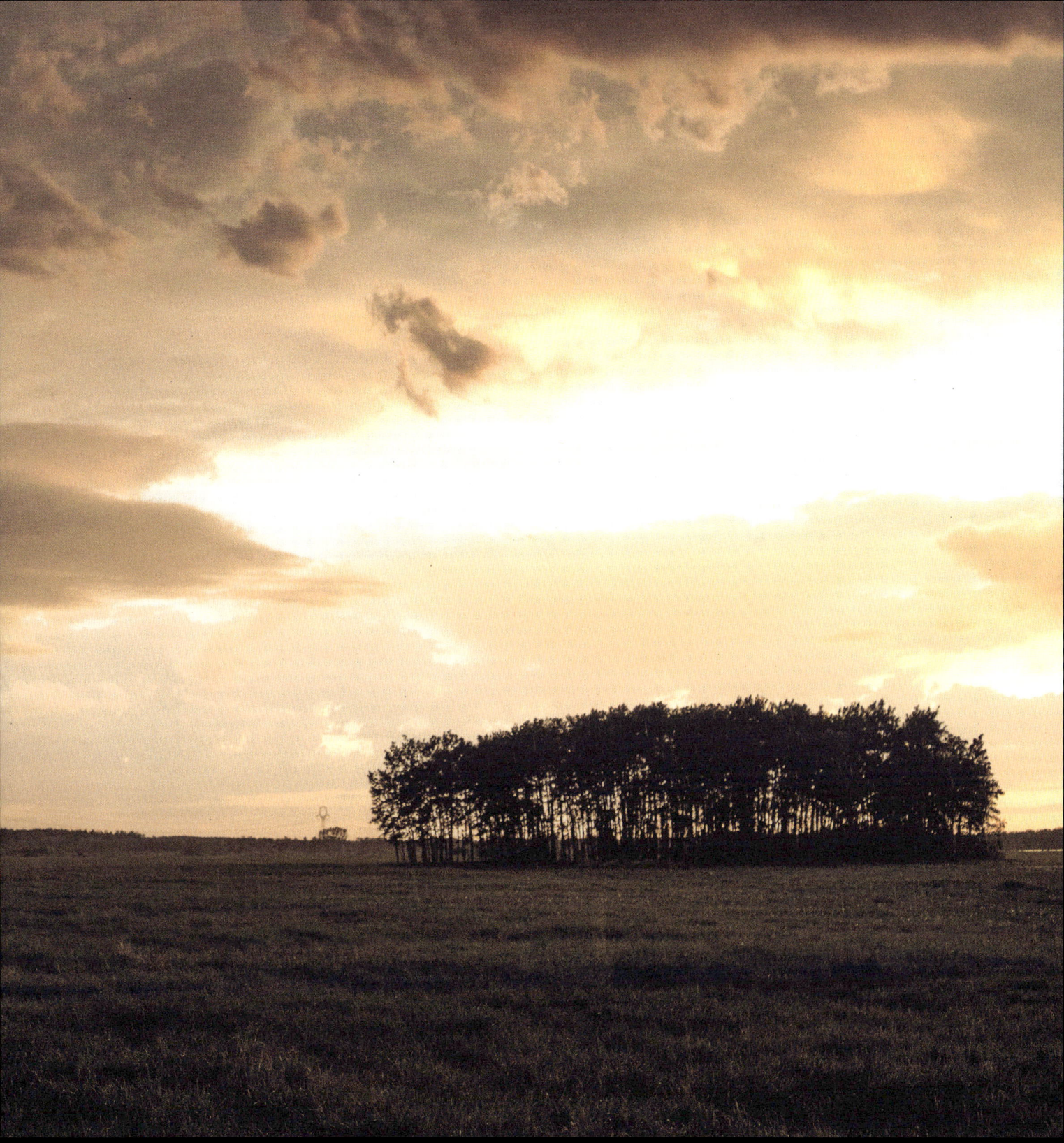

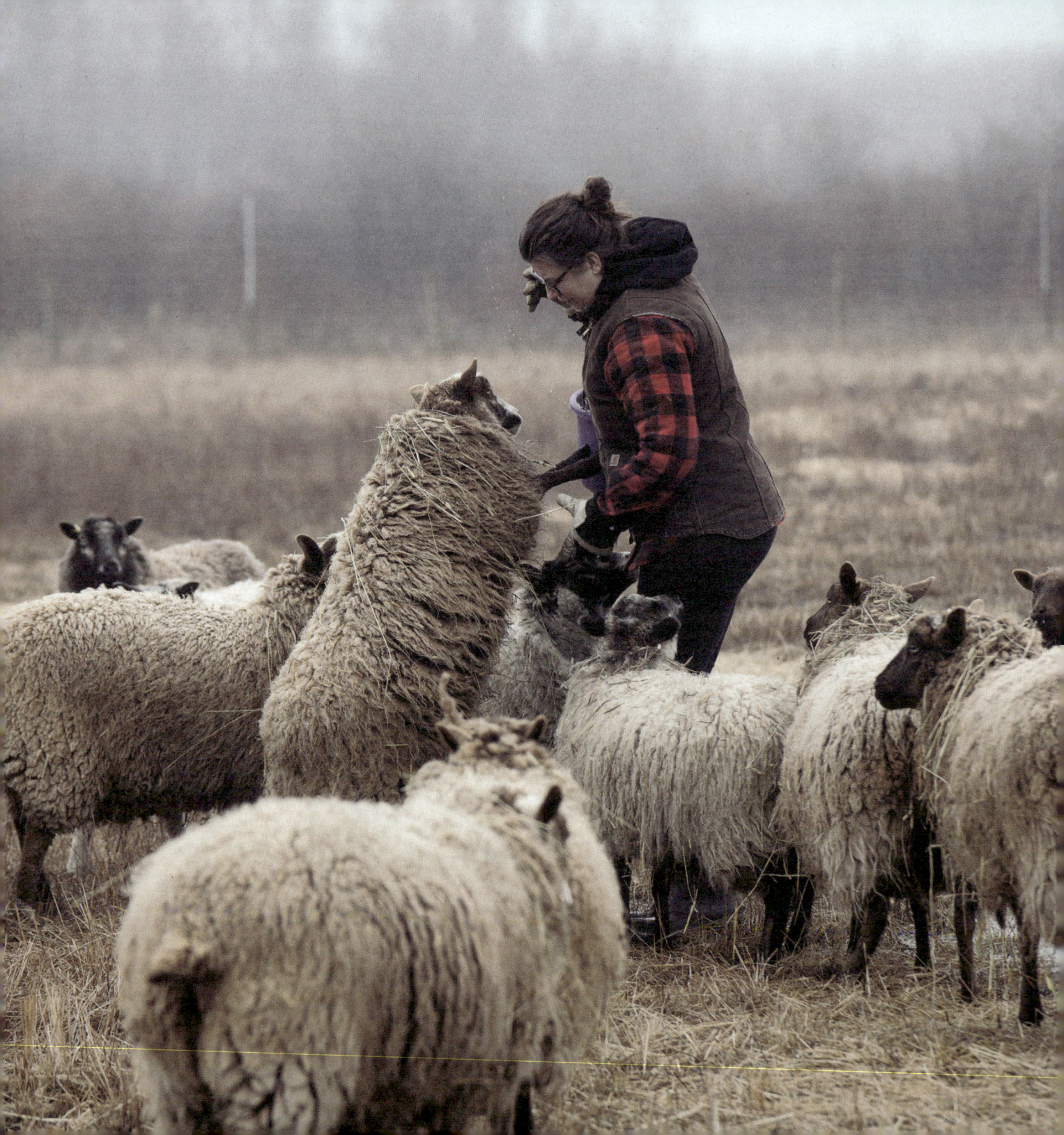

A Journey in Wool

I HAD NO IDEA I WANTED TO BE A FARMER. In fact, at one point in 2003, when I was invited out to a farm in rural Nova Scotia for a summer of food growing and land stewardship, I defiantly announced that I was a city girl, and that urban struggle was more important than growing organic tomatoes. Apparently, the universe still had some lessons to teach me.

I started knitting during the Christmas of 1998, while I was working as a nanny in Switzerland. I was supposed to spend that holiday skiing in the Swiss Alps, but my dear friend and skiing buddy had broken his pelvis the week before, and all our plans fell through. So instead of screaming down the mountains, I was cozied up on the couch with some plastic PONY straight needles and acrylic yarn from the local grocery store as Tammy, the generous and patient sister of the family I worked for, taught me how to knit and purl. The first thing I cast on was the back of a sweater. Yes, my first ever knitting project was a sweater. I fell in love with knitting and never looked back.

Over the last few years, as my entire life has become consumed with wool, I often think back to that winter—how things might look a little different for me now if I had spent the week skiing instead of learning the skill that would eventually lead me to becoming a sheep farmer.

But I did become a sheep farmer, and then a wool mill owner, and through both of those things I began to connect with other farmers and to hear some of the incredible and heartbreaking stories of growing wool in Canada. Many of the stories I've heard have similarities to my own: a desire for greater connection to food and fibre.

Anna feeding her flock of Shetland sheep.

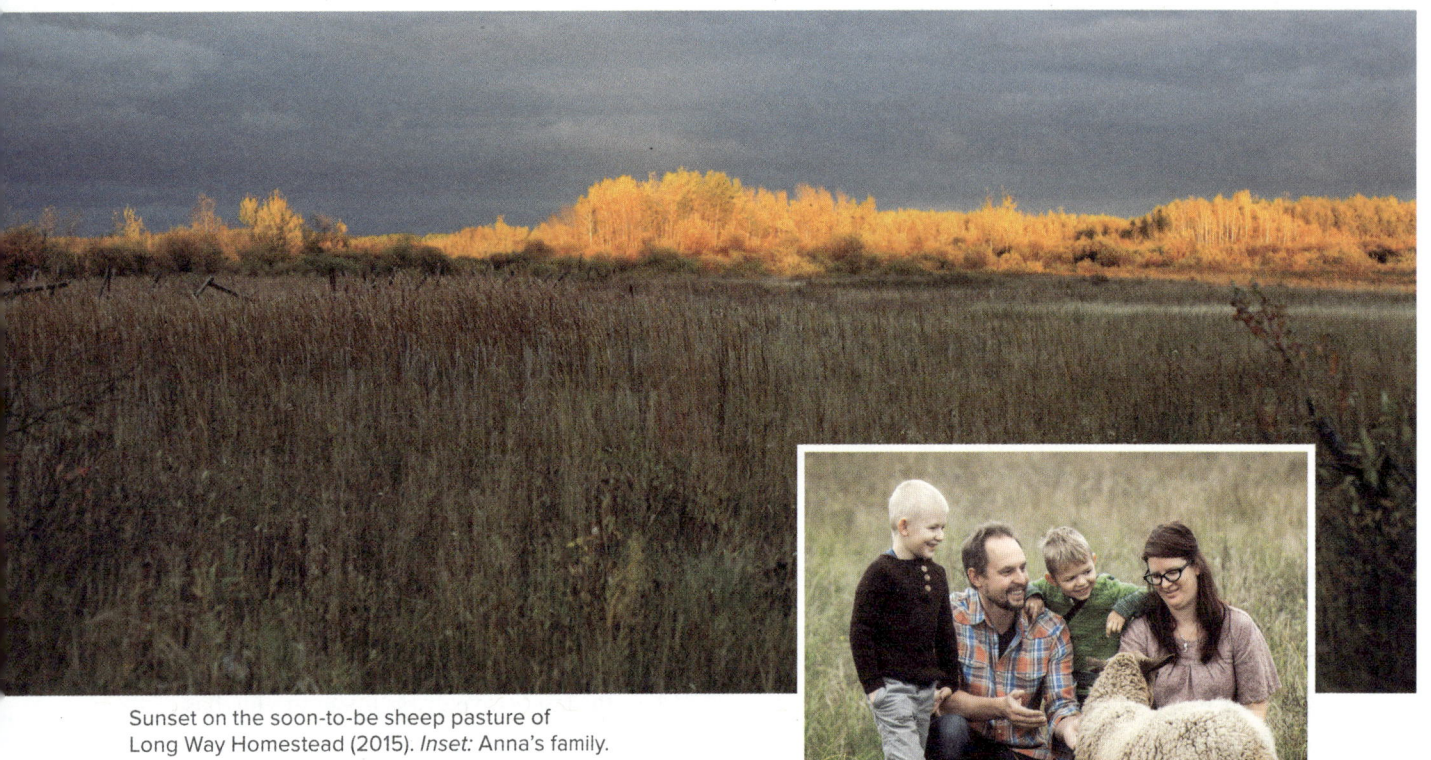

Sunset on the soon-to-be sheep pasture of Long Way Homestead (2015). *Inset:* Anna's family.

MY STORY

Manitoba – Shetland and Long Way Homestead

It is challenging to pick a starting point for your own story, but perhaps this chapter of my story started in 2008, shortly after I married my husband, Luke Palka. I was burnt out from my work as a frontline anti-poverty advocate in Vancouver, and I needed a change. Luke suggested I do something with my knitting. I can see now that this was his subtle way of trying to perhaps channel my ever-growing yarn stash into something else. I sat with the idea for about a month and then declared that I was going to open a 100-mile yarn store in East Vancouver. My goal was to source and sell yarn and fibre that had been grown and manufactured within 100 miles of the Fraser Valley in British Columbia.

I got to work, creating a business plan, finding a location in the Hastings-Sunrise neighbourhood of Vancouver, and looking for farms that would sell me their yarn. After months of dead ends, I realized that my shelves would be empty if I only sourced local wool. This was the first seed that was planted for me: the realization that even though we have sheep farms across the country, there is a disconnect between our production of wool and the growing local communities of knitters, crocheters and fibre artists. I opened up Baaad Anna's Yarn Store in 2009 with a commitment to community-building and sourcing yarn that was "as local as possible."

Fast-forward five years, add on two babies and a growing housing crisis in Vancouver, and Luke and I were ready for a change. We wanted our boys to have a stronger connection to the source of their food and we wanted to get our hands dirty growing that food. Luke and I had dreamed of a small homestead away from the city, where we could grow our own food and of course have a sheep or two. I wish I could tell you that it came from a well-thought-out commitment to regenerating land, but honestly, I think we'd watched too many post-apocalyptic zombie movies, and we wanted to have a place that would give us a fighting chance.

Regardless of the motivation, we started looking for a new home—and ended up in the middle of Canada. Like, the actual middle. We live fifteen kilometres from the longitudinal centre of the country! I think many of our friends and family thought we were losing our minds, but we did it anyway. We moved in the spring of 2015 and found our farm shortly thereafter. The farm is 140 acres of mixed forest, bush, and wetland at the edge of the Boreal Plains region just east of Winnipeg, Manitoba, in Treaty One Territory.

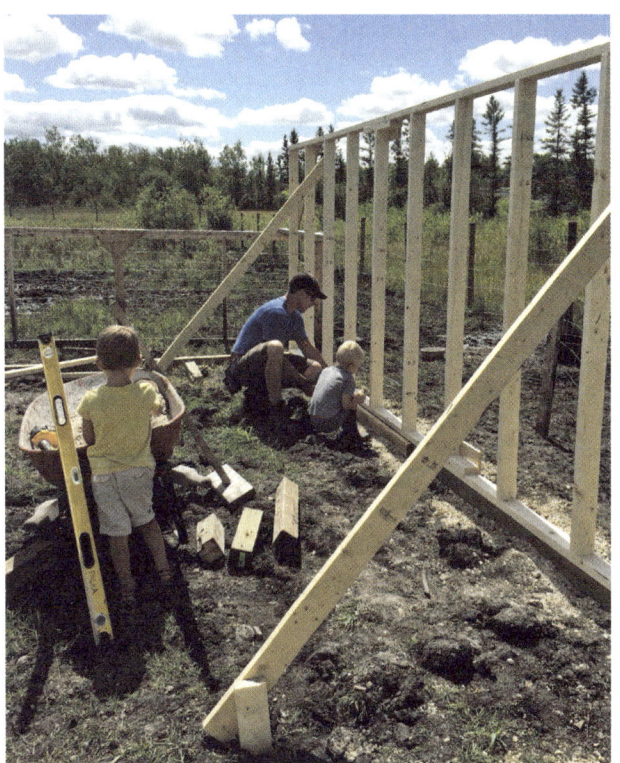

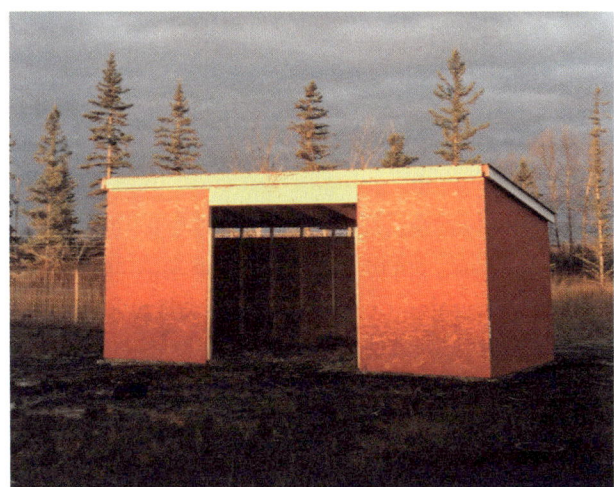

Top: The three-sided sheep shelter under construction by Luke, Anna and their sons. *Bottom:* The completed shelter (2016).

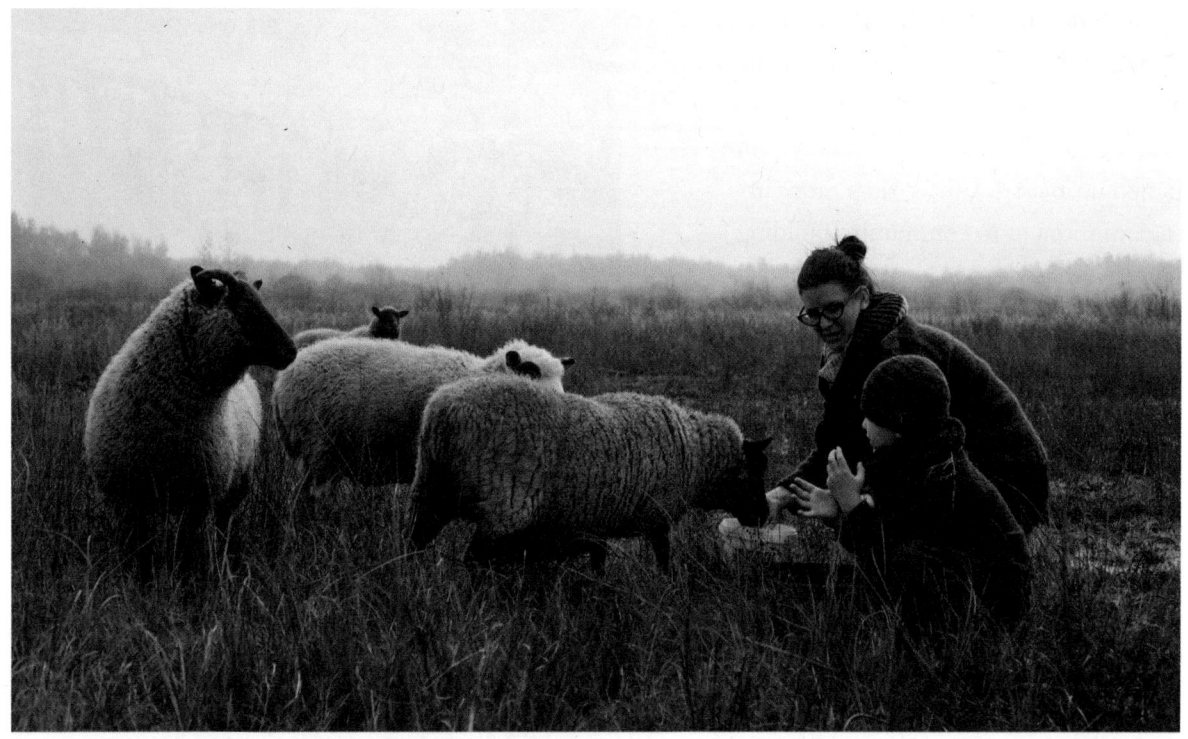

Anna and her son Bohdan feeding their first four sheep (2016).

We had a five-year plan to figure out how to farm, how to provide for our family from farming, and I hoped to find a shepherd-mentor to help me learn what I needed to know about sheep. But I was impatient, and I spent our first winter in Manitoba reading everything I could get my hands on about sheep farming, wool, and regenerative agriculture. I had no idea there were so many different ways to farm, and I was inspired by the opportunity for land regeneration through grazing animals. In the summer of 2016, we brought home our first four Shetland sheep. I wish that I could say our breed choice for Shetlands was based on a thorough study of breeds and a well-thought-out marketing plan for their unique and quality wool. In reality, I bought Shetlands because local shepherd and Shetland breeder Margaret Brook was willing to sell them to me, and I trusted her.

We took a book out of the library with instructions on how to build the best sheep fencing. Luke built a three-sided shelter for the sheep and we thought it would take years to fill it up with enough sheep. Then the day finally came when we loaded the kids into the truck, picked up the

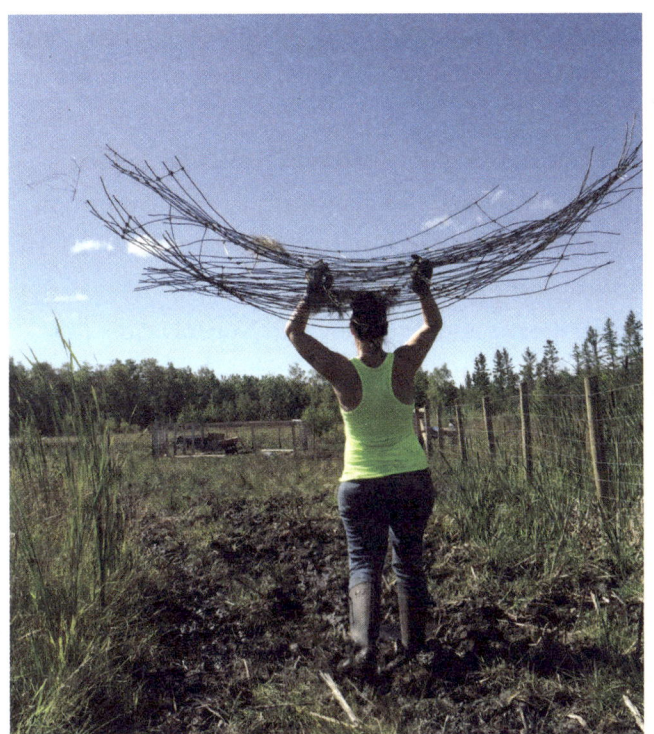
Anna removing old fencing from the pasture to prepare for their sheep to arrive (2016).

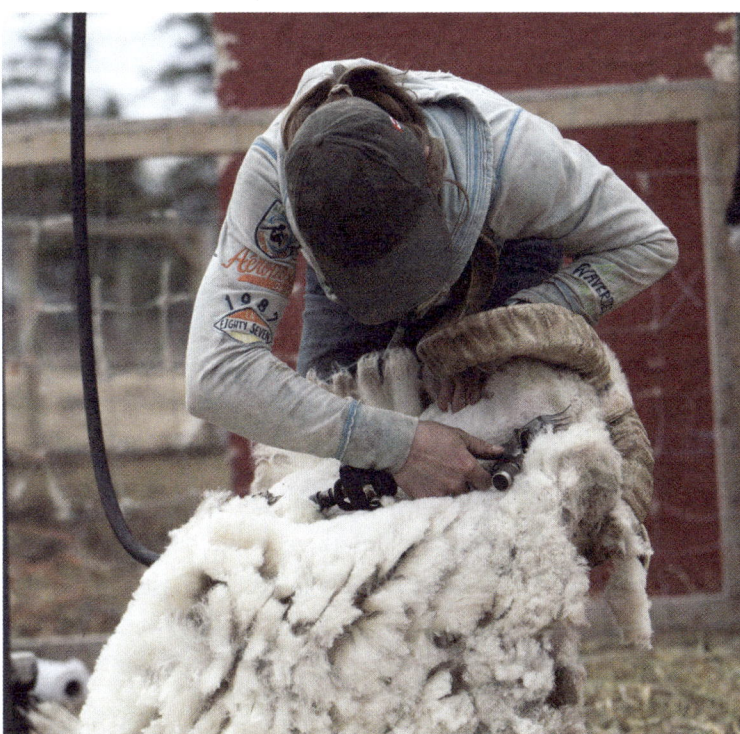
Local Manitoba shearer Stacey Rosvold shearing Anna's sheep (2017).

sheep, transported them home, and let them loose in our newly fenced-in pasture.

We had no idea what we were doing, but we did it anyway. That first year was filled with every mistake in the book: not feeding the sheep enough quality forage, feeding the sheep too much grain to overcompensate, losing a baby llama to a lowland parasite called liver flukes—and subsequently realizing that we have to treat for worms. We realized that managing animals is so much more involved than we had planned for, and that to grow good wool, we needed good management. We learned from our mistakes, and little by little we built better infrastructure for stress-free animal handling. We changed our feeding systems to limit the vegetable matter in our fleeces and to ensure our sheep were getting the proper nutrition. Perhaps most importantly for our long-term goals, we realized that the most important thing on our farm is the health of our soil and ecosystem, and we began implementing techniques to work with the land base rather than against it.

That was just year one of having sheep. Little did I know we hadn't even come up against our

A Journey in Wool **17**

largest hurdle: there was nowhere to process our wool. In April 2017, we hired a local shearer to shear our tiny little flock, and it might have been the best day thus far on our farm. I looked at the growing pile of beautiful wool and imagined all the sweaters I would make out of it. My excitement turned to panic when I realized that there were no wool processors in Manitoba. The closest Canadian processor was in Alberta, and they had a forty-pound minimum. We had only thirty-two pounds of wool. I couldn't believe that I hadn't discovered this sooner; I'd just assumed that with the huge sheep farming community in Manitoba, there would be at least one wool processor. I finally found a fantastic mill in North Dakota, in the United States, and Chris from the Dakota Spinning Mill was willing to process my wool and walk me through those early ignorant days of not knowing how to properly skirt my fleeces. (Skirting is the removal of vegetable contamination and manure to prepare the fleece for processing.) So, Luke and I packed the kids and twelve dirty fleeces into the car and drove down to North Dakota to check out the mill.

As Chris gave us a tour of her mill, I'm pretty sure Luke witnessed the moment when the lightbulb above my head started blinking. I needed to open a mill. I'm still not totally sure how I convinced him it was a good idea for us to jump into a manufacturing

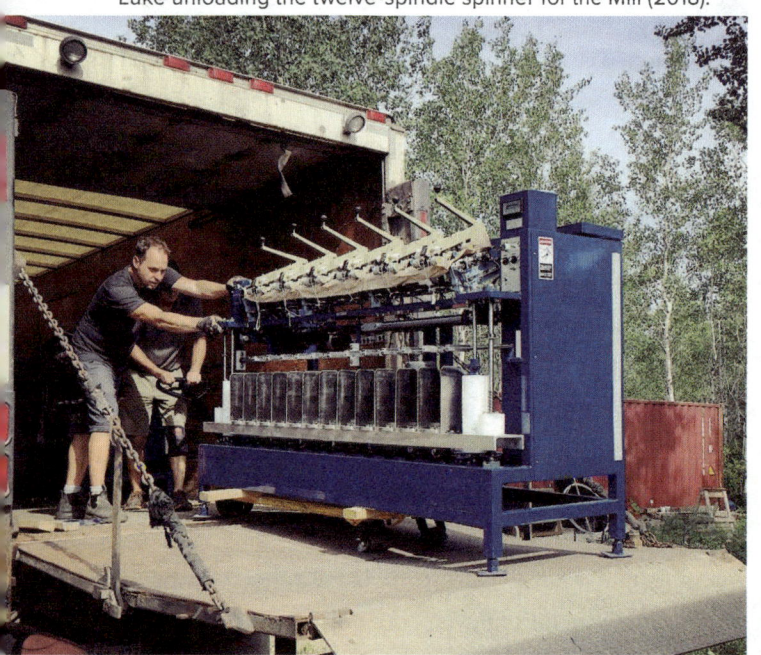

Luke unloading the twelve-spindle spinner for the Mill (2018).

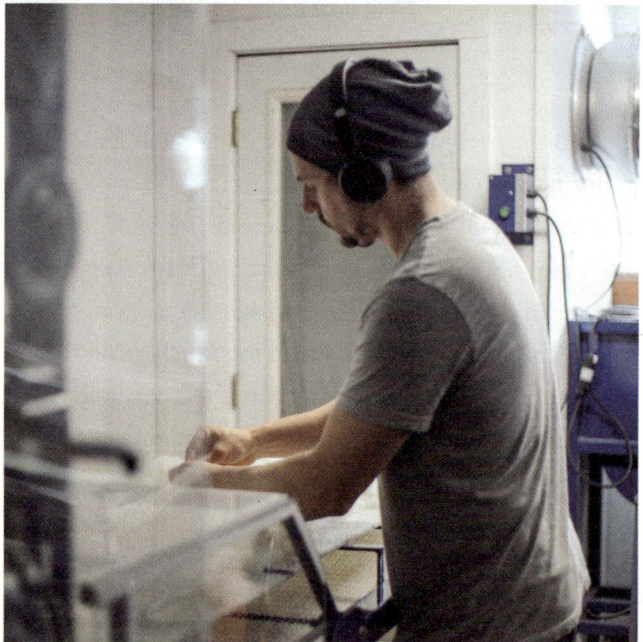

Luke loading the carder with wool for processing (2019).

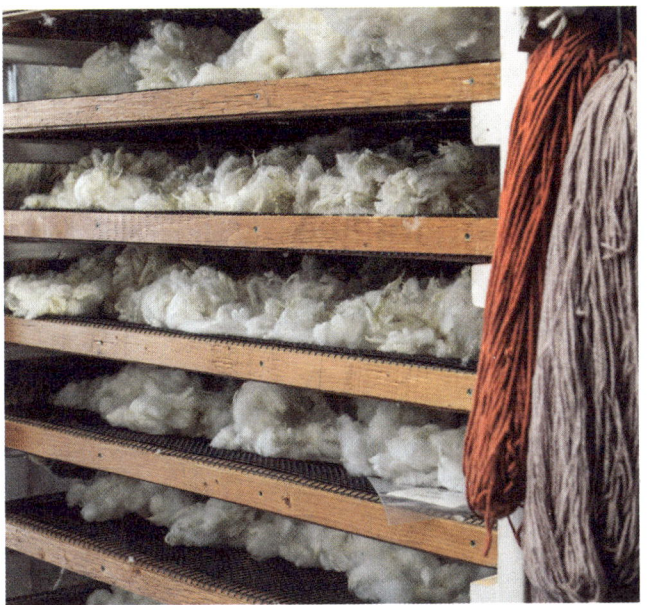

Raw, clean wool drying on the racks in the Long Way Homestead mill (2020).

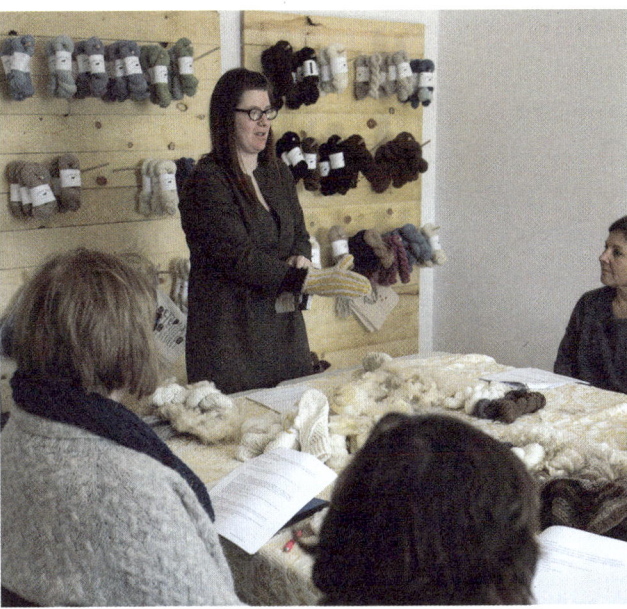

Anna teaching a breed-specific knitting class at the Long Way Homestead Field School (2019).

business while we were still knee-deep in trying to learn how to be farmers. But he agreed, and by the summer of 2018 our fibre processing mill had arrived from Belfast Mini Mills, based in Prince Edward Island.

In the year leading up to the arrival of the mill, I started my deep dive into sheep breeds. I wanted to be as prepared as possible for processing wool, and my understanding of sheep breeds was extremely limited. I took a wool-judging course to understand how to evaluate the quality of raw fleece. I started collecting every kind of sheep breed fleece I could get my hands on, and I hunted down every book I could find about sheep breeds and wool and what makes them all unique. At some point during that year, I realized that my knitting and fibre arts journey had been somewhat shallow because of my limited understanding of the variety of wool in the world, and from that moment on, I couldn't stop talking about sheep breeds to anyone who would listen.

I began teaching workshops on sheep breeds and knitting, and I started a breed-specific wool subscription exploring sheep breeds that thrive on the Prairies of Canada. The more I talked with farmers and learned about their own journeys to sheep and working with different sheep's wool, the more I wanted to share these stories with others.

Wool Mills in Canada

Production of cloth and clothing has been an important part of Canada's manufacturing history. Less than 150 years ago, we had the ability domestically to process the majority of all clothing and textiles we consumed. In 1880, thirteen percent of all Canadians working in manufacturing were employed in the textile industry, and cloth or clothing manufacturing ranked third in the gross value of production. Textile manufacturing has impacted our labour history and architectural legacy and has helped to shape our early understanding and navigation of tariffs and international trade.

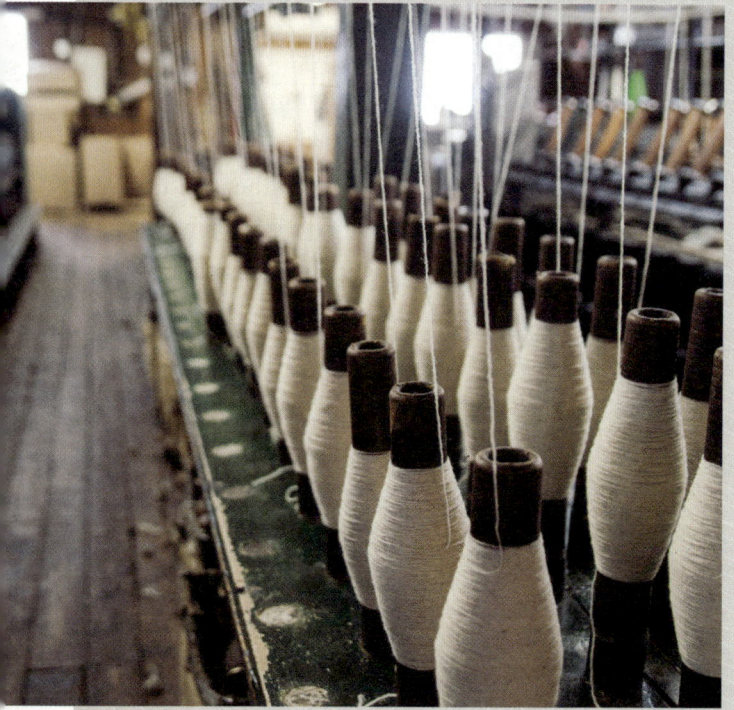

Bobbins of spun wool at MacAusland's Woollen Mills, PEI.

Between 1750 and 1850, wool manufacturing moved from small, home-based, subsistence-type carding, spinning, and weaving practices to a more industrial, factory-scale system. This was mostly due to the introduction of large, mechanized machines. Carding and fulling mills were the first to emerge and were very popular until the early twentieth century, when knitting and hosiery mills began to cater to the fashions of the day and there was a shift away from the woven or fulled wool fabrics of the past.

Increased pressure from British imports led to the National Policy of 1879—a strategy designed to assist Canadian wool mills by limiting imports. High tariffs on imported cloth, plus demand for wool fabric from the Canadian Department of Militia and Defence, resulted in sustained growth for the wool manufacturing industry. But, ultimately, this would not last.

A decline in demand for woollen textiles, an increase in imports, in addition to inefficient organizational models within the industry and obsolete machinery, resulted in significant losses for the textile manufacturing industry over the first half of the twentieth century. The introduction of synthetic fibres and increased trade liberalization through the formation of the General Agreement on Tariffs and Trade (GATT) dealt the fatal blow to the domestic textile manufacturing industry. By the 1970s, the industry was barely hanging on to what was left of its infrastructure, labour force, and the market share for textiles.

Canada now has just over forty small- to medium-sized wool mills, processing wool and other protein-based fibres across the country. The majority of these mills are mini mills, consisting of small-scale fibre processing equipment intended to complement a cottage wool industry. Most mini mills are working to fill in the gap created when the majority of the large mills shut down, and in many cases mini mill equipment is the only infrastructure available for new mills to purchase.

Canada still has three larger mills operating and producing exclusively Canadian-grown wool: Briggs & Little in New Brunswick, Custom Woolen Mills Ltd. in Alberta, and MacAusland's Woollen Mills Ltd. in Prince Edward Island. MacAusland's produces their iconic woollen blankets, and the other large mills produce knitting and crochet yarn. Canada also has a vibrant and expanding mini mill and small mill industry as shepherds and artisans recognize the economic opportunity in producing their own wool and answering the incredible need for more processing.

Access to, and cost of, machinery, as well as incredibly steep learning curves with slow return on investment are just a few of the barriers to more mills being established in Canada. However, with more movement towards valuing and sourcing local fibre and wool, there is a growing awareness of the need for enhanced processing services.

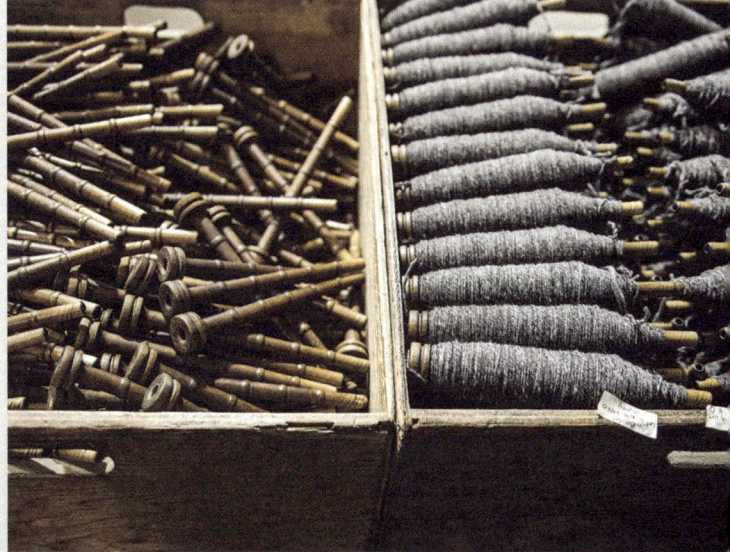

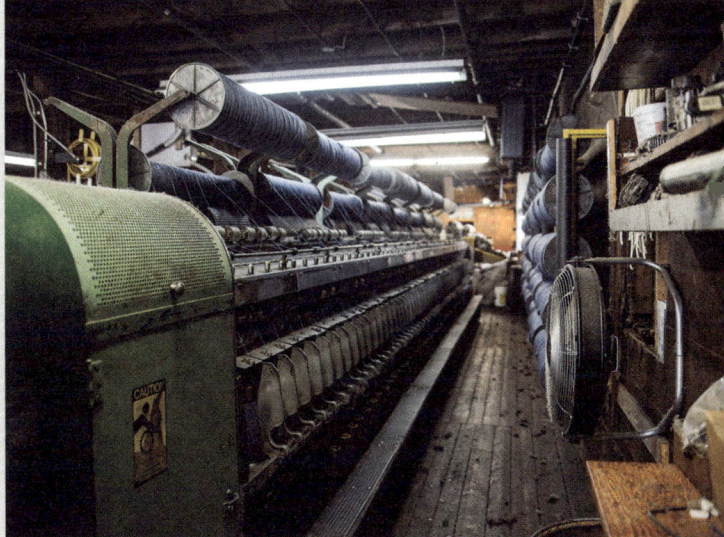

Top: Empty bobbins and bobbins wound with grey yarn at Custom Woolen Mills, Alberta. *Bottom:* MacAusland's Woollen Mills, PEI.

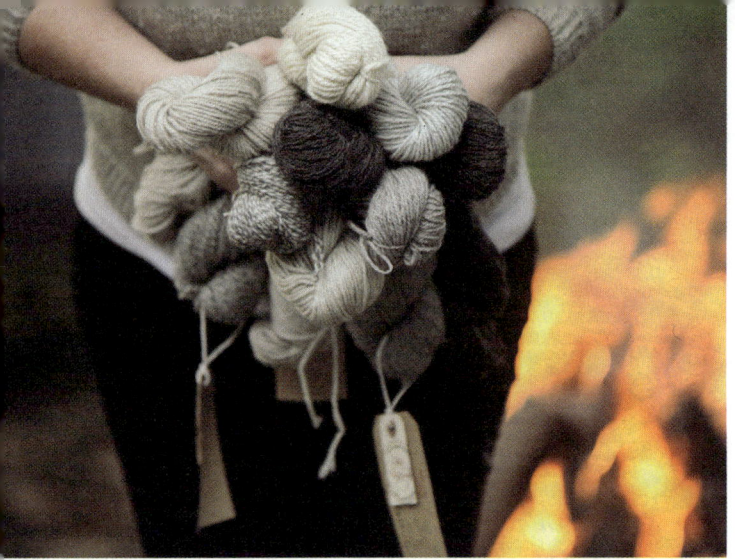

THIS BOOK

This book emerged from my desire to share what I've learned about sheep breeds with others, and to celebrate the breeds that exist across our country and the diversity of our land base. It explores the beauty of Canadian-grown wool and the ways in which it intersects with our daily lives. Most importantly, this book tells the story of Canadian farmers and ranchers and outlines the potential for sheep and wool to help us stabilize the climate crisis.

I want fibre artists across the country to get a glimpse of the history of the sheep that thrive here, as well as to meet and connect with the farmers that are working so hard to grow their wool. I wasn't expecting the themes of fibre friendship, breed conservation, and climate change mitigation to percolate to the surface the way they did during my interviews, but they did. The wool we grow, the sheep breeds we raise, the textiles we create—these all intersect with some of the most important aspects of our lives.

AN INDUSTRY IN CRISIS

The Canadian wool industry is in crisis. Many sheep producers see no value in their wool and therefore some will burn it, compost it, or trash it—they see shearing sheep as a necessary expense, and wool is simply a way to keep feed bills lower in the winter. I was shocked the first time a farmer told me they drag their yearly wool clip into the bush to let it slowly break down; now, I hardly blink, it is so commonplace. The remaining wool is sold to the Canadian Co-operative Wool Growers Limited (CCWG), the only large-scale, national wool buyer in Canada.

Approximately ninety percent of this wool is then marketed and shipped overseas for processing, the majority going to China. We know that fourteen percent of all greenhouse gas emissions are from the

Arlette Seib needle felting in her studio in Saskatchewan.

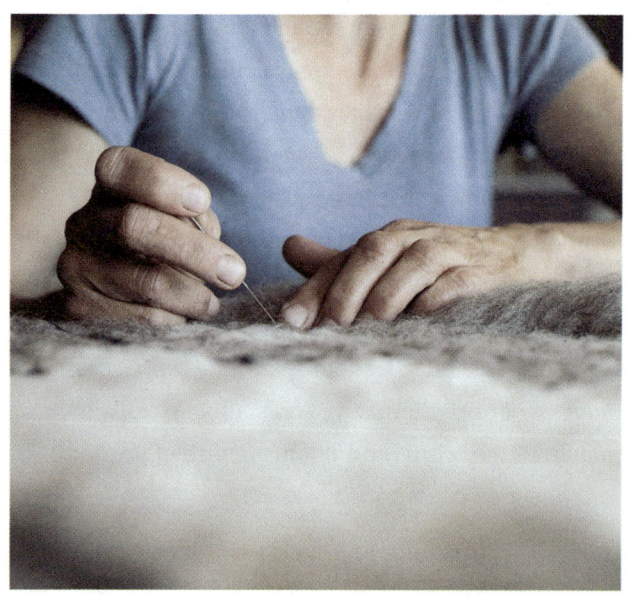

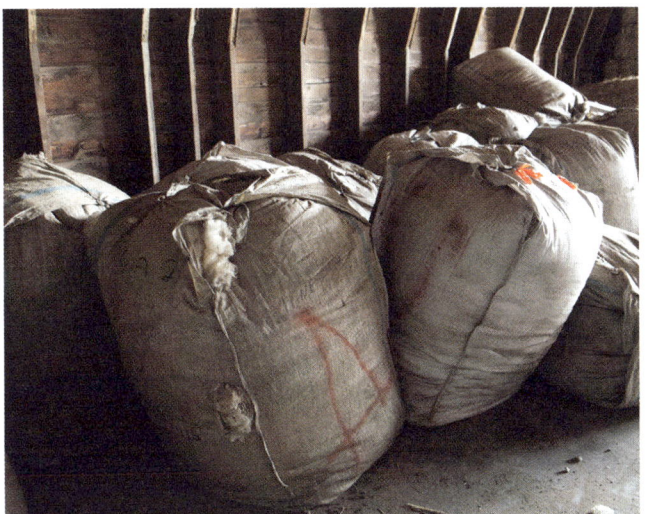 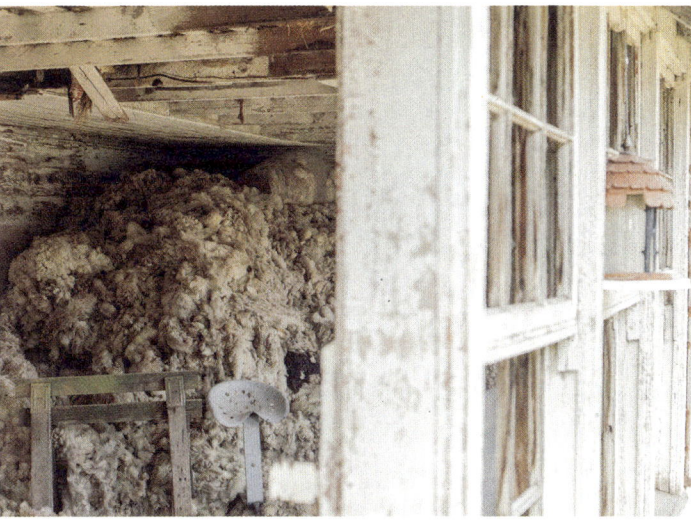

Wool stored in wool bags (left) and in an outbuilding (right). Much of the Canadian wool clip is underutilized.

transport of raw materials and finished products[1], and wool is contributing to those emissions. What is staggering is that the number of knitters, crocheters, weavers and spinners has grown dramatically in Canada in the last fifteen years. Fibre artists are hungry for more wool—we will flock (pun intended) to fibre festivals and knit shows and spend millions of dollars annually on wool, the majority of which cannot be traced to the farm it was grown on. Much of that wool is Merino grown abroad.

We have a globalized system for our yarn and wool products. It's a system that inherently seeks out the most cost-effective way to source raw materials and convert them into finished products while ensuring the highest profits for corporate shareholders. This system leaves behind the farmers that care for the sheep and steward the land. It ignores, or pays rock bottom prices, to the workers that convert the wool into usable products. And this system relies on the exploitation and extraction of resources from our ecosystems with impunity. But we do not have to continue this trajectory.

I strongly believe that when we feel more connected to the source of our wool, when we understand the stories and people behind the wool we love, we will seek out a different path. This book aims to be a starting point of connection: between land and sheep, sheep and farmer, fibre artist and wool. 》

---

1 Plumptre, Bora, Eli Angen and Dianne Zimmerman. *The State of Freight: Understanding greenhouse gas emissions from goods movement in Canada.* The Pembina Foundation, 2017.

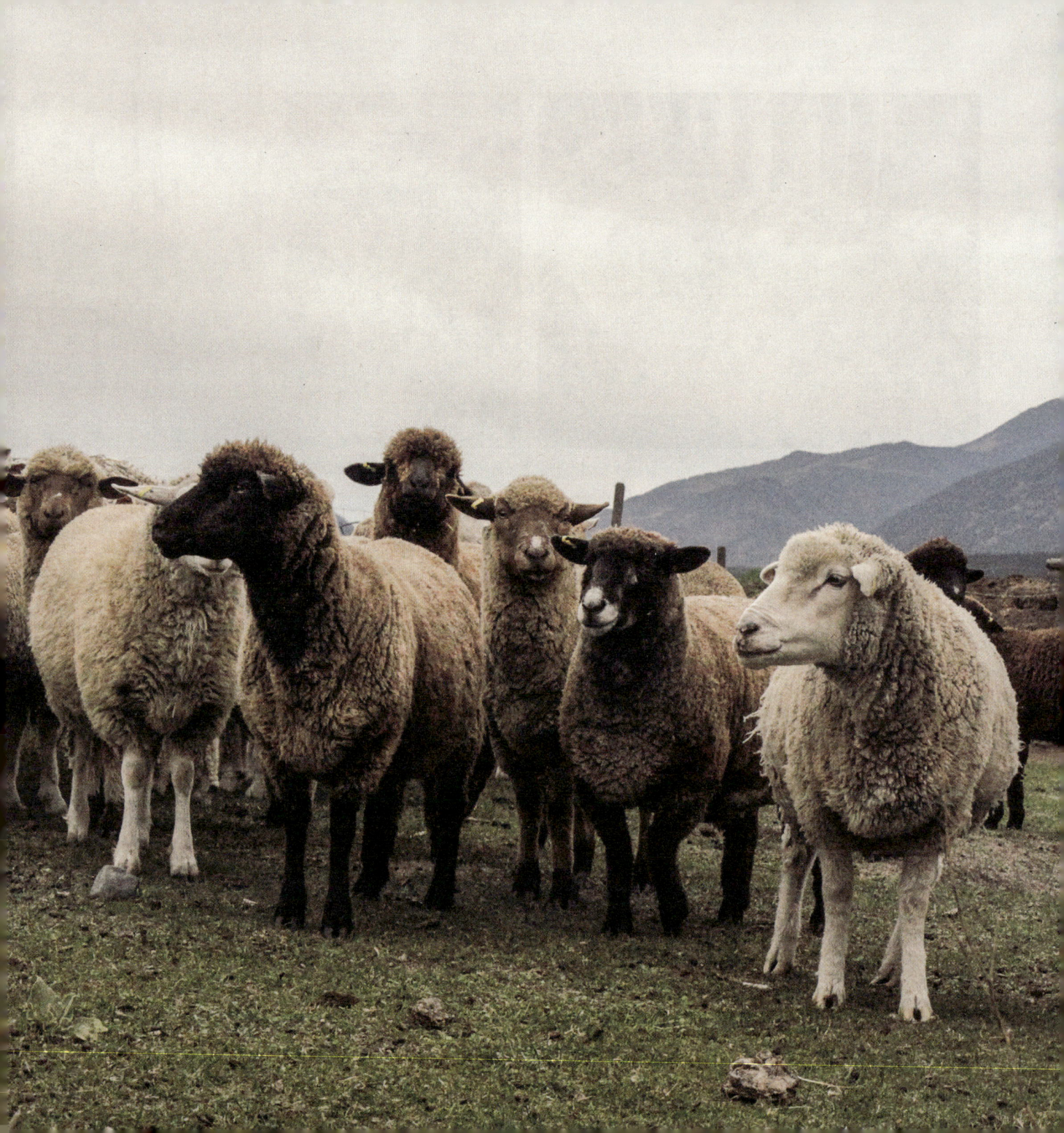

Sheep Breeds
AND WHY THEY MATTER

When I opened my yarn store in East Vancouver in 2009, I knew that I wanted to focus on local Canadian wool. But if you'd have asked me, I couldn't have named more than three sheep breeds worldwide. It was still another seven years before I started learning about the sheep breeds in Canada and the different wool that they produce.

I remember being shocked the first time I heard someone mention that sheep were on the endangered species list. I truly believed that was a status reserved for exotic animals like Bengal tigers or orangutans—not livestock.

Not only are sheep at risk, but a number of my favourite breeds to work with are at serious to critical risk, including the Shetland, Corriedale, Rambouillet, Jacob, Cotswold and others.

Mixed flock of Corriedale and Romney sheep at Disdero Ranch in BC.

Discovering this put me on a path to doing what I could to raise awareness among fibre artists about the unique wool qualities of particular sheep breeds, with the sole purpose of encouraging their use, purchase and preservation.

When we seek out or purchase breed-specific fibre and yarn, it has a direct impact on the preservation of that breed and supports the shepherds who raise the sheep. Generally, it is small-scale producers, as opposed to large-scale industrial farmers, who raise purebred, registered fibre sheep and work to maintain and propagate the genetics of that specific breed. Purchasing raw fleece or value-added product from those shepherds makes it possible for them to continue raising sheep.

In 2020, I conducted a research study specifically to capture data about farmers across the country raising sheep specifically for wool (not for meat). Recognizing a serious gap in the agricultural data around sheep and wool farms from Statistics Canada and the various livestock organizations, I wanted a better look at who is raising wool and what they are doing with it. (The full results of the survey can be found at qrco.de/survey-results [1].)

One of the key findings from this research is that most Canadian fibre farmers are selling directly to consumers. They are not working with a large-scale buyer, such as the Canadian Co-operative Wool Growers, or selling through mills or other organizations. They are dependent on word of mouth, on-farm sales, and wool-show sales directly to fibre artists. The greatest barrier cited to selling more wool is marketing: reaching customers and finding the time to actually sell wool.

Our Canadian fibre farmers are working hard to preserve sheep breeds and we have the opportunity to help them, to be engaged in the work of building a resilient and diverse fibre industry in Canada. If we expand our fibre palette beyond the well-known Merinos and non-breed-specific wools, our fibre arts practice will be all the richer for doing so.

SCAN FOR SURVEY RESULTS

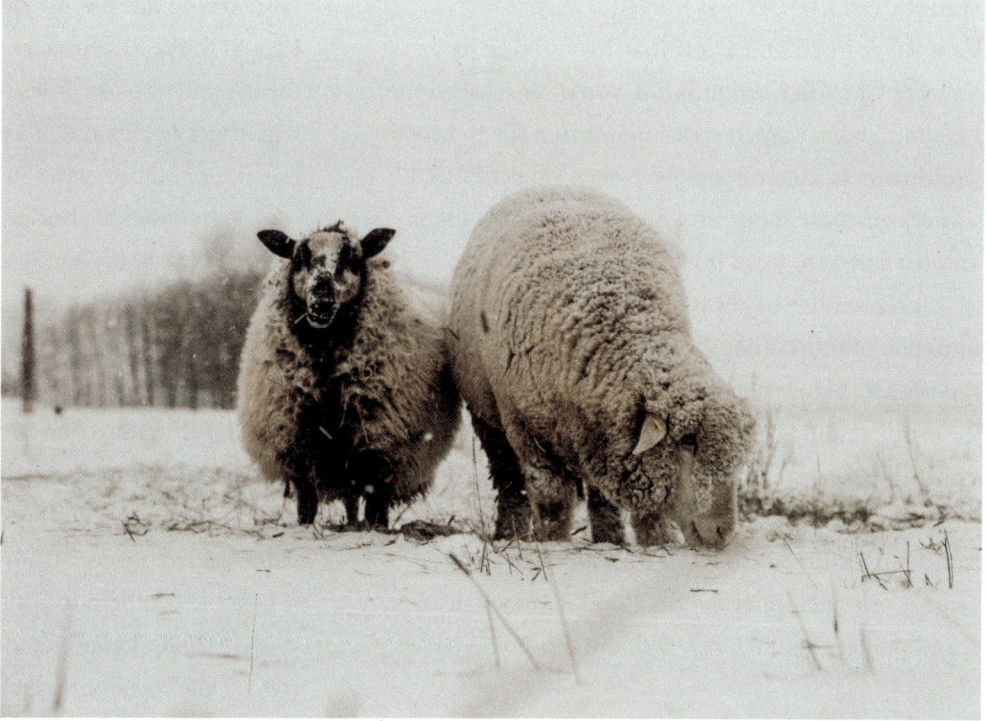

---

1 Hunter, Anna. *Wool in Canada Survey Results* https://www.longwayhomestead.com/survey-resultus. December 10, 2021.

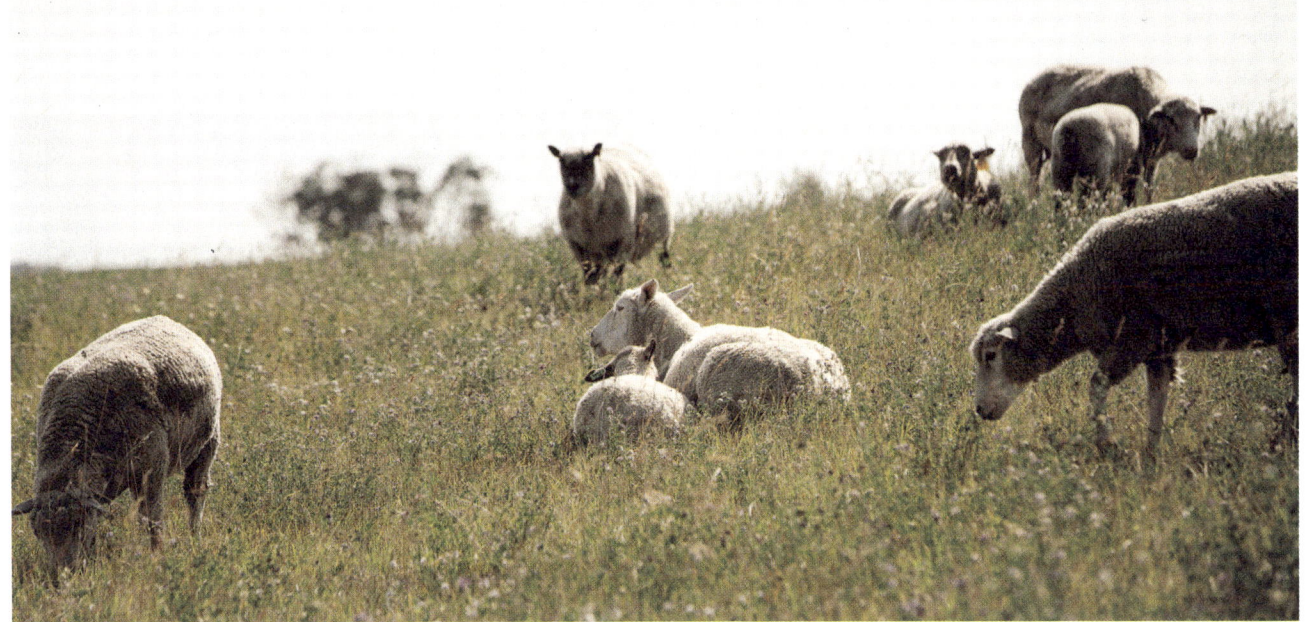

DIVERSITY OF WOOL

Wool is incredibly diverse. There is so much variability among the different breeds and how their wool will react with our needles, hooks or spinning wheels. We have down wools, full of elasticity and body; long wools with their resilience, lustre, and density; fine wools that are soft and insulating; and the "other": wools that don't fit neatly into any category.

When you open your craft up to the wide world of breed-specific wool you will learn that the characteristics of each breed are unique and varied (and I daresay you might never use superwash Merino again). You will learn which breed's wool is best suited for a sweater that you want to wear next to your skin, versus the practically bomb-proof sweater that will keep you warm on the coldest or wettest days. You will discover that long wools, despite their slightly coarser feel, will add durability to those harder wearing projects, and drape completely differently when used in a shawl or sweater. You will find yourself seeking other uses for wool too, knowing that down wools are excellent as bedding or insulation, that long wools can be used in furniture and carpets and even for horse blankets, and you will see that we haven't even scratched the surface of all the innovative ways we can use wool in our daily lives.

So why does genetic diversity in our sheep matter? Why should fibre artists and wool lovers care about protecting different sheep breeds?

When we focus on sheep breeds or seek out their fibre, it protects sheep diversity and prevents the loss of heritage breeds. Heritage sheep breeds represent the genetic diversity within the species that is reflected in the characteristics of the wool we love to work with. If we only seek out wool from a handful of breeds, we risk losing the diversity and genetics of those other breeds, and, ultimately, we risk the genetic diversity and health of the entire species.

The historical relationship between sheep and shepherd has resulted in the development of many different breeds. This has allowed sheep to meet a variety of our needs (both cultural and practical) and to adapt to diverse climates and environments. Wool quality has been important in the development and propagation of heritage sheep worldwide. According to The Livestock Conservancy, "Heritage breeds are traditional livestock breeds that were raised by our forefathers [sic]. These breeds were carefully selected and bred over time to develop traits that made them well adapted to the local environment and they thrived under farming practices and cultural conditions that are very different from those found in modern agriculture. Traditional, historic breeds retain essential attributes for survival and self-sufficiency—fertility, foraging ability, longevity, maternal instincts, ability to mate naturally, and resistance to diseases and parasites." [2]

Integrating wool from different sheep breeds informs our experience as fibre artists and adds a depth to the materials and projects we choose. It also informs how we interact with and navigate the land base we inhabit.

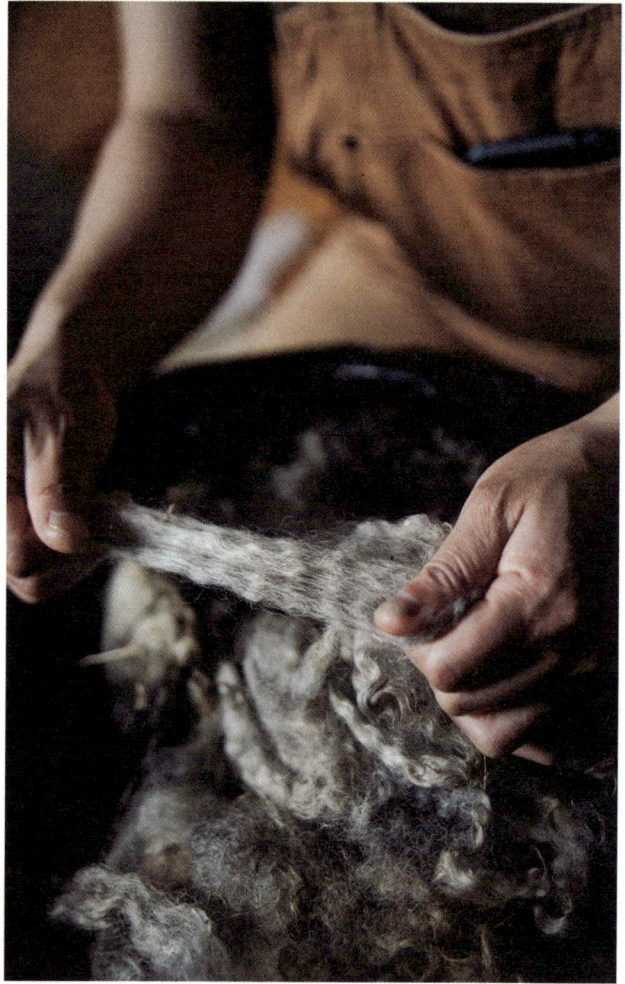

Testing the strength of wool from a Gotland sheep, Ontario.

---

2 Livestock Conservancy. *What are Heritage Breeds?* https://livestockconservancy.org/heritage-breeds/ July 21, 2022

Terminology

There are some terms I use in this book that refer to different traits or aspects of sheep and wool. There can be some variation in the way these words are defined and used, so I've included the definitions that I use for these terms. I think open conversation about terminology can work to help us better understand this industry, and I welcome any feedback on my interpretation of these words.

CRIMP

Crimp describes the natural wave or curl in a fibre. (Picture the crimping we did to our hair in the eighties—well, at least what I did to my hair in the eighties.) Crimp is what helps fibre absorb and balance twist and trap air.

DOWN WOOL

In this book I use *Down wool* to describe the wool from the Down sheep families that originated in England in the nineteenth century. I don't cover any of the original Down wool breeds in this book, but I do focus on some breeds that are Down wool descendants (like North Country Cheviot), and their wool has similar characteristics (elasticity, resiliency, lack of lustre, resistance to felting). I recommend the *Fleece & Fibre Sourcebook*[3] (Robson and Ekarius, 2011) for a more in-depth study of the Down wool breeds.

LONG WOOL

A category of wool that generally has a staple length longer than four inches and has a more curl-like crimp.

MICRON

This refers to a specific unit of measurement for the diameter of a fibre when viewed under a microscope. Coarser wool has a larger micron count; finer wool has a smaller micron count. It is important to remember that fibre has inherent variability throughout, and the micron count won't necessarily be uniform across a fleece or a breed.

SOUNDNESS

Describes the strength of wool fibre. A fibre is considered "sound" if it is free from breaking or tenderness. The soundness describes the strength of the staple length.

STAPLE LENGTH

The natural length of a fibre from tip to tip.

---

3 Robson, Deborah and Carol Ekarius. *The Fleece & Fiber Sourcebook*. North Adams, USA. Storey Publishing LLC, June 6, 2011.

Sheep and the Land

Domestic sheep are not native to Canada. They were introduced to the land that we now call Canada during settler colonization. There is documented evidence of the first two sheep arriving in Nova Scotia in 1604. The first small flock of forty-five sheep, resembling what was most likely the Cheviot breed, arrived in New France (Québec) in 1667. A few years later, in 1671, records show that 407 sheep were brought to Nova Scotia. Sheep were initially brought for the subsistence needs of early settlers, mostly for food and clothing.

Records of how many sheep arrived over the next hundred years are spotty, but by the end of the 1700s there were many sheep in the colonies that were settled in the maritime provinces, Ontario and Québec. Many of these colonies brought sheep up

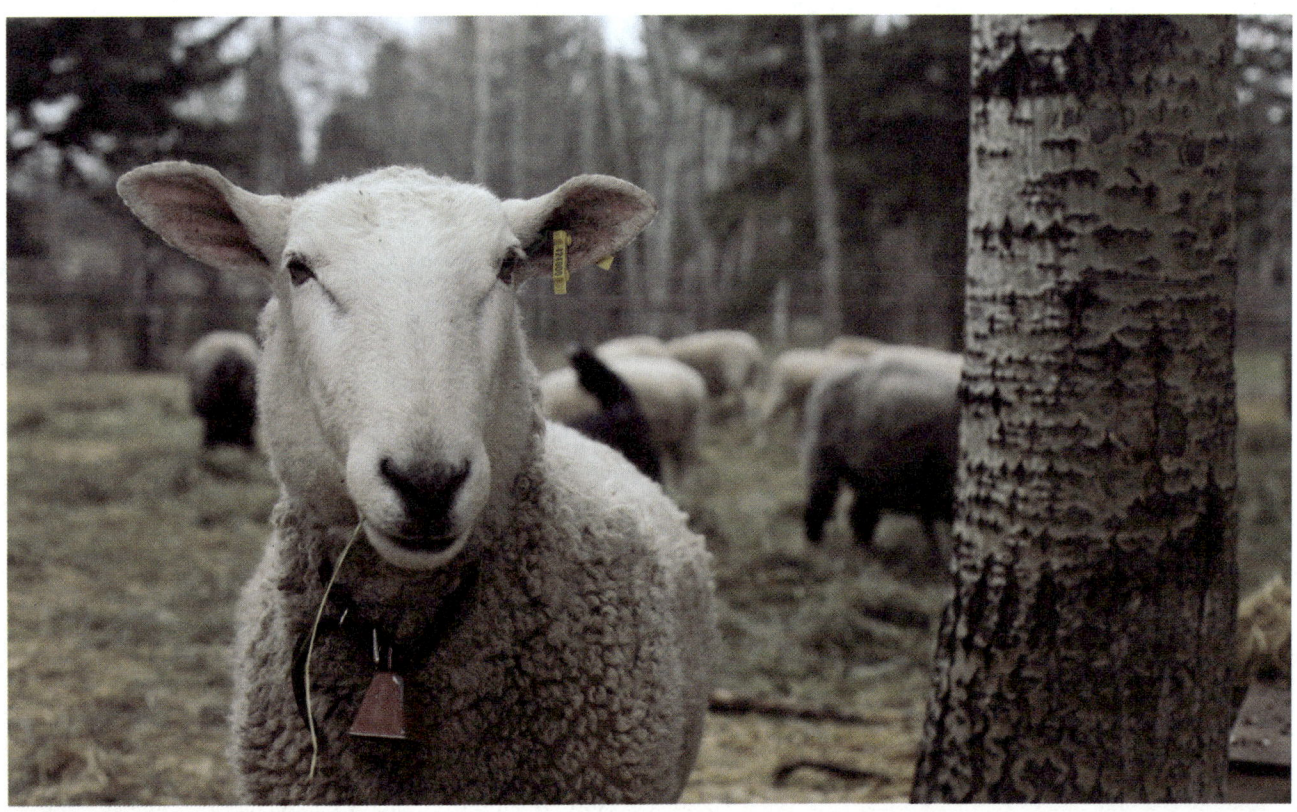

from the U.S. They were common English breeds: Cotswold, Leicester, Hampshire, and Southdown. In 1830 there was an influx of British immigrants that brought purebred flocks of sheep that were then crossed with existing sheep flocks to improve the stock and quality. It was during this time, from 1827–1871, that our textile industry shifted from subsistence-based clothing production to factory output. As the number of sheep grew, so did our ability to transform that wool into textiles with carding, fulling, and weaving mills.

The first documented Provincial Exhibition for sheep was held in 1846 in Toronto, with the Leicesters and Southdowns taking the prize money. Sheep had become both profitable and popular within Canadian agriculture during this time. The sheep population grew and travelled west along with settlers. Canada reached its peak sheep population in 1931 with a recorded 3.6 million sheep across the country.

This growth in the sheep population did not last, and, after World War II, the population began to decline significantly. There isn't extensive research to explain exactly why this happened, but it is likely linked to the demise of the domestic textile processing industry. Prior to the twentieth century, Canada had the infrastructure and milling capacity to manufacture into clothing the roughly twelve million pounds of wool grown every year. Near the end of the nineteenth century there were more than 639 carding and fulling mills producing textiles in Ontario and Québec.

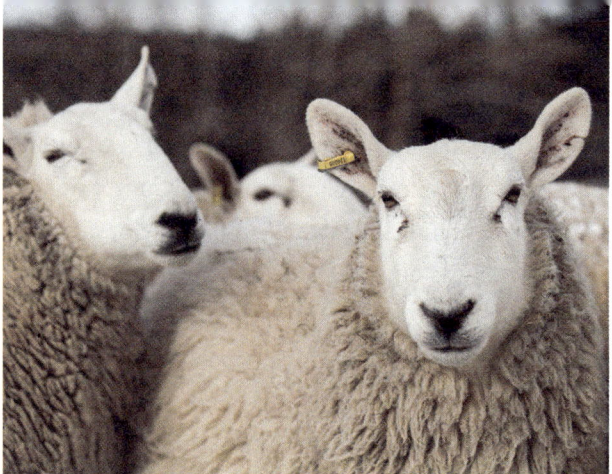

There are many factors that may have contributed to this decline:

1. Changing fashions and increased exports of finer wool fabrics from Britain and the U.S. Those who could afford imported fabrics preferred the fine cloth from elsewhere rather than the more coarse wool being grown and manufactured in Canada.
2. Canadian mills did not have the organizational capacity or the capital to modernize equipment and keep up with the changing trends and domestic demand.
3. Increased reliance on synthetic fibres. Starting in the mid-1920s, rayon, nylon, and acrylic became more popular and cheaper to produce, and soon took more of the market share for textiles.
4. Trade liberalization and the removal of barriers on cheaply made clothing after World War II. Canadian manufacturing could no longer compete with the prices of imported textiles.

These shifts in the textile processing market decreased the value of Canadian wool until it was no longer a financially viable commodity for farmers. When wool was devalued, the only commodity from the sheep industry was lamb meat and breeding stock. Lamb was not as popular with Canadian consumers as other meats, and sheep populations declined. Canada had a record low population of 560,000 sheep in 1977, and the population has been slowly growing since, due at least in part to an increase of lamb in our diet. Statistics Canada recorded just over one million sheep in Canada in 2020.

Agricultural Product

The sheep and lamb industry in Canada is focused almost entirely on lamb meat production, with dairy and then wool far behind in importance and market share. The Canadian Co-operative Wool Growers (CCWG) is the only large-scale wool buyer in Canada. They buy wool from Canadian sheep farmers and sell 90% of it on the international market, with the majority going to China for processing. The rate per pound for farmers is dismally low and often doesn't cover the cost of shearing. This lack of financial compensation for Canadian wool has resulted in the ongoing devaluation of wool to the point that many farmers simply burn or compost their years' wool to eliminate the transport costs to CCWG.

Textile Agriculture

Humans have been harvesting plants and animals for clothing for as long as we have been harvesting them for food. However, we are increasingly disconnected from the agricultural processes that grow our clothing and textiles, as fast fashion trends provide an ever-changing stream of clothing. Moreover, the increase in the use, availability, and development of synthetic, carbon-based textiles such as nylon, Lycra, polyester, and acrylic, has furthered the disconnect between clothing and agriculture.

One hundred and fifty years ago, much of our clothing and textiles were grown and manufactured in Canada. It was predominantly wool and linen, with some imported cotton, wool, and silk. Clothing was made on a subsistence basis, and by the late nineteenth century Canada had over 600 textile mills to process wool, flax, and cotton. We had the knowledge and infrastructure to grow, harvest, and manufacture much of what we consumed. Canada does not have adequate growing conditions for cotton, but flax (for linen) and hemp thrive in various regions across the country.

The twentieth century saw a complete dismantling of infrastructure for processing wool and other fibres.

As the focus of the Canadian sheep industry shifted to meat, our wool lost its value on the international market. This devaluation occurred for two major reasons. First, because of our climate we do not have access to year-round pasture and must feed sheep hay for six months of the year, which results in heavy vegetable matter contamination and makes Canadian wool quite dirty when compared to wool produced in other countries. Second, the focus on meat breeds in Canadian agriculture means that Canadian sheep farmers focus less on raising breeds that produce fine wool, which is the more valuable wool for textiles internationally. As Canadian wool lost value on the global market over time, and our domestic capacity for fibre

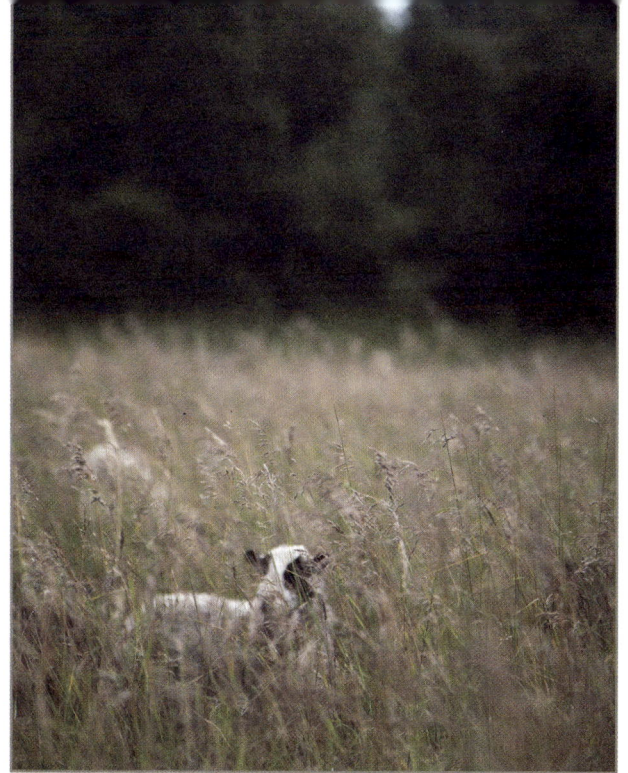

This downturn was caused by the introduction of synthetics, increased trade liberalization and imported textiles, and slow adaptation by existing mills to new technology (especially to the finer worsted fabrics). Ultimately, the textile manufacturing industry in Canada was not nimble enough to accommodate the changing trends in fashion and desirable materials (fine wools and synthetics) and it could not compete with the costs of overseas processing.

The move to a globalized supply chain for textiles has decimated our understanding of clothing as an agricultural product. Raw materials like wool, flax, and hemp are exported from our country to be processed in nations with less stringent environmental and labour laws, then shipped back to us as finished products. There are few opportunities to connect with the source of the fibres that make our clothing, and we no longer recognize that our clothing comes from the soil. Once we collectively recognize that textiles are also an agricultural product, we can change the fast-fashion attitude and begin to acknowledge and value the resources and labour required to produce our clothing.

Sheep Breeds and Why They Matter

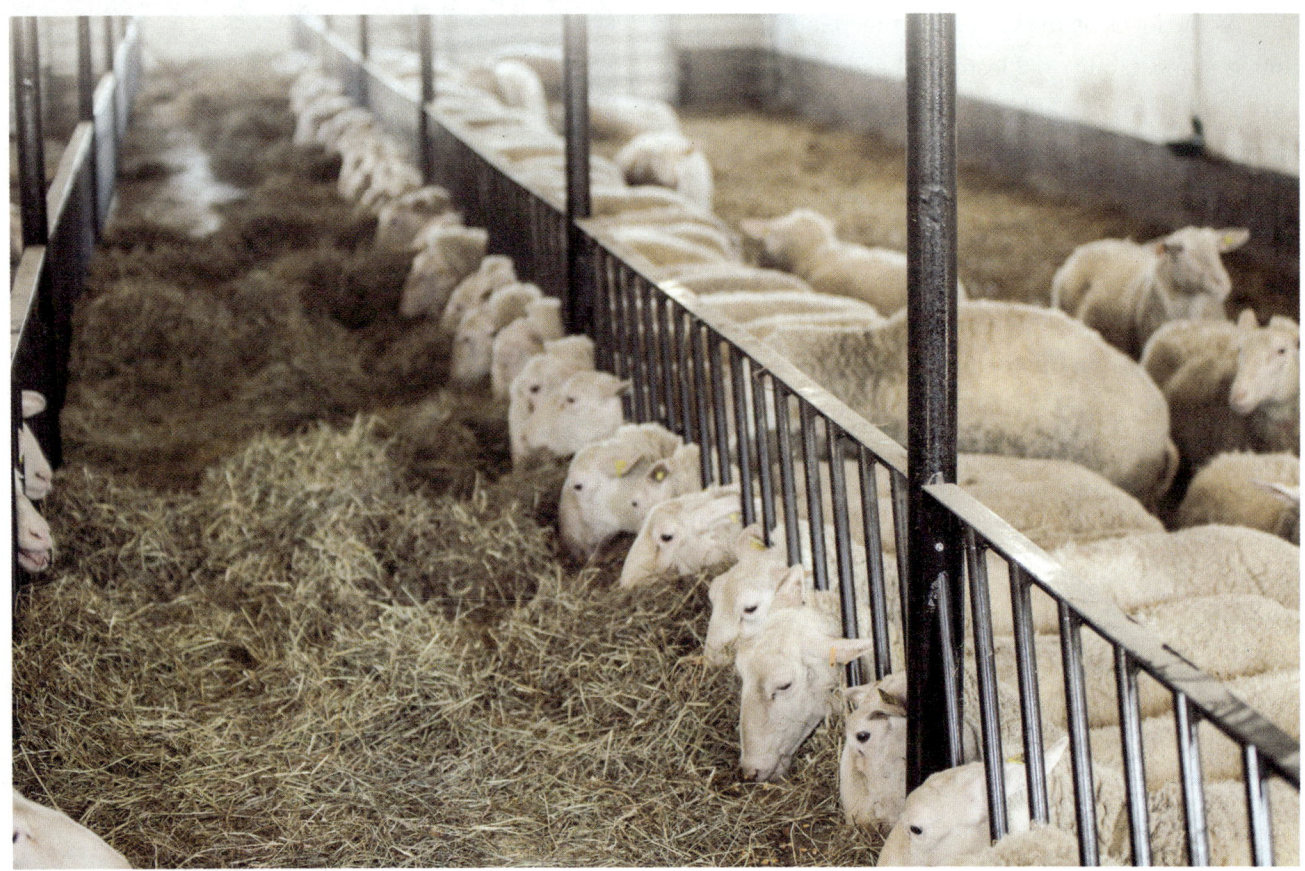

production was decimated, our wool industry has fallen into crisis.

The domestic wool industry has been left out of the larger conversation about Canadian agriculture, and the growing, processing, and marketing of wool has fallen on the shoulders of fibre-focused producers, small- to medium-sized mills, and industrious entrepreneurs who still see value in selling Canadian wool. It is challenging to find locally grown and manufactured Canadian wool in many local yarn stores (although, thankfully, we are starting to see a renewed interest in this from retailers), and it is almost impossible to find ready-to-wear textiles that have been grown and manufactured with Canadian wool.

We are disconnected from where our clothing and our food come from. Many don't realize that textiles, wool, linen, cotton, and hemp are actually agricultural products. Canada is not a cotton-growing region, but we can grow flax (for linen), hemp, and wool and other protein-based fibres. It is challenging, as a fibre farmer, to convince the agriculture industry that textiles are also agriculture and that growing or raising the materials that go into them should be treated with the same urgency as that of ensuring food security.

In many ways we have lost the knowledge, infrastructure, and economy to process the wool that we grow in Canada. Meanwhile, the fibre arts industry is burgeoning with interest. At some point, perhaps around the time I decided to become a sheep farmer with zero experience in agriculture, it became my mission to connect fibre artists with the source of their wool, and to convince our government that as a society, we need to support the growth and resilience of this agricultural sector.

More to Wool than Knitting

What I discovered through my own journey connecting to the sources of my fibre is that there is so much more to wool than knitting. When managed well, sheep can nourish our soils and contribute to ecological health and climate change mitigation in many of the land bases across Canada. Despite the bad rap that sheep and other ruminants get for contributing to greenhouse gas emissions through "farts and burps," ruminants are a requisite component for healthy grassland ecosystems.

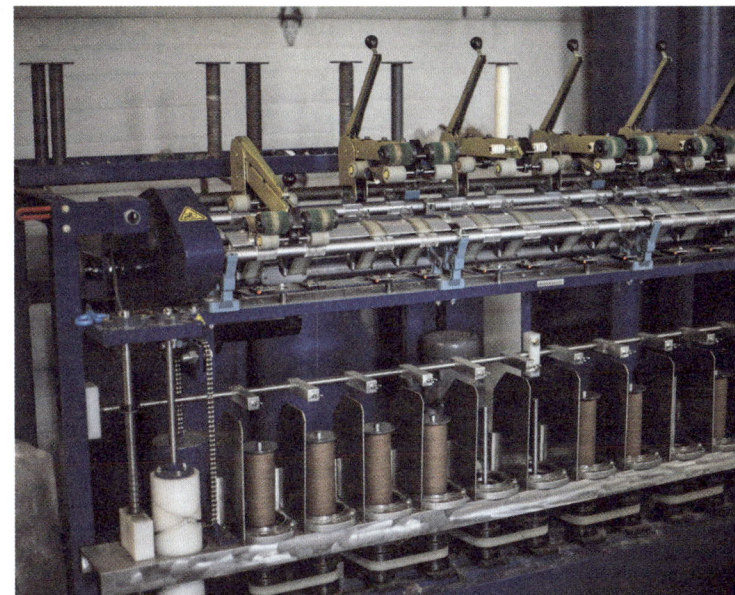

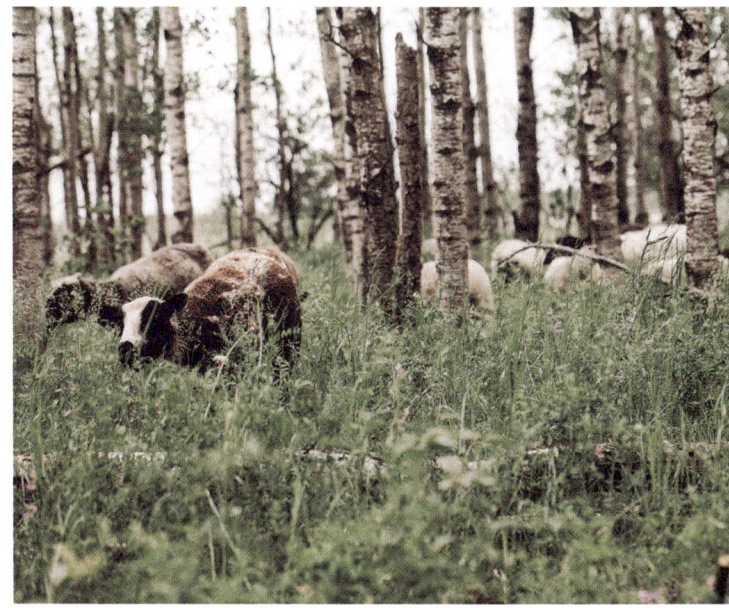

Carbon Sinks

Carbon dioxide (CO_2) is a natural part of our atmosphere and is taken in by green leafy plants. Through the process of photosynthesis, the two oxygen molecules are separated from the carbon, and oxygen is released back into the atmosphere for us to breathe. The carbon is then transformed into a simple carbohydrate that the plant uses to feed both its own structure and the soil ecosystem through its roots.

When sheep, alpacas, goats, llamas, and other ruminants eat those plants, they are taking that carbon and turning it into various types of protein, like wool or other fibre. That wool or fibre is sheared and turned into our clothing or other textiles and (hopefully) used for many years.

When that clothing is no longer useable it can be composted, and that carbon (still fully contained in the wool fibres) will be returned to the soil along with other nutrients to feed soil microbes and nurture other plants, starting the cycle again.

It is a truly radical thought to consider our clothing and textiles within a circular model such as this. So often our clothing and textiles are only considered in a linear way. When I speak to knitting groups about the wool industry and climate change I pull on my favourite wool hat. It's made of grey wool, from one of my first sheep, named Shirley. And I say to the group, "If you need another reason to love wool, think of it this way: This is a grass-fed hat that I'm wearing. It is basically a mini carbon sink. Is there anything more amazing than that? We are all wearing a LOT of carbon sinks in this room."

The rest of the book will be less about climate and more about sheep, but bear with me—this is good shit (literally).

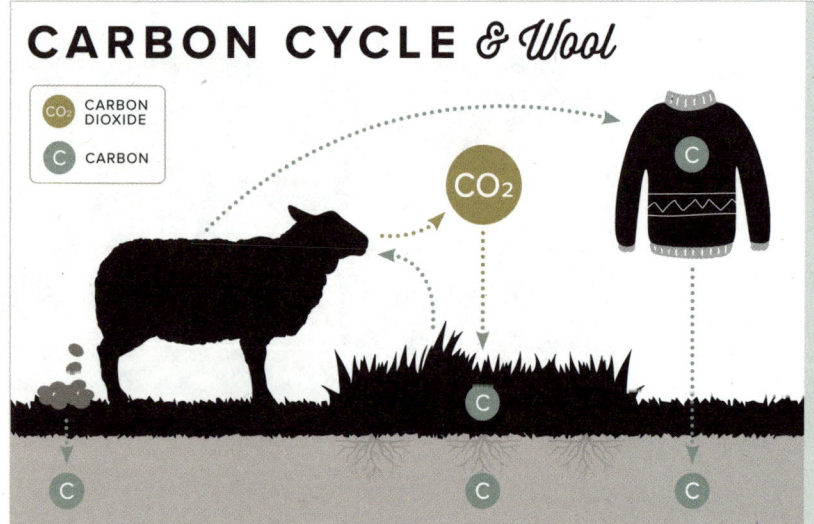

CARBON CYCLE & Wool

- CO_2 CARBON DIOXIDE
- C CARBON

Wool is a carbon sink:

- Pasture grasses take **CO_2** from the atmosphere and sequester it in the grass, roots and soil (as **carbon**).
- Sheep eat grass and use the **carbon** to grow wool.
- Items made from wool store **carbon** until they are returned to the earth to compost. This **carbon** then returns to feed soil and new plant growth.
- Well managed grazing sheep stimulate increased growth of pasture grasses, while their manure fertilizes the soil, resulting in more **carbon** being stored in the ground.

Healthy Grasslands and Ecosystems

Not only are sheep taking carbon out of the atmosphere and turning it into fibre that we can turn into clothing, but sheep can also contribute to the health of our grasslands and ecosystems. Sheep can be housed and managed intensively or extensively. **Intensive management** means they are housed predominantly in an indoor, controlled environment (like a barn) and they are fed and bred to increase the production of meat, milk, and wool, to maximize return on investment. **Extensive management** is a system in which sheep are raised outdoors on pasture and left to graze in the summer and fed hay in the winter. Within extensive management operations there are many different approaches and strategies that can be used to benefit our grasslands, restore ecosystem health, and ultimately affect the climate in a positive way. These strategies can be called regenerative agriculture, holistic management, adaptive planned grazing, or rotational grazing. For me, this is the exciting opportunity we have to use sheep to clothe us *and* to heal the land.

Regenerative agriculture is not a one-size-fits-all approach to farming. It is a place-based approach that identifies what strategies would be required to regenerate soil health. These methods are applied to build more soil organic matter so that our soils can sequester more carbon from the atmosphere, increase water holding capacity thus decreasing our reliance on aquifers and other water sources, and provide healthy ecosystems for other species.

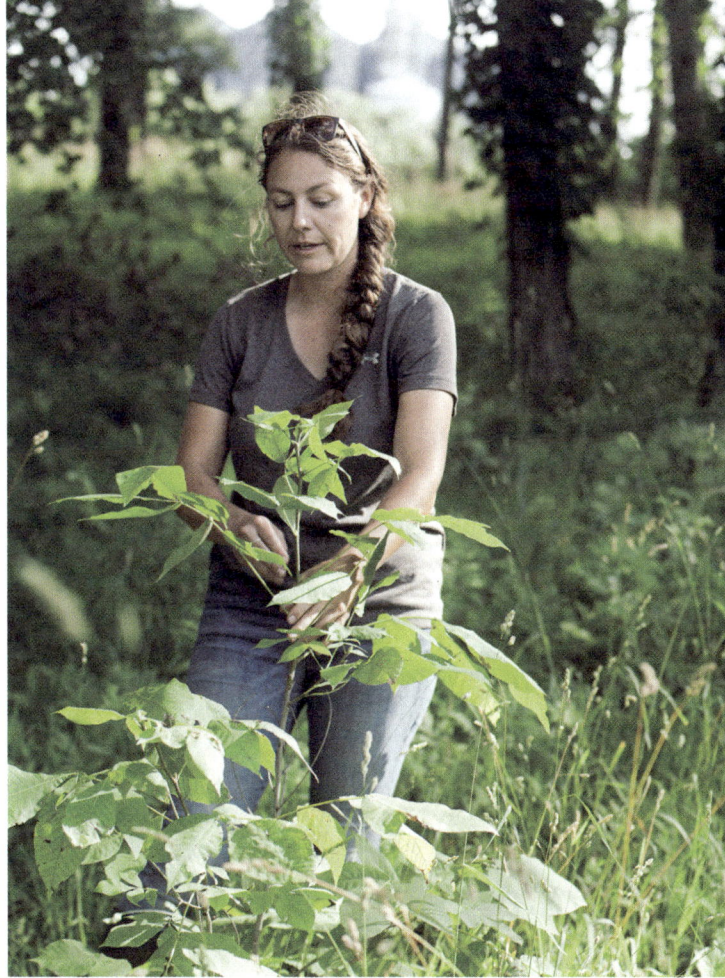

Carrie Woolley explaining the benefits of her silvopasture operation, Ontario.

While some of the atmospheric carbon taken in by plants is utilized by animals to grow wool and fibre, the rest of the carbon stays in the soil and is used to feed the microbes in the soil and promote the development of mycorrhizal fungi. The microbes and fungi work together to produce humus, the rich

Sheep Breeds and Why They Matter 37

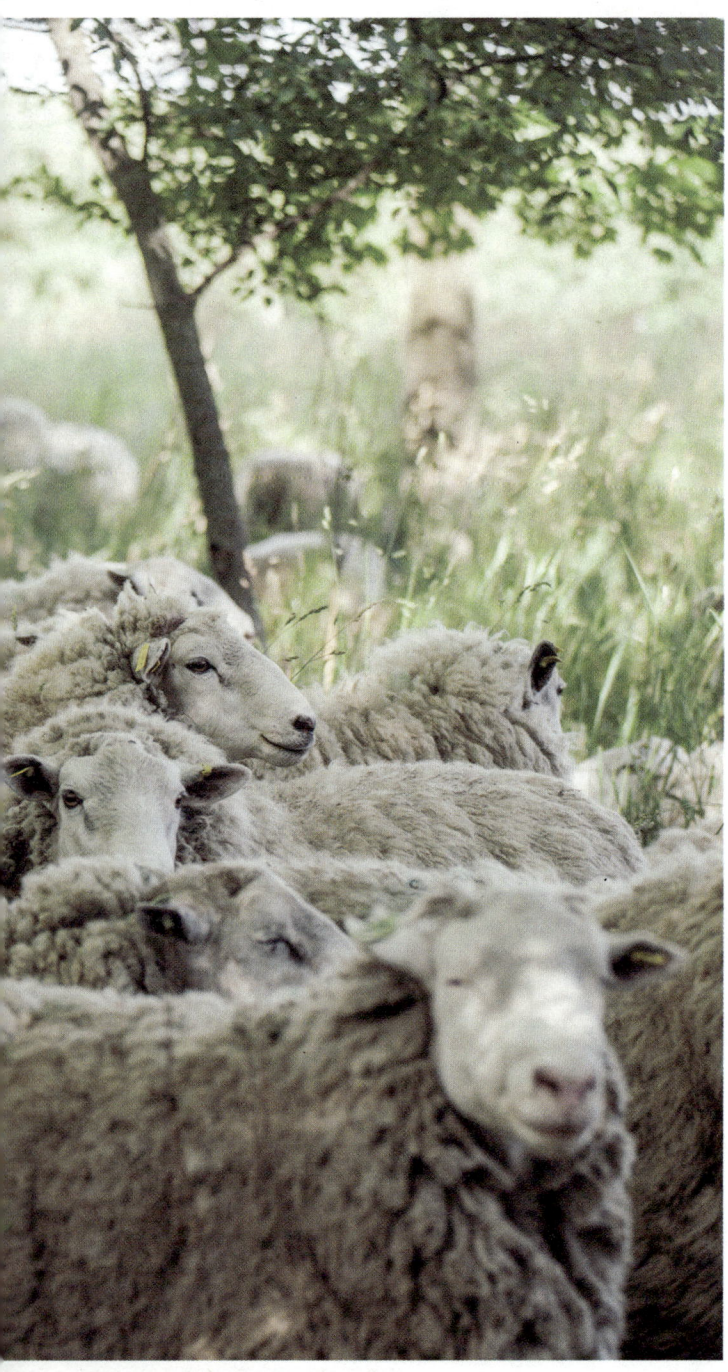

soil that is essential for growing healthy plants. Carbon that is stored in humus can stay sequestered in the soil for a very long time. Managed grazing of sheep on grasslands and pasture can encourage plant growth and increase drawdown of carbon into roots and soil. As sheep turn grass into wool and encourage plant growth, they also leave nitrogen-rich fertilizer, in the form of manure (that's the shit!) that further builds health and resilience in the soil.

When shepherds utilize grazing animals to imitate the movement of wild ruminants or historical herds of bison through managed adaptive or planned grazing, they provide the disturbance necessary to reduce dead grass or overgrown forage and allow for new growth. Sheep can be used to clear out overgrown brush to mitigate fire risk in wildfire-prone areas and to keep invasive species at bay. When we as consumers understand the vital role that sheep can play in building healthy soils, resilient grasslands, and biologically diverse ecosystems, we can support the shepherds in our region who are committed to promoting and regenerating the vitality of our land, by purchasing their fibre, yarn, and clothing.

Land and Sheep and Wool

With this book I want to link sheep to the land in the important way described above, and I also want to demonstrate how diverse sheep breeds are best suited to the diverse landscapes across

Coopworth sheep grazing the woodlot in the silvopasture operation, Ontario.

Canada. It is not one-size-fits-all when we talk about sheep: each breed is unique in the way it affects the land through grazing, the way its wool reacts to moisture—or lack thereof—and the nutritional requirements available.

The conditions on the Prairies of Saskatchewan require different breed management than the rocky central lowlands of Nova Scotia, or the dry scrublands of the Okanagan in B.C. The origin of sheep breeds often directly correlates to the environmental conditions in which they thrive. Land and sheep and wool are linked. Range sheep flourish in dry regions and can spread out over vast sections of land to graze on sparse forages, so they're well-suited to the Prairies. They, in turn, grow beautiful fine fleeces that are best used as next-to-skin insulating layers—just the type of clothing that shepherds on the Prairies need during a stretch of -40 °C weather.

In contrast, a long-wool breed like Romney has natural resilience to foot rot (they came from salt marshes after all) and they are resistant to parasites that thrive in wet conditions, so a coastal climate or a river valley farm that is constantly dealing with flooding and receding water is an excellent choice for that breed.

This inextricable link to the land is yet another reason why preserving the genetic diversity of our sheep population is so crucial, and ultimately, it's why we should wear more wool, give wool to our friends and family, and never stop talking about the wonders of wool! »

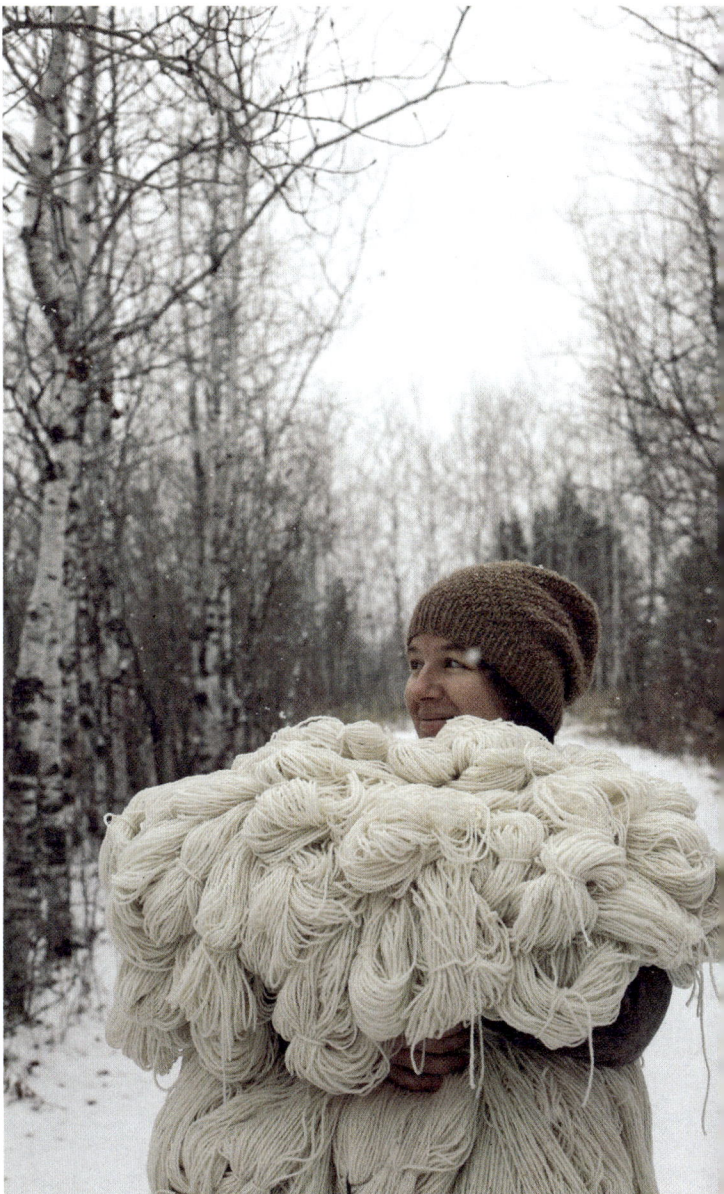

Anna holding a large batch of Corriedale wool yarn, Manitoba.

Sheep Breeds and Why They Matter

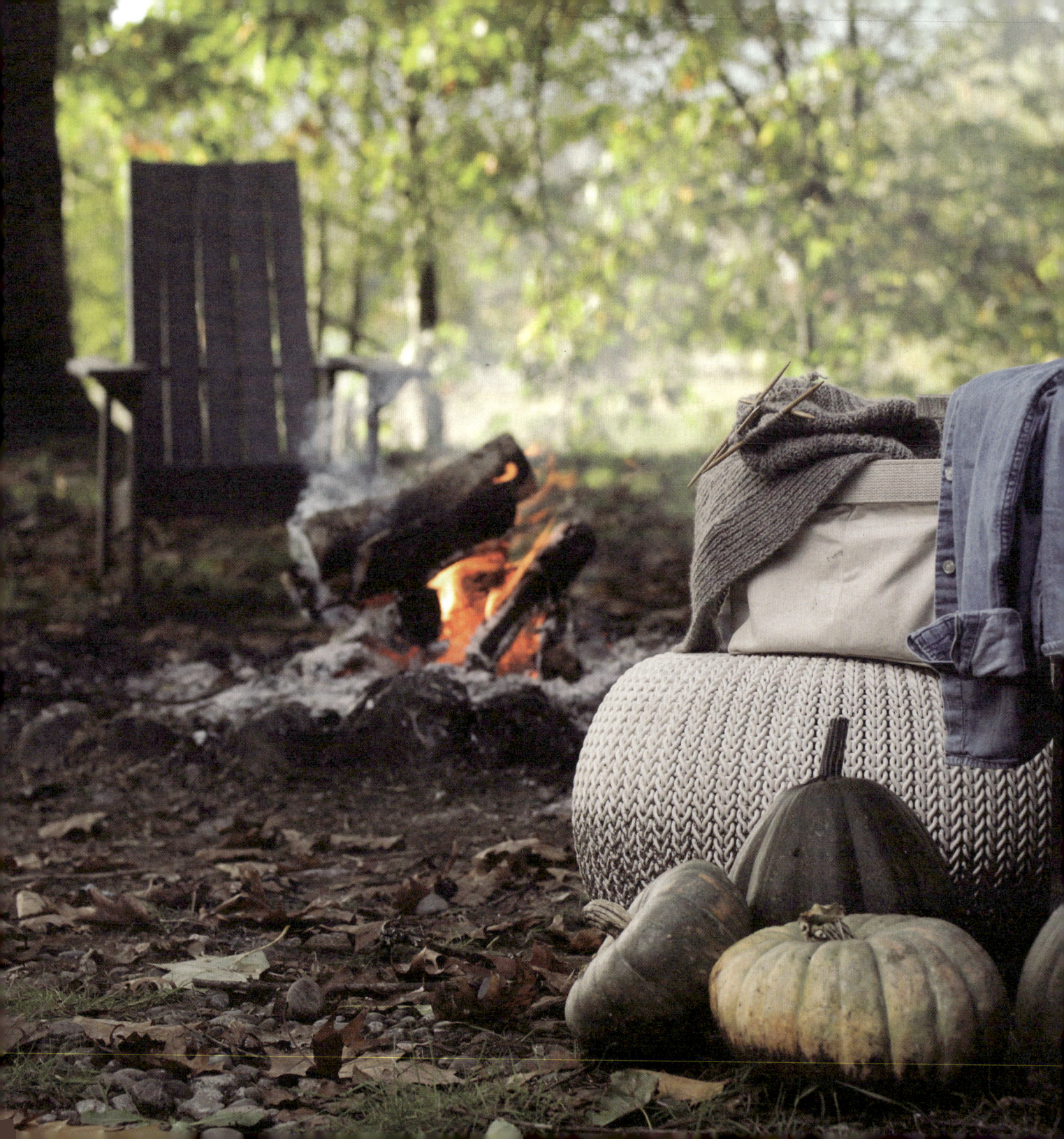

West Coast

When I first envisioned this book, I knew it had to be equal parts deep information, captivating interviews, and beautiful pictures of sheep and landscapes. I'm so fortunate that my dear friend, fellow fibre farmer, and neighbour Christel Lanthier is also an incredible photographer. She was integral to this book project coming together. Her pictures have captured the beauty of the sheep breeds explored in this book, and I couldn't have chosen a better travel companion for this project. You can read more about how Christel and I met, in the profile of her own farm that you'll find in The Prairies chapter.

The interviews I conducted took place over the two years between 2020 and 2022. The reality of health and travel restrictions due to the COVID-19 pandemic meant we had to navigate lots of cancellations and interruptions. We shoe-horned interviews into other trips, like picking up wool from farms in the Prairies, or attending yarn festivals. We tried to interview farmers in every season we experience in Canada, and to visit as many regions as we could.

The Yukon, Northwest Territories, and Nunavut do not have large sheep populations (if any at all), so they are not included in this book, but a more inclusive fibre book could feature the beautiful qiviut fibre that is grown and harvested in Canada's northern regions. Sadly, we did not get to Newfoundland and Labrador, but I've recently come across the story of shepherds that ferry their sheep on boats from the mainland to islands for grazing every year, and I think that could be an incredible story in and of itself. They were featured in a CBC story, available at this link: qrco.de/newfoundland.

We could have spent another two years interviewing many other incredible fibre farmers who are growing beautiful wool, and there are other stunning breeds that are not included in this book.

Fibre & Forge Farm in the fall.

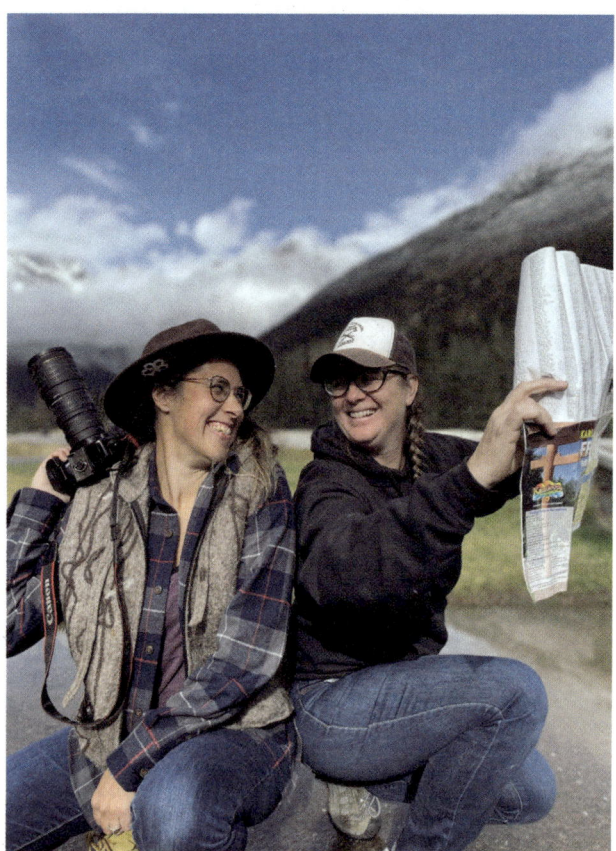
Christel and Anna during their travels in British Columbia.

Their omission is only because of time and resources, and even as I write this, I'm wishing that I could sneak them in under the wire of my deadline.

To create this book, we travelled 16,632 kilometres by plane, truck, and car. We hit every kind of weather imaginable, including a tornado in Saskatchewan! Often it was only Christel and me, fuelled by coffee and endless conversation about how to ignite a wool revolution in Canada. But sometimes we had other passengers, either literally travelling with us, or figuratively joining us on social media—so many of you providing us with ongoing support and encouragement. Wool really is an incredible thing. Not only does it provide warmth, protection, entertainment, dexterity, and carbon sequestration, but it has also brought so many fantastic people into my life. I'm so honoured to share some of their stories.

It seemed fitting to start this journey on the West Coast of Canada, as that is where so much of the foundation of my own wool journey was laid. When I launched Baaad Anna's Yarn Store with a hope that someday I could fill the shelves with local yarn raised by local shepherds, I couldn't have imagined that someday I would be that local farmer, albeit in another province, and that I would write a book about so many of the other farmers I've met along the way.

British Columbia
BLUEFACED LEICESTER AND FIBRE & FORGE FARM

It was October 2021, and I was still in the post-fibre festival haze, exhausted yet exhilarated in a way familiar to wool vendors, after setting up, running, and breaking down what amounts to a small yarn store in a ten-by-ten-foot space in a matter of hours. This iteration of Knit City Vancouver was especially exciting, as it was the first one since the pandemic had forced the cancellation of all large fibre festivals for two years, so I didn't really mind the exhaustion.

Christel and I, along with our friend and "honorary farmer" Nicole, piled into the rental van, armed with coffee and cinnamon buns, and said goodbye to Vancouver as we headed east along the south shore of the Fraser River towards Abbotsford, B.C. With the looming Golden Ears Mountain to our north and the various cranberry, blueberry, and vegetable farms lining the highway, we followed the road along the river until we pulled into the picturesque driveway belonging to Beatriz and Glen Remple of Fibre & Forge. Even though we had literally spent the entire weekend fawning over the beautiful yarn and fibre at Knit City,

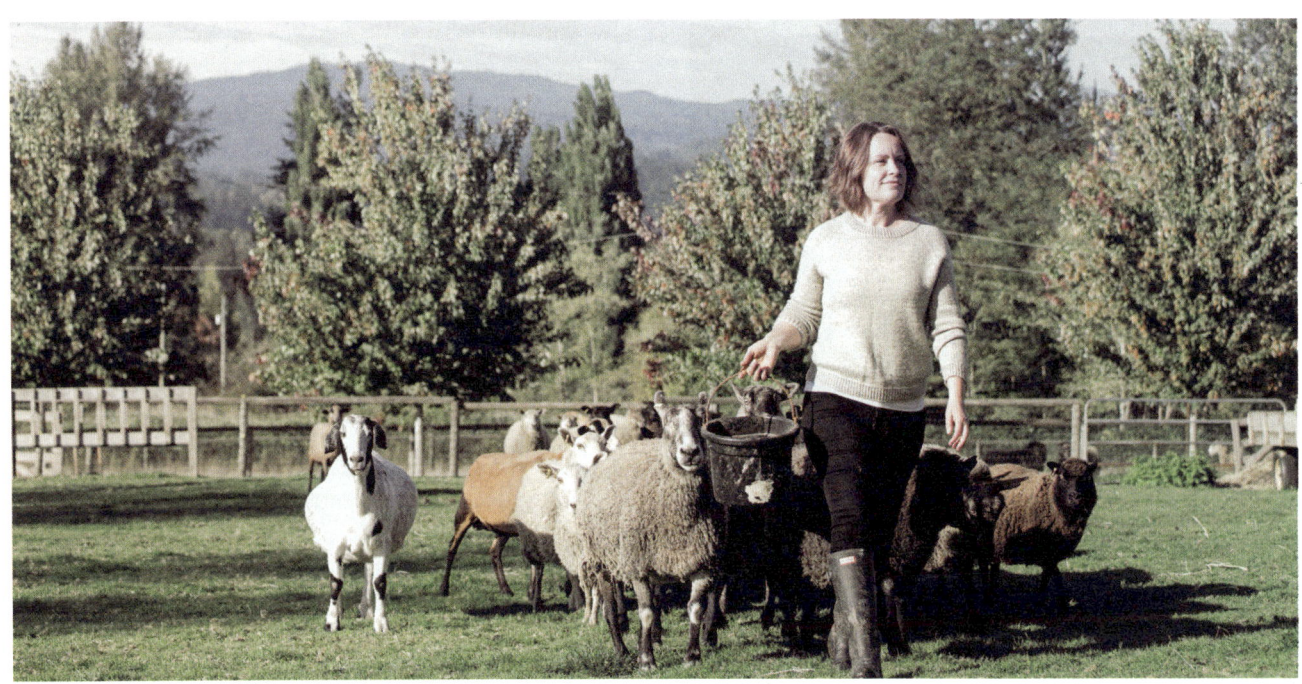

we all squealed in unison when we saw the farm stand at the entrance to Beatriz's farm. Filled with jam, candles, knitted fall leaf garlands and other treasures, the stand was a sign that we were about to experience this farm in more ways than one.

It was early afternoon on a perfect fall day, with only a slight chill in the air and the sun at our backs. The vibe of Beatriz's farm could be described as "country chic" or maybe "modern farmhouse," featuring a perfectly aged table filled with green, white, and orange pumpkins and gourds they had grown in their garden. I think the three of us could have stayed all day. We sat around a campfire with fresh coffee and delicious homemade cookies that almost made the air smell like pumpkin spice. Beatriz wore a simple but stunning raglan sweater she had knit from the wool from one of her Bluefaced Leicester (BFL)-Shetland cross sheep named Dave's Mom. She told us the story of Dave's Mom and how she came to be on the farm, and in that brief origin story the sweater somehow became more stunning. The crackling of the campfire and the occasional chortle of the turkeys in the barn provided the backdrop as Beatriz shared her own origin story.

Beatriz has a degree in interior design (which is evident throughout her beautiful farm) and worked in that field for a while, before becoming sick and having to leave her work. During that time her sister-in-law taught her how to knit and she was instantly captivated. Beatriz and her husband, Glen, lived in Burnaby, B.C., just east of Vancouver. They had a dream of living on a farm but knew that the prohibitive cost of land in the region made it impossible. During a fortuitous open-farm driving tour in 2013, they came upon a dead-end road and a "for sale" sign, and the spark of that dream was once again ignited. They found out it was a foreclosure, and, within ten days of accidentally coming across the nine-acre property, they had a court date, had put in an offer, and were awarded the place.

In 2014, they brought home their first sheep. It was actually a free sheep that came along with some goats they had purchased, but Beatriz knew this was meant to be. She then saw a Facebook post for a flock dispersal in the town of 100 Mile House, and she purchased the entire flock: a mix of Shetland,

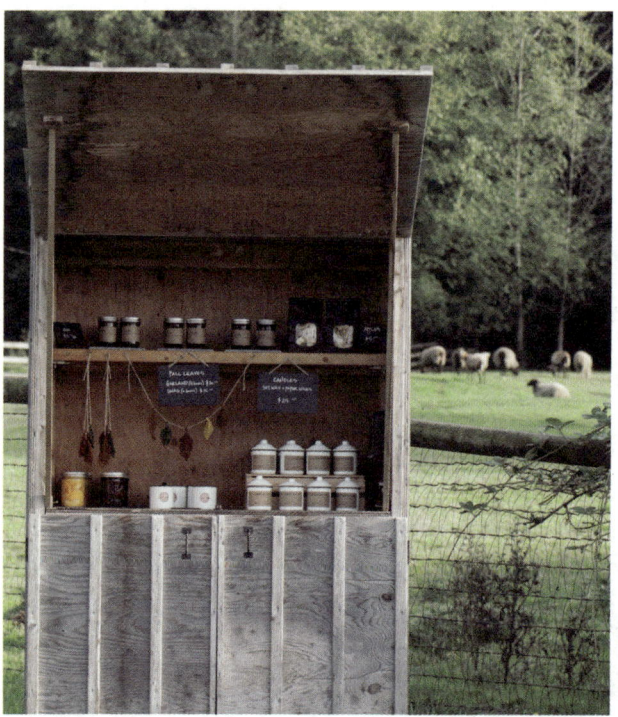

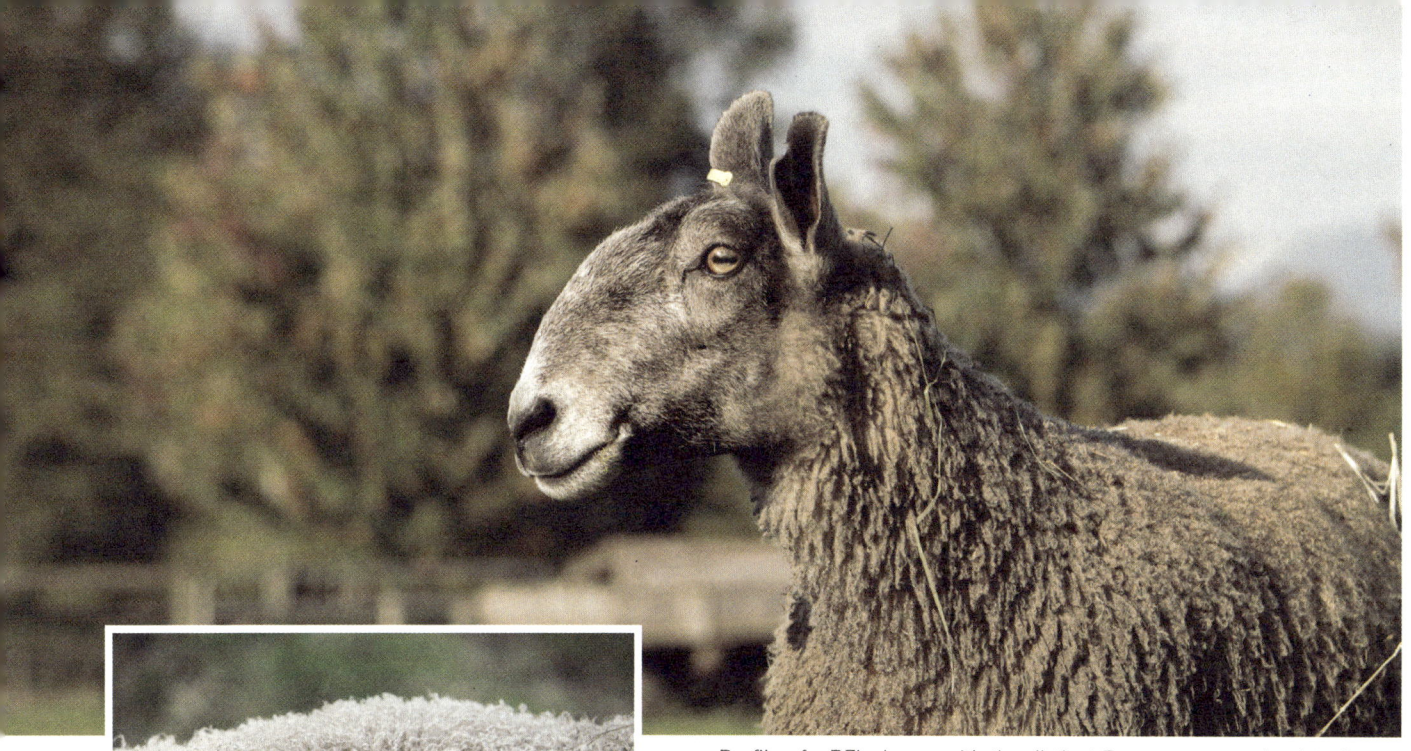

Profile of a BFL sheep, with the distinct Roman nose and pointed ears.

BFL, Merino, and Gotlands. Beatriz jumped in with both feet to raise sheep for fibre, using her keen eye for beautiful things to seek out more sheep, with the express purpose of growing beautiful fleece and stunning natural colours.

After we ate a few too many cookies and a enjoyed a second cup of coffee, Beatriz introduced us to her flock. She lovingly described each of their personalities and unique fleece qualities. I was struck by how authentic her affection for each of them was—it was evident she absolutely loves her sheep and has truly developed a connection to the source of her wool. I asked her what it was like, the first time she was able to use wool from her own flock. She stared off towards the mountain range in the distance, absently scratching the chin of her partially blind BFL Helen, and then said, "I wish I could put that into words. I took one of each [skein] and I just sat on the couch hugging my own yarn. I knit it so slowly, revelling in each stitch."

This love of fibre quality and colour has been the driving force behind the development of her flock, and the breed choices she has made. Like many fibre farmers she has a mix of purebred and crossbreeds to develop yarn of stunning colour and quality. She purchased a BFL ram from Alex

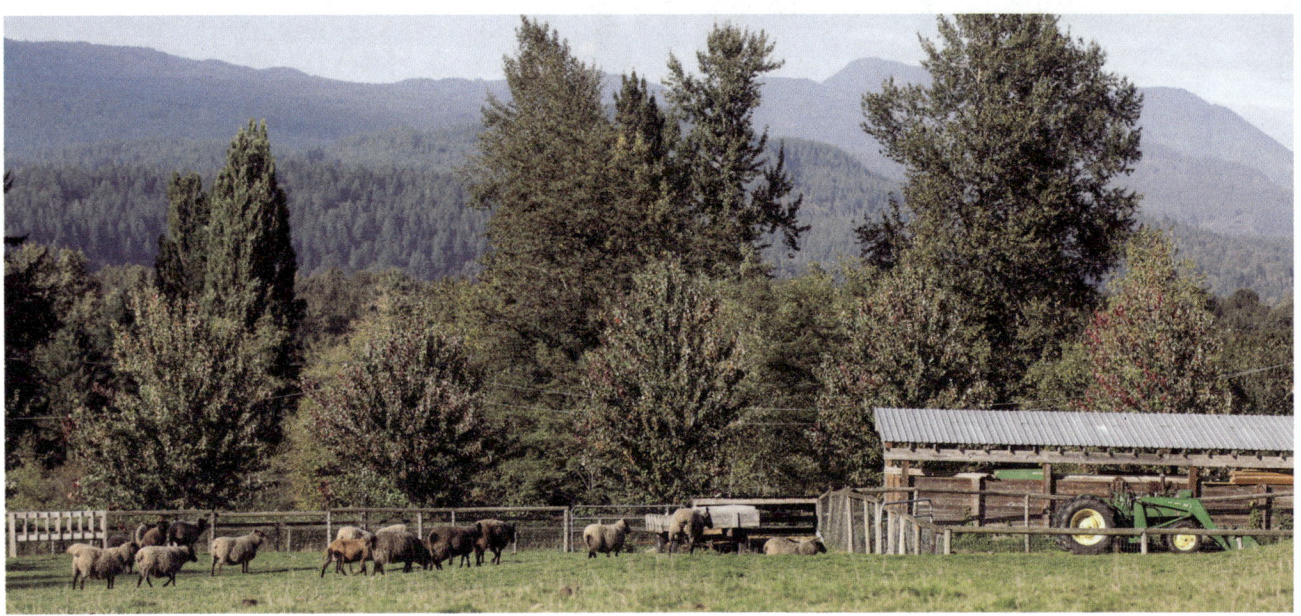

of Rosebud River Fibre Mill (who also processes Beatriz's yarn) and the BFL influence in her flock and yarn is evident.

Bluefaced Leicester wool is the finest of the longwool breeds. It has the durability and lustre typical of longwools, but with next-to-skin softness usually found in some of the finer wools. It is a dependable wool that feels great and is resilient to harder wearing. My favourite use of BFL is in socks, but it is also a great fit for sweaters or mittens and is a fantastic fibre to play around with on your spinning wheel or your loom.

Bluefaced Leicester sheep are very distinctive with their Roman noses and alert ears and, most strikingly, their blue-appearing faces (hence the name). The white hair on their faces exposes the dark skin underneath, making it appear blue. They produce fairly small fleeces, only about 2.5–5 pounds per animal. Their wool grows in beautiful tight curls and can be white, grey, or black.

It makes sense that the first breed in this book is from the English longwool family, as so many of the fibre breeds come from this family. The BFL is relatively new compared to other Leicester breeds. It was developed in the early twentieth century to assist in the production of mules. Mules are a three-way crossbreed to ensure both high-quality grass-fed lamb meat and excellent wool.

The BFL breed was first introduced to North America in 1970 when one ram and three ewes were transported by boat from Scotland to Nova Scotia, with a few other breeds, including Scottish Blackface, Clun Forest, and North Country Cheviot. They were accompanied by veterinarian Dr. L. Brian

Nettleton, who was very passionate about sheep and dedicated to importing quality stock to influence Canadian sheep flocks. The second importation of BFL happened by air travel in 1974 when one ram and ten ewes were shipped from England. The sheep were used by many British expats in the production of mules in Nova Scotia and eventually some of the Nova Scotian BFL were sent to the United States. Canada saw a decline in BFL stock in the mid-1990s and it wasn't until 2007 that the breed became popular once again in Ontario, Alberta, and Nova Scotia. The breed thrives on a variety of land bases and is a very popular choice for both lamb operations and fibre farms.

Beatriz raises some purebred BFLs along with Gotlands, Shetlands and some crosses. She focuses on "single source" processing and marketing of her yarn. This means that every skein of yarn has a specific story behind it. The story is of that sheep's personality and origins, and of the beauty and imperfection of that fibre. "Each sheep is so different," she told me, "I'll leave the 'not perfect' bits of fibre in the yarn. I don't need perfection. It is what it is, and I love them for it."

Every fibre farmer I've met has defined their own goals or values for what breed they raise, how they manage their flock, and how they market their wool. It is such an individual motivation and I feel truly honoured to have witnessed so much care. Beatriz finds joy and contentment in just connecting with her sheep and leaning into the connection she now has with the wool she uses. She feels it on a visceral level every time she comes out in the morning to do chores. "I love it," she told me. "Even if there are gross, cold, rainy days and I think, 'Oh I don't want to do chores today,' as soon as I'm outside and I see my sheep it's just, 'Oh yeah, I love this.'"

After meeting the sheep and fawning over the luscious locks from her most recent shearing, we went into her house and fawned all over the finished yarn. Beatriz, whose attention to detail is exceptional, had put together the most incredible little gift for us: candles, handknit wrist warmers and homemade lip balm. I bought some beautiful grey BFL yarn that I cannot wait to make socks with. We said goodbye and made our way down the driveway just as the sun was setting, but of course we had to stop at the farm stand and buy just one more jar of jam.

Beatriz knitting with wool from her flock.

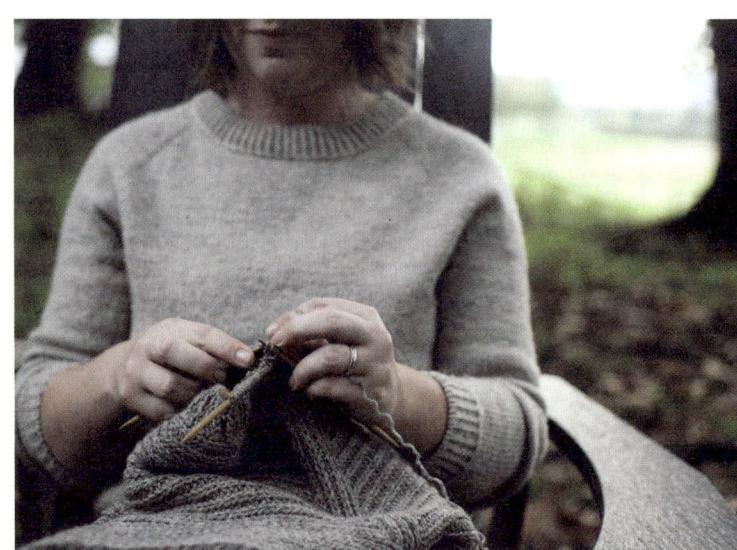

British Columbia
ROMNEY AND DISDERO RANCH

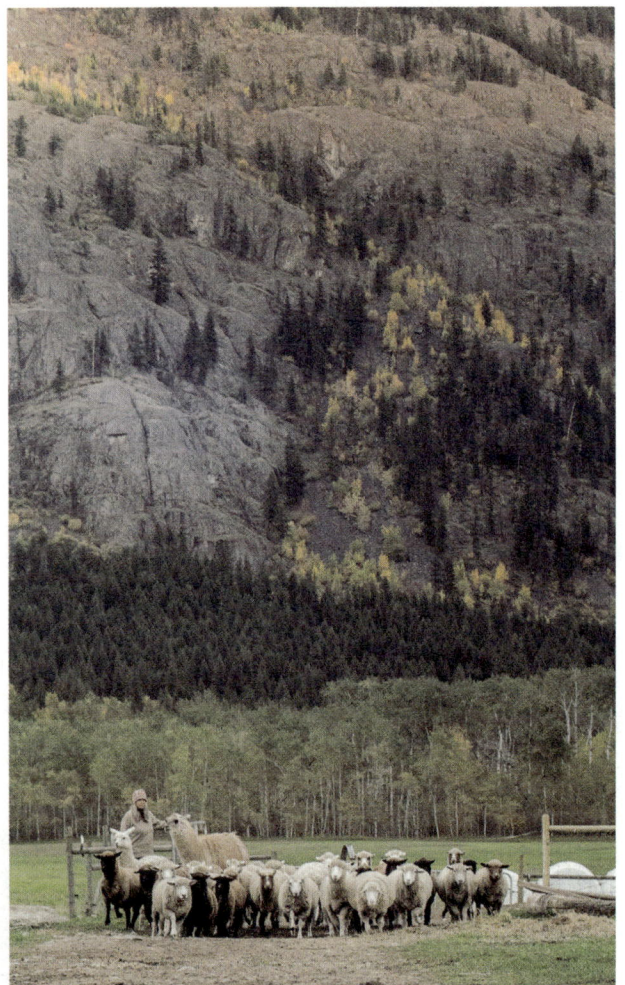
Laurie moving her sheep as the sun sets over the valley.

It was a postcard-worthy sunset over the North Thompson River Valley just north of Kamloops, B.C., though we couldn't fully enjoy this particular golden hour as we were watching precious minutes of ideal photography light literally slip behind the mountains.

I sped up as the winding road straightened out, and I silently cursed the tire problems we'd had earlier in the day. Photo shoots of sheep happen best when there is natural sunlight before the sheep are brought in for the evening, and we were racing the clock to get to Disdero Ranch before our window of light slammed shut.

We drove down the driveway and I threw the car into park at the locked chain-link fence. The chorus of barking from guardian and herding dogs only made our rush feel that much more hectic. We were met at the gate by Laurie Morris, owner and operator of Disdero Ranch, and her fibre friend Mona Fischer. We blurted out the need for photos first and talking later as Laurie walked us to the pasture while calling out directions to working dogs and farm hands.

We opened the gate to her flock of Romney and California Variegated Mutant (CVM) sheep just as the sun hit the mountains on the opposite side of the valley and cast the region in a magical golden glow, almost as though we had planned this beautiful display of light and livestock.

Disdero Ranch is 180 acres on the North Thompson River, a floodplain that rises and falls with the melting of the snow from the mountains surrounding it. The river flows south and is fed by the Thompson Glacier. Even with the drought the region (and indeed, all Western Canada) experienced in the summer of 2021, it was possible to imagine the way this land base would change with the rising river as the snow and ice melt every spring.

"Needing land and wanting land is in my genetics, so I'm just doing it," said Laurie when I asked her how she got started with sheep. Laurie grew up with horses and has always had a love of animals. She attended school in Alberta to become an animal nurse, specializing in horses. Her connection to and love for animals is at the core of why she started her farm in 2011. She originally purchased some Great Pyrenees dogs and realized they needed something to do. So, she volunteered on a sheep farm and it wasn't long before she brought home her first eight bottle lambs (lambs fed with a bottle rather than nursing from their mom) and a ram.

Her first few sheep were Corriedales and then she found a CVM ram. Like many other fibre farmers, it took her a few years to decide on a breed and to determine what she was looking for. She determined that her "...vision was natural coloured wool," a quality that she found in the Romney breed. Disdero Ranch now houses eighty breeding ewes and lambs, Angora goats, and many working dogs.

Romney sheep are undeniably cute. It's perhaps a combination of the long droopy locks framing their face and their full noses, or perhaps it is their friendly demeanour and willingness for a chin scratch.

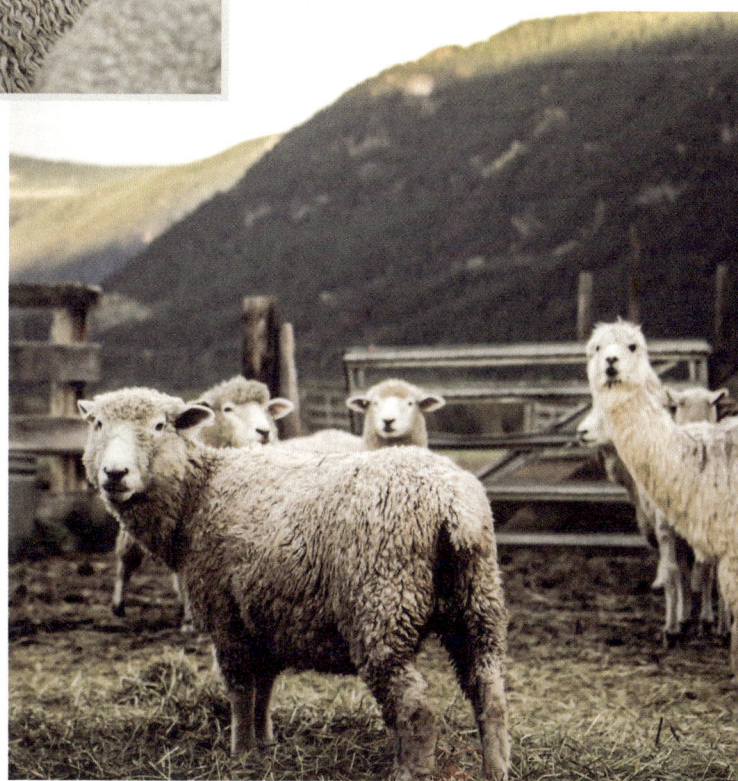

Romney sheep of Disdero Ranch.

West Coast **49**

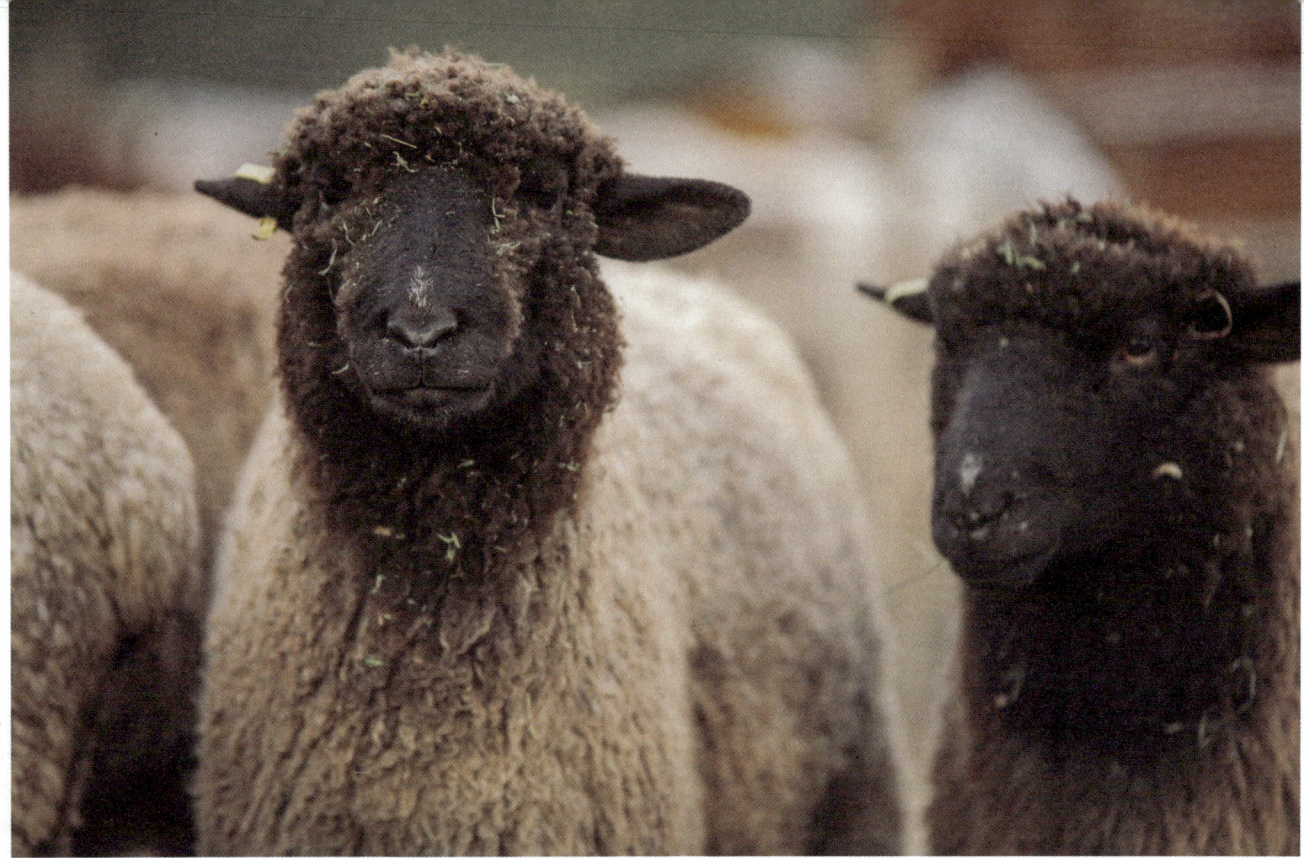
The undeniably cute faces of the Romney breed.

Either way, both their wool and their personalities are a must for any fibre enthusiast.

The Romney sheep originated in the Romney Marsh in England, which has a fascinating history of sheep husbandry and wool smuggling. Drainage ditches, dikes, and sea walls were all used to drain the marsh while maintaining significant soil fertility, and it was an excellent place for grazing sheep. Romneys were popularized in New Zealand and first imported to North America in 1904. Romney sheep are often found on farms in coastal or humid areas, as they are well suited for wet and humid climates. "Romneys are built to last. They are a heritage breed and they've been around for a long time. Their hooves are naturally resistant to foot rot, and they are parasite-resistant," Laurie explained. These features are key to their ability to thrive in a flood plane.

Romney wool is very versatile in terms of how we experience it next to our skin and how we use it. It has strength and durability, and is a great choice for sturdy outerwear, household textiles, mittens, and socks. The fine fleeces are excellent for clothing and the more coarse fleeces are best suited for carpets or furniture coverings. Romney is an excellent fibre for handspinning and can be prepared and spun using many different methods. The natural colours of Romney wool are white, black, silver, grey, and brown. The range of colour, combined with the lustre of the wool, adds a sheen and a depth to clothing and other textiles.

Laurie has her wool processed at Custom Woolen Mills and at Exotic Fibers, both in Alberta, and she markets the yarn at fibre shows and online. Laurie wasn't a fibre artist when she started with sheep; in fact, she didn't have any experience working with wool. She explained, "I've concentrated more on the animals. It's made me more happy, it's made me more peaceful. I love my animals. I get a lot of laughs from them, and it's been a really enriching experience."

Thankfully she found her community and her fibre friends. Many of the fibre farmers I've met have a fibre friend, or a few fibre friends if they are really lucky—someone who perhaps raises sheep themselves, or someone who understands the challenges of raising sheep and working with wool: someone who shows up no matter what. I've been fortunate to have Christel and Nicole, and I often see the strength of our fibre friendship reflected in those of other farmers. This is how I felt when I met Mona Fischer that evening at Laurie's farm. Mona and Laurie met through a local fibre arts guild. Laurie needed someone on her team who knew something about knitting and could help her market this beautiful wool and show her how to use it. They laughed as they shared that Mona has taught Laurie how to knit and that their friendship has grown around wool.

Mona and Laurie took turns telling me the story of a blanket that Mona knitted. She chose a specific fleece on shearing day and brought it home.

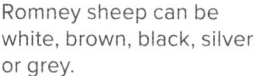

Romney sheep can be white, brown, black, silver, or grey.

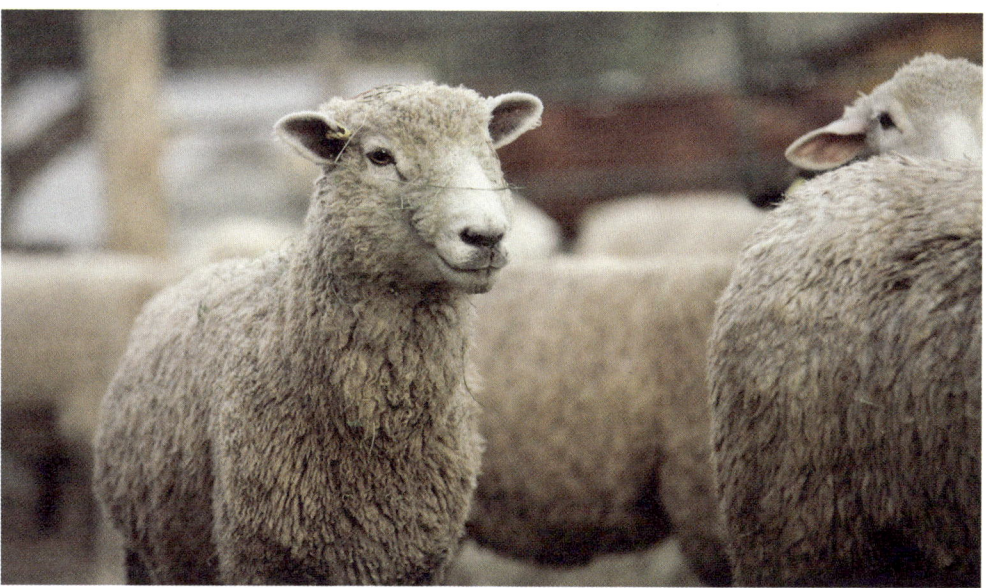

She washed it and carded it and it made her house smell like the sheep it came from. Then she decided to knit a blanket with the wool. As she knit it, it kept her warm when she was cold and cooled her down when she was hot; it changed her experience of working with wool. "When I get Laurie's wool in my hands, all of a sudden it comes alive and I'm having a conversation with it. Rather than this thing that was in my hands and I was manipulating it, now it's working with me." It is clear that Mona believes in the wool that Laurie is raising on her farm and is committed to getting it into the hands of knitters so they can experience the fibre come alive and enjoy a little piece of Disdero Ranch.

Mona and Laurie come as a pair to many of the fibre and yarn shows I've attended. Laurie talks about the sheep, how she raises them, and why they are important, and Mona jumps in with the benefits and beauty of the wool, and what sort of patterns it should be used for. Most folks walk away buying more than they had planned.

As Christel and I hopped in the rental van and navigated our way back to the highway in the dark, I said to her, "They are kind of like us. They have each other to talk about all the sheep stuff, the wool. They probably like to drink cold radlers after a long day of moving fence, too."

Like I said, wool really can bring the best people into our lives.

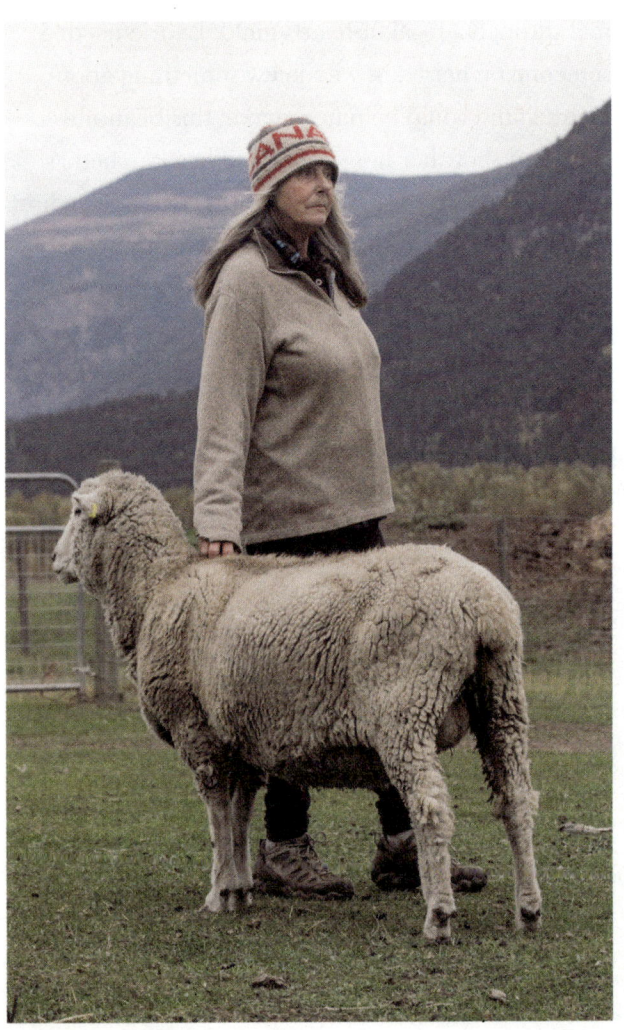

Laurie Morris, shepherd at Disdero Ranch.

British Columbia
NAVAJO CHURRO AND LONE SEQUOIA RANCH

"I just don't understand how you farm sheep with all these hills and mountains." I must've exclaimed twenty-five times in the thirty-five-minute drive up to Lone Sequoia Ranch in Lumby, B.C. I felt like a Prairie girl who had never seen the mountains, which couldn't be farther from the truth since I grew up in Calgary, in the foothills of the Rocky Mountains, and spent every weekend skiing. I also spent a year living in the Swiss Alps, where I learned to knit at the age of eighteen while working as a nanny there. I also lived in Vancouver, surrounded by mountains, for the decade before moving to the flat lands of Manitoba. So, I'm not sure why the mountains were such a big deal for me, other than that I couldn't comprehend how to manage sheep and land on such a slope.

Despite my serious confusion about the extreme landscape of this farm, I could not stop staring at the beautiful backdrop for Leanna Maksymiuk's beautiful flock of Navajo Churro sheep. It was late September in the breathtaking Okanagan Valley, and the leaves were just starting to take on the beautiful red, orange, and yellow glow of fall. The clouds were rolling over the Monashee Mountains and through

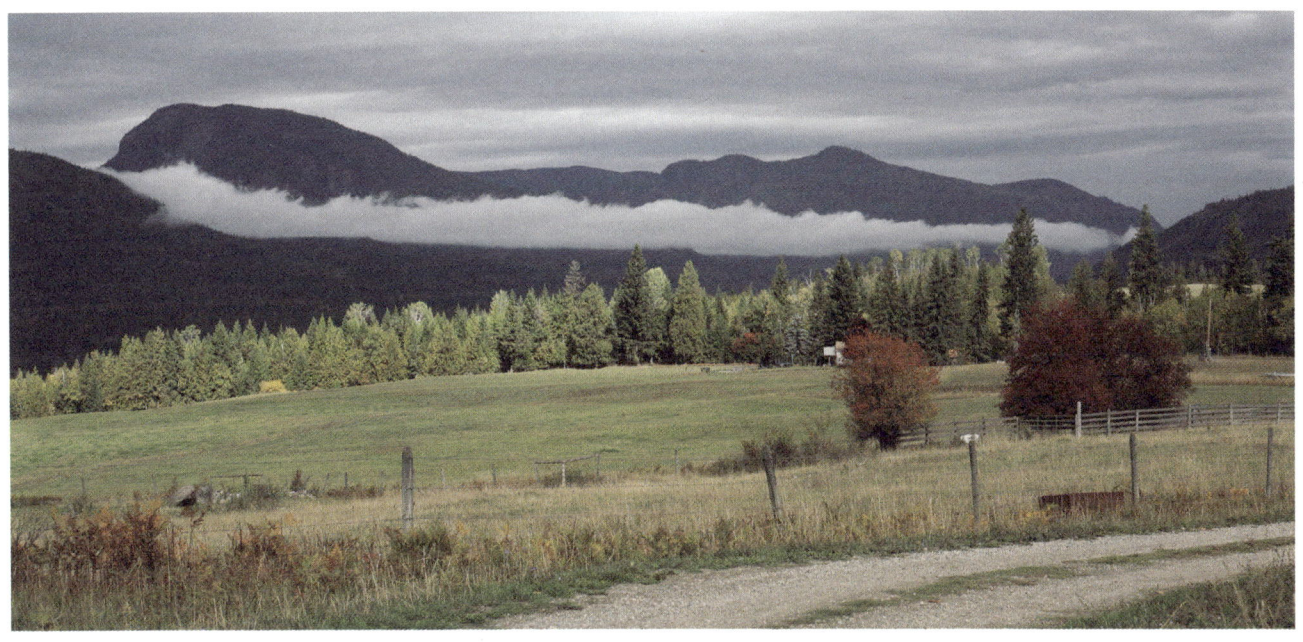

the valley during our visit. A foreshadowing that winter, with its snow and fog, was just around the corner.

I first met Leanna on Instagram (@lonesequoiaranch), the same way I've met so many of the fibre farmers across our country. I really liked her enthusiasm and her innovative approach to working with wool. So, when we headed west, I knew I had to stop at her farm. Leanna and her family moved from Langley, B.C., to the Okanagan in 2017. As a lover of fibre, she initially thought she would get a few alpacas and use their fibre for her own practice. It wasn't until her daughter Poppy started a 4-H project with sheep that she considered actually raising sheep for fibre. Poppy raised one sheep that first year and Leanna purchased some companion sheep for the project. It snowballed from there.

Leanna spent a year researching different sheep breeds and trying to figure out what would work best for their land base and her fibre aspirations. In the spring of 2020, she brought home her first Navajo Churro sheep, purchased from a breeder in Alberta.

The Navajo Churro breed is considered "critical" according to the Livestock Conservancy organization in the U.S. This critical status means

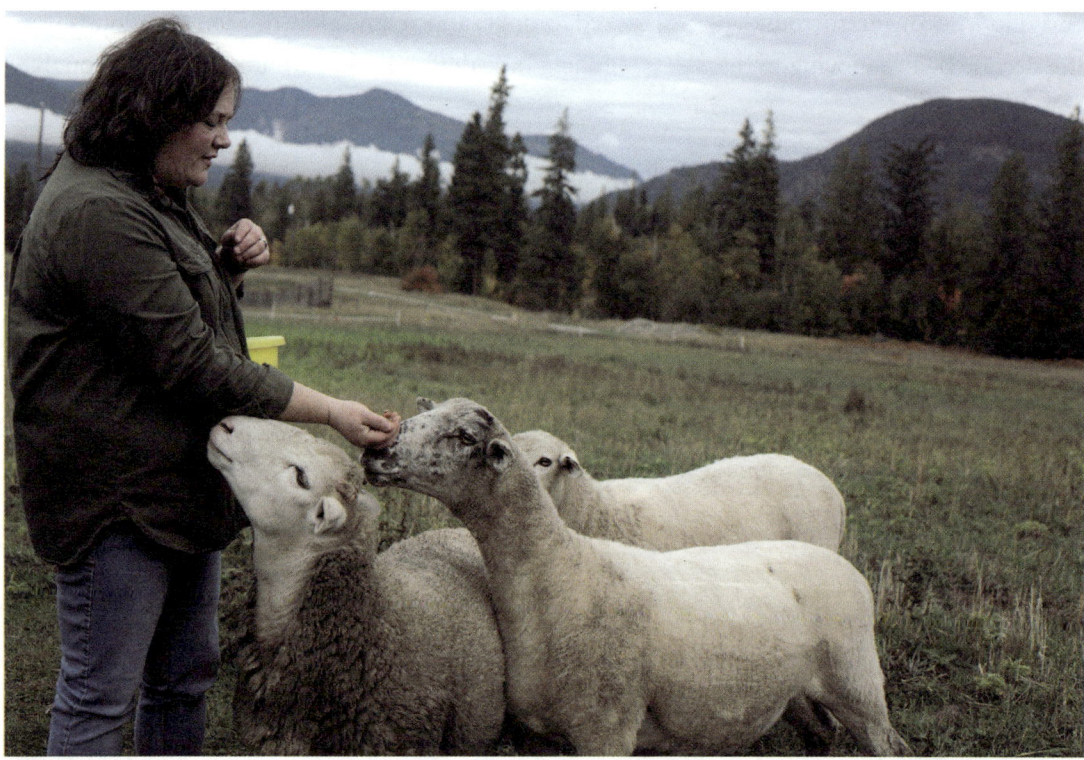

Leanna Maksymiuk of Lone Sequoia Ranch, with some of her flock.

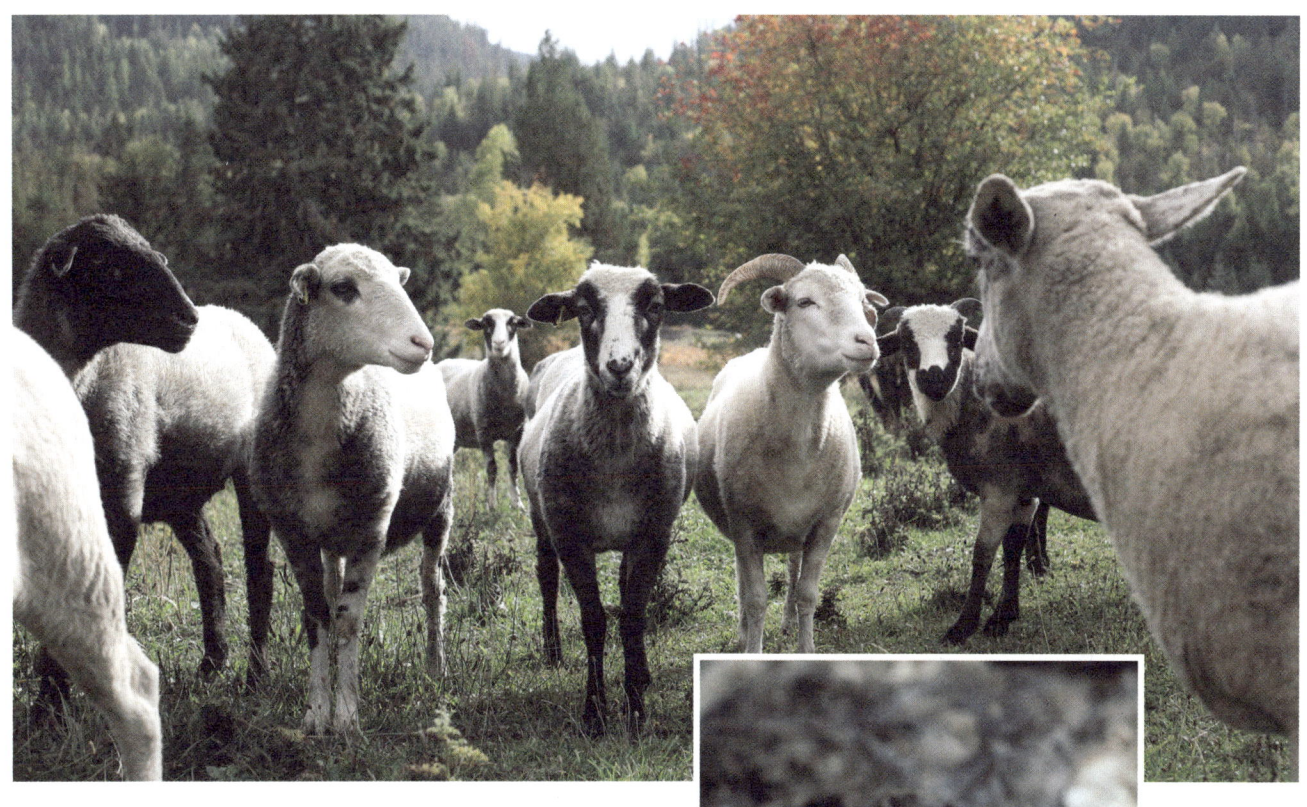

the breed is at risk of extinction and should be considered a priority for conservation.

Leanna stewards 160 acres of mixed forest and pastureland through which they rotationally graze their flock of thirty-five Navajo Churro sheep during the hot, dry spring and summer. The climate in which these sheep thrive is an important part of their connection to land and provides the starting point for their story.

The history of the Navajo Churro breed is not specific to our land base in Canada, although there are a handful of farms in Western Canada, including Leanna's, working to protect this species

Leanna showing the staple length of the Navajo Churro wool.

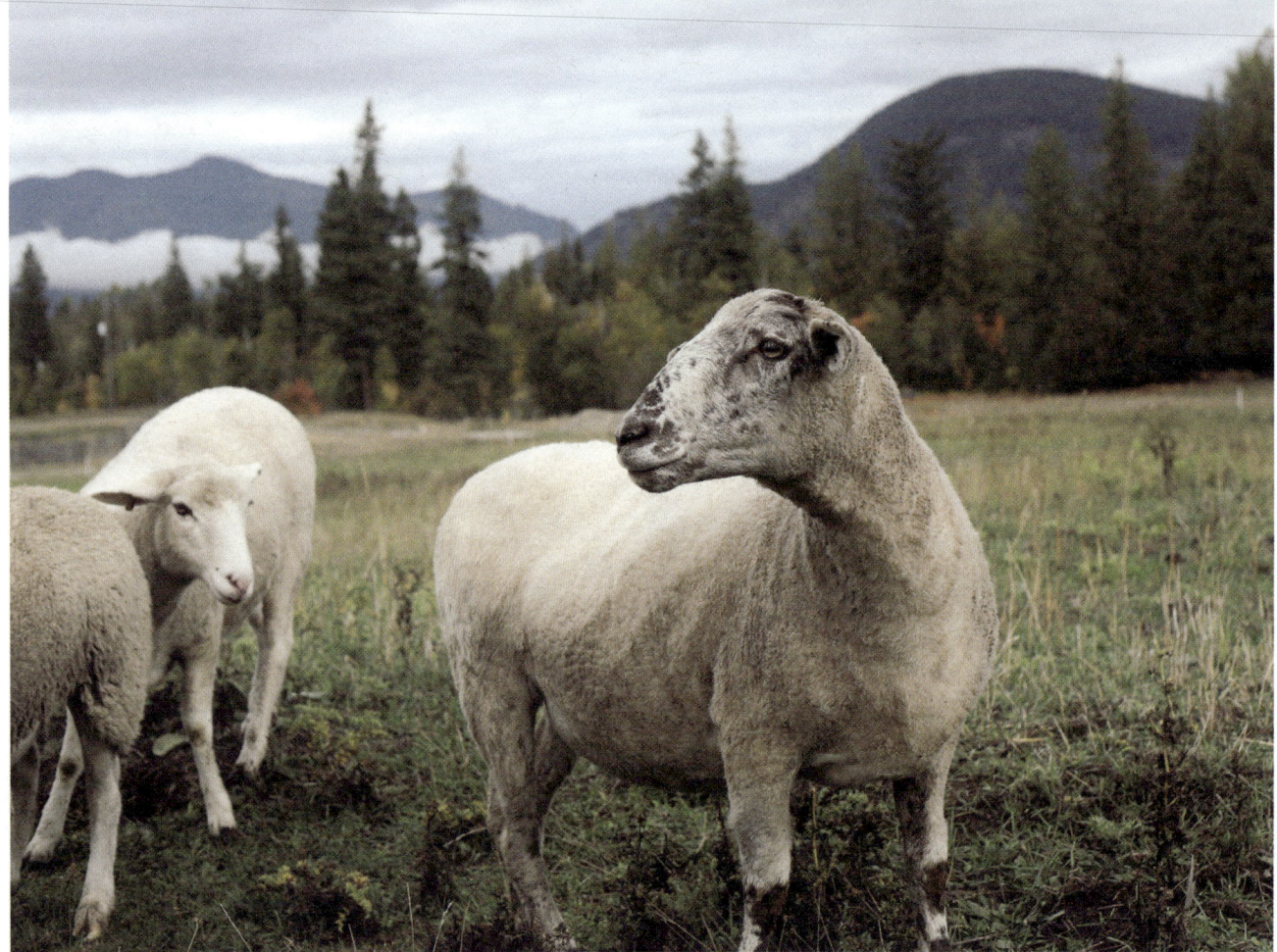

Navajo Churro ewe at Lone Sequoia Ranch.

of sheep. The story is enmeshed with the history of colonization and assimilation of the Indigenous Peoples of the U.S. and the myriad ways that colonizers worked to control and limit their farming and economic opportunities.

Spanish settlers first brought the Churro sheep to the southwestern part of what is now the U.S. in the sixteenth century. The sheep were used to feed and clothe the conquistadors and Spanish settlers. During the seventeenth century the Churros were an important part of Spanish ranches and villages along the upper Rio Grande Valley. This is when Indigenous communities first acquired the sheep for food and fibre. Within a century they had developed a distinct form of weaving the wool into cloth and it became a major economic activity for the Diné. As more European settlers arrived in North America, they brought with them the use of and demand for finer textiles, and the Churro was cross-bred with Merino and other English longwool breeds. During this time some of the original Churro breed were isolated within the Diné (Navajo) communities and they became recognized as the breed standard which is now referred to as Navajo Churro, acknowledging both the Spanish and Navajo influence in the management of the breed.

Navajo Churro sheep are considered a heritage breed, meaning they have not been "improved" or cross-bred to accentuate certain characteristics. This makes the breed extremely hardy and resilient to harsh weather (both extreme heat and harsh cold) and they can thrive on sparse grassland or forage. They have a long outer coat of coarse fibre and a very soft downy undercoat. Most often these two are spun together to create a luxurious, strong yarn that is perfect for weaving and is resilient to repeated wear. The Navajo Churro have twenty-three different colour variations within the breed, making the use of their wool desirable in coloured patterns such as weaving blankets or tapestries. Navajo blankets were prominent in the spiritual traditions of the Diné.

Unfortunately, the Churro breed and the Diné communities that cared for them were repeatedly targeted by the U.S. government as part of its ongoing colonization and assimilation programs. In the late 1800s, many Diné resisted European settlement on their homelands. In response, the government ordered a massive military action to destroy their economic opportunities by killing their livestock and destroying their orchards. Thousands of Navajo Churro sheep were slaughtered and over 9,000 Diné were forced to walk 300 miles to an internment camp in New Mexico. During this time, some small flocks and shepherds were able to escape and hide in the remote canyons of New Mexico and Arizona. Three years later the Diné returned to the land and were each issued two sheep to begin growing their flocks again. Then, in the 1930s the government launched a livestock reduction campaign in an attempt to curb the effects of the dust bowl and the assumed erosion and deterioration of the land. They again slaughtered hundreds of thousands of Navajo Churro sheep and decimated the flocks and businesses of many Diné. Many never recovered all that was lost during this horrific assault.

The breed was maintained at critically low numbers by some farmers in the Navajo Nation until 1977, when a researcher named Dr. Lyle McNeal began the Navajo Sheep Project to protect and revive the breed. He and his team worked with

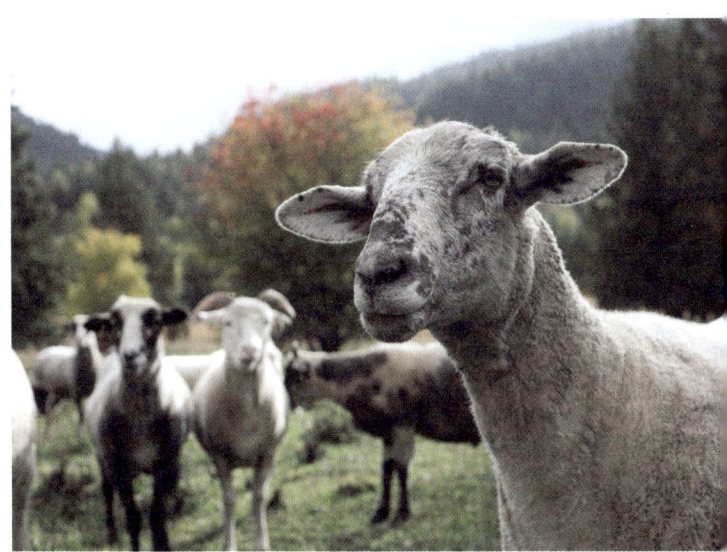

Navajo farmers to purchase single sheep and then return a breeding pair to the ranchers that wanted to participate. This program was successful in reviving the breed, and in 1986 the Navajo-Churro Sheep Association (N-CSA) was formed.

There are now over 4,500 sheep registered with the association in the U.S., 1,500 registered on Navajo reservations, and hundreds of undocumented sheep throughout Canada, the U.S., and Mexico. There are also individual farms and organizations, such as the Rainbow Fiber Co-Op, that are Diné led businesses and farms working to revive not only the ancestral flocks of the Navajo Nation, but to reinvigorate Navajo weaving and fibre businesses using the Navajo Churro wool.

Leanna was drawn to the Navajo Churro breed for its resilience in hot and dry environments like those of the Okanagan. But she was also committed to preserving a breed that is still listed as critical by conservation organizations such as Rare Breeds Canada. She recognizes that as a non-Indigenous person she can never fully understand the historical and cultural significance of the breed and its history to the Diné. She does believe that she can contribute to reviving the breed by raising the sheep, building awareness about their wool and its uses, and promoting Diné organizations and farmers who sell the wool and yarn.

In addition to raising Navajo Churro sheep and processing their wool, Leanna has started an

Rainbow Fiber Co-Op

There have been many projects and individuals that have worked to preserve the Navajo Churro breed against extinction in North America. The Rainbow Fiber Co-Op was formed in 2020 as a Diné-led agricultural co-operative. They work alongside Diné shepherds to purchase and manufacture Navajo Churro wool and provide marketing and a website to sell value-added wool products including weaving yarns.

The proceeds from the sale of wool and yarn are funnelled back into the co-op to support the purchase of more wool from shepherds the next year. As of 2022, they had worked with thirty-two farms to pay equitable prices for the wool and to promote the value of Navajo Churro wool products.

For more information or to find Navajo Churro wool and support the co-op, check them out at rainbowfibercoop.org.

incredibly innovative project in the Okanagan region called Waste Not Wool. In response to so many meat farmers discarding their wool due to the dismally low prices of wool nationally, she began collecting this wool, sorting through it, having it processed at Custom Woolen Mills, and selling it as roving and yarn. "I'm taking this wool out of the waste stream and selling it to consumers who are looking for local wool. I don't have enough room to keep more sheep at the moment, but at least I can keep wool out of the landfill and get it into the hands of people who want it."

As Leanna walked me back to the car, I asked her what was behind the name of her farm, Lone Sequoia Ranch. She told me that it was her husband's favourite type of tree. They had one planted in their yard in Langley as a wedding gift, but when they moved to the farm, they had to leave the tree behind, so Leanna bought him a single sequoia tree. She pointed it out to me at the entrance to the yard. In some way, that sequoia tree felt emblematic of all that Leanna is doing with her farm and fibre aspirations. Sequoias are one of the largest tree species on Earth. They require fire, stress, or disturbance to regenerate and create new life. Leanna's Waste Not Wool project is helping to revitalize the Canadian wool industry and create new markets for Canadian wool. 》

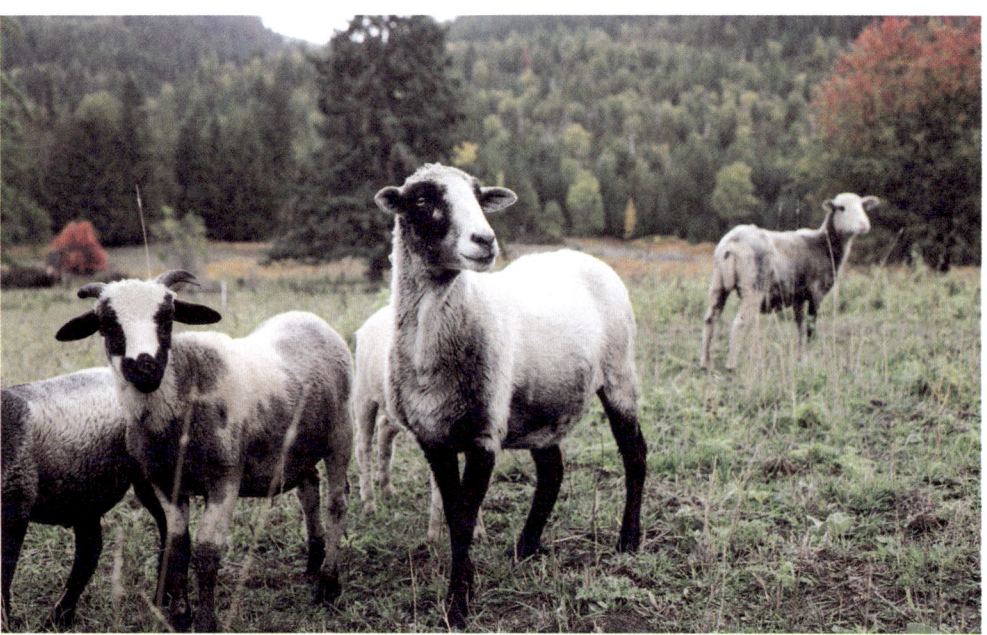

Navajo Churro sheep and the changing fall foliage at Lone Sequoia Ranch.

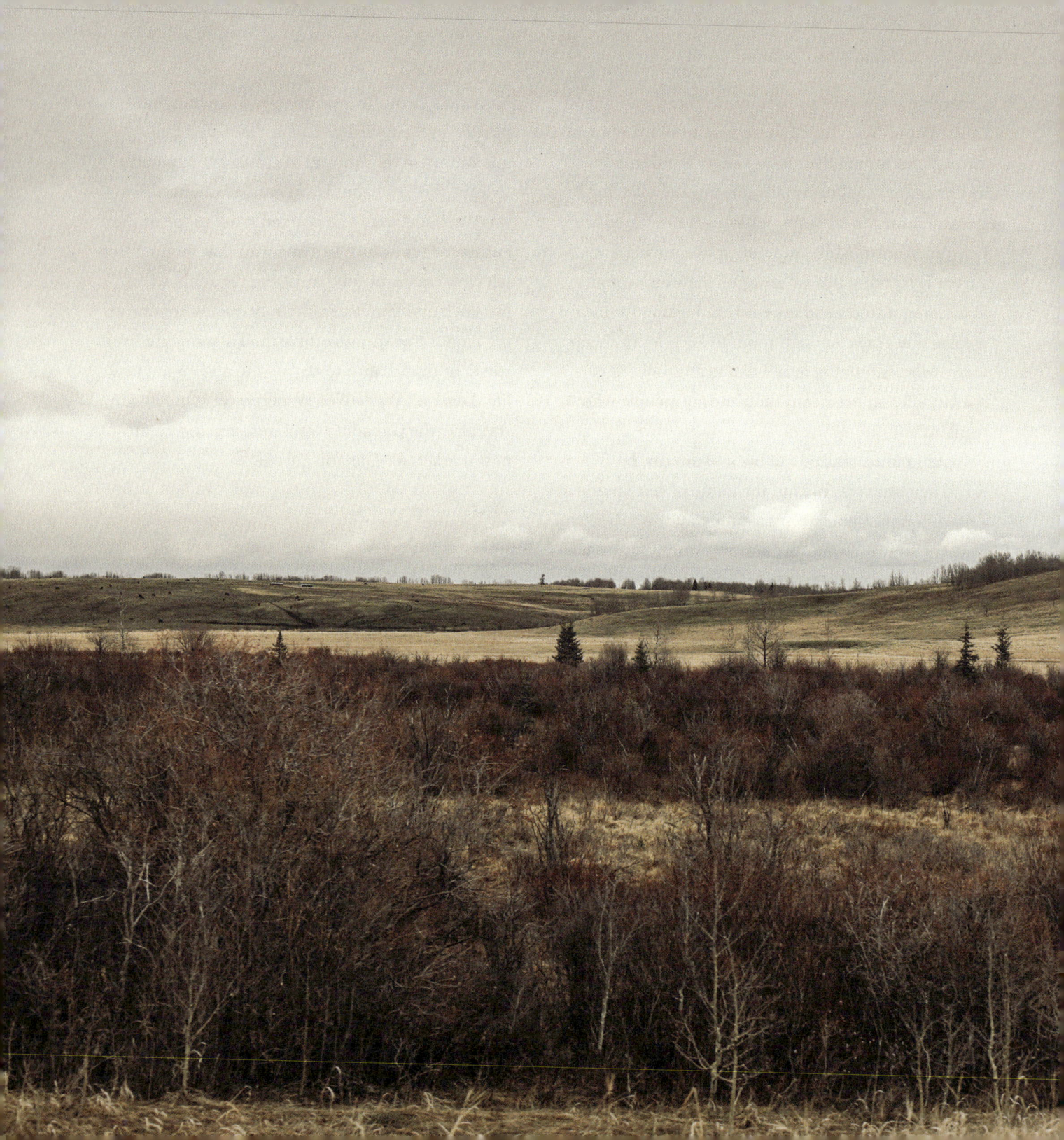

The Prairies

As a child, I spent much of each summer visiting the grain farm where my dad grew up, in Shaunavon, Saskatchewan. I would ride on the seeder or the combine with my dad or uncle for hours on end. I can still recall the smell of that combine, the feeling of dirt in my mouth, and the refreshing taste of cold iced tea from a Thermos. We picked rocks in the spring and we hid in the tall wheat fields in the late summer. It shaped my early understanding of agriculture.

I never imagined that I would farm later in life, and I certainly didn't picture farming as happening on vast ranges with grazing sheep. Meeting sheep farmers across the Prairies and hearing their stories of land management and shepherding has given me a new understanding of what agriculture is. Canada's grassland and prairie ecosystems provide the right conditions for raising fine wool breeds. Many of the fine wool breeds can resist cold, heat, drought, and sparse forages, and produce excellent quality wool. Some of these breeds are Rambouillet, Targhee, Corriedale, and Polypay.

The Prairie provinces are some of the fastest growing sheep-producing regions in Canada for both meat and wool. There is great opportunity to produce more fine wools on the Prairies and to manage those flocks in a way that can restore health and diversity to ecosystems that have become defined by monoculture crop farming.

In this chapter, we'll meet Tara Klager, who, with her flock of Border Leicesters, has provided a different narrative on what land management can be and how important livestock can be to restoring native grasslands; Arlette Seib, who has taken an ecosystem health and diversity approach with her flock of Corriedales; and Christel Lanthier, who shares her perspective on using and respecting the entire animal, and the numerous benefits of diversifying farming operations.

These farmers, with their unique approaches to land and animal management, are forging new paths for Canadian sheep farmers.

Prairie landscape.

Alberta
BORDER LEICESTER AND PROVIDENCE LANE HOMESTEAD

Tara Klager is passionate about wool, sheep, soil health and animal welfare. Whenever I visit Tara, I barely have time to stir the honey into my tea before we are both fired up, talking about the challenges facing the wool industry and small-scale sheep farmers in Canada. I find her "don't take shit" attitude and unwavering commitment totally inspiring, and I knew she had to be a part of this book. Despite knowing Tara for a few years and visiting her farm and sheep before, I really didn't know that much about her story.

Tara grew up in the town of Ayr, in southwestern Ontario, on a small farm owned by her grandparents but run collectively by her parents, aunts, and uncles, with a spirit of cooperation. They grew their own beef and had a large market garden that produced enough food to feed their family and many people in their community. Tara's grandfather was a big part of the Co-operative Commonwealth Federation (CCF), a Depression-era progressive political party, and his attitude towards workers' rights and community shaped her formative years and her understanding of community. Tara remembers going to her grandpa's farm and finding it filled with people harvesting veggies to supplement their strike-pay wages. This sense of community, place, and sustenance was a normal part of her life that she has been trying to re-create ever since.

It took a little while for her to arrive back on the land. She went to university in Ontario, took some time to travel in Europe, and then finished her journalism diploma at a college in Kitchener, Ontario. Then she met and married Bob and they moved all over Canada as they started their family. But that sense of place and community back on the farm stayed with her.

"It was bucolic," she told me. "It was perfect. It was idealistic and romantic, because I was just a

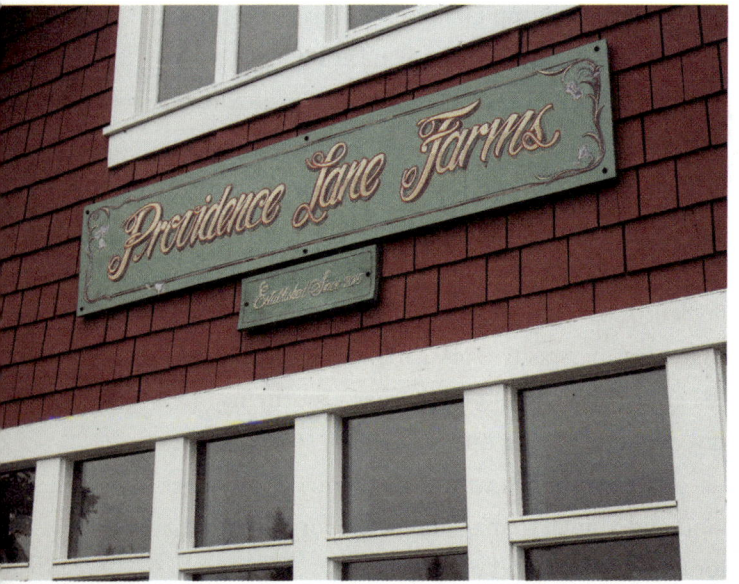

The sign welcoming visitors to Providence Lane Homestead, Alberta.

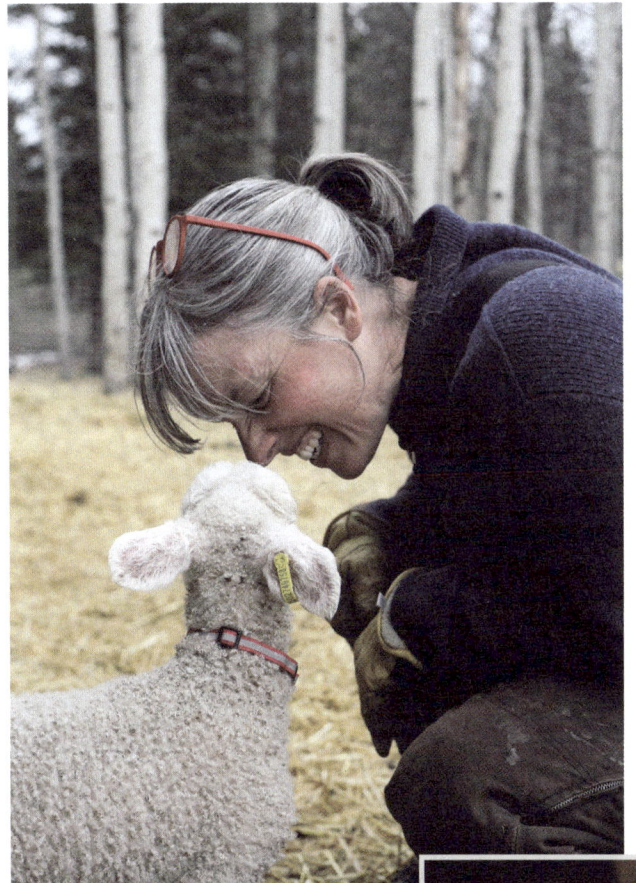

Tara Klager enjoying a moment with a bottle lamb named Juniper.

kid, but it was awesome. I've always loved that it was a place that people could come to, they could hide in, where their needs would be met, whether that was for food or companionship and community, or whatever it was. Grandma and Grandpa had a firm belief in community and the ideals of the CCF and the Regina Manifesto [its founding policy statement]. I saw that all lived out and I've been looking for ways to recreate that in a modern context. So that's how we ended up here."

In 2010, they moved to Calgary with their two boys, and they were happy. Then, one day in 2015, Bob brought home a magazine from the airport lounge with a real estate listing in the back for a pretty little green prairie farmhouse. The house was "so cute," and it was located in Cochrane, about a half-hour northwest of Calgary, where Tara boarded a horse. They decided to go take a look. Two weeks later they owned that cute little prairie farmhouse.

Raising sheep wasn't the goal when Tara founded Providence Lane Homestead, their farm in Rocky View County, Alberta, aptly named for its breathtaking view of the Rocky Mountains. Her principal goal for the forty-acre farm was to restore the land to its original state of tall grass

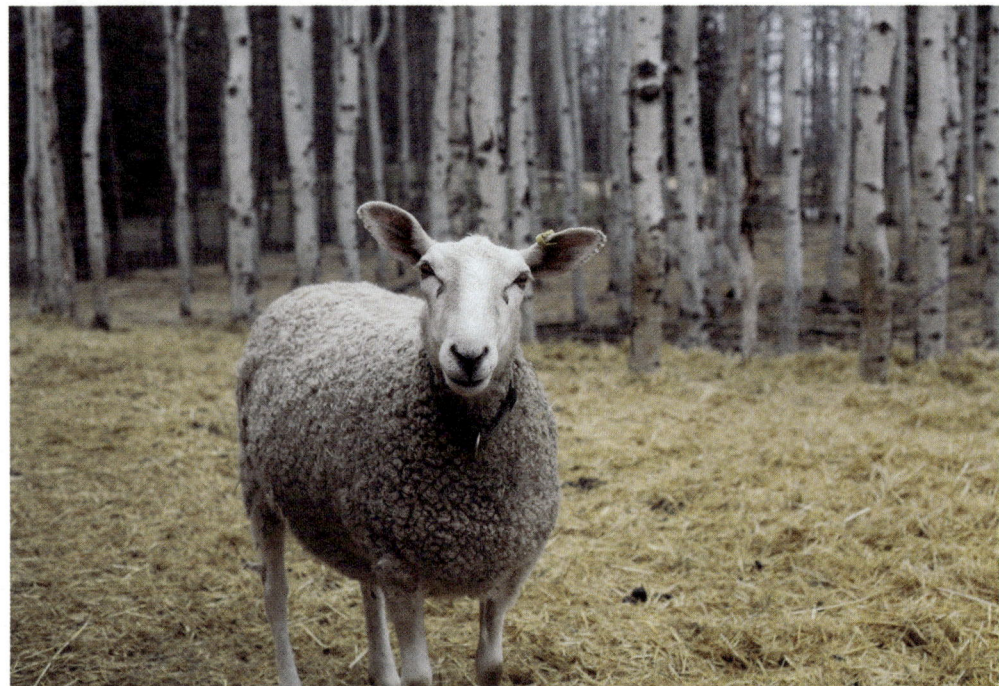

Border Leicester sheep at Providence Lane Homestead.

fescue prairie. "The most endangered ecosystem in our world is the tall grass fescue prairie, and it's in Canada, and we've lost seventy-five percent of it." Tall fescue is a cold-, heat- and drought-resistant forage grass. Restoring the prairie is not an easy task, as the tame grasses that have become prolific across the region will out-compete the fescue. "If you look at the root system of the fescues it'll be four to six feet compared to maybe one foot to sixteen inches for Timothy or other tame grasses. The implications for a dry land ecosystem: obviously, the fescue is far more desirable. The natural actors historically on that land would be bison. I can't have bison, so who can I have instead? Sheep is what I wanted."

Tara sought out the advice and mentorship of a fellow sheep farmer in Alberta, Nicole Schieck, and decided on a starter flock of Border Leicesters and Cotswold sheep. Border Leicesters are easy on the land if they are well managed, and they are excellent foragers. They will thrive on marginal feed, and they are indiscriminate about what forages they will eat. Tara explained that this is a beneficial trait when you are trying to stimulate a return to the native flora of a region.

The Border Leicester breed was developed in 1767 by two Scottish brothers, George and Matthew Cully. They had some Dishley rams from Robert Bakewell (a revolutionary figure who altered the

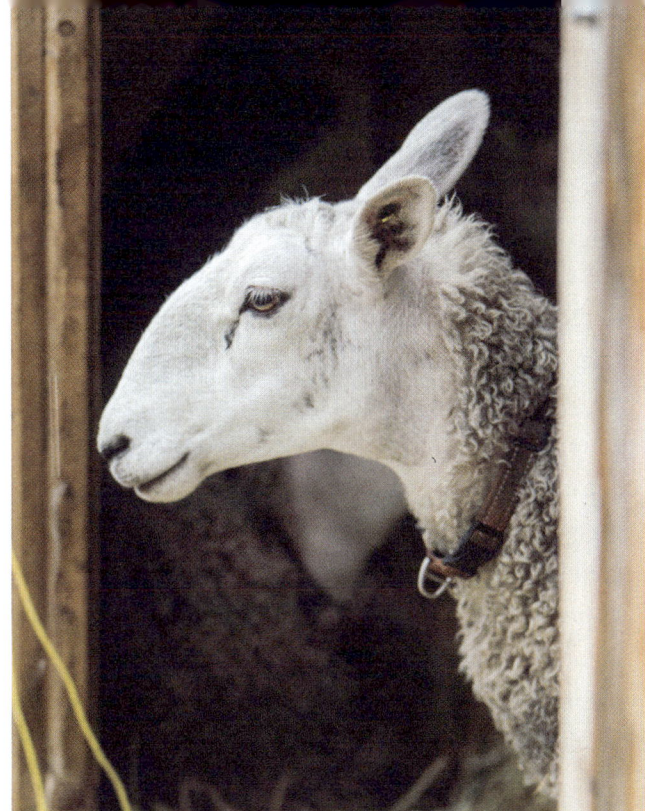 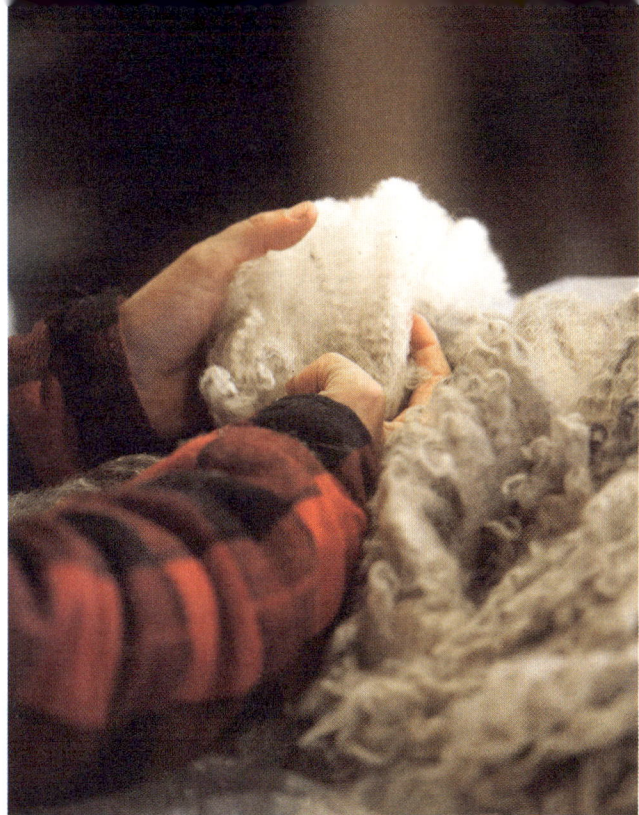

way farmers breed cattle and sheep) and cross-bred them with either Teeswater or Cheviot ewes (no one is really certain which). The Leicester line is present in many of our modern breeds today. They are an excellent all-purpose breed and produce excellent quality wool, good carcass size (an industry term that I know may sound harsh for those who don't like to think of sheep as food), and are known for making use of rough landscape—like the Northumberland County landscape in Northern England where they were developed.

Border Leicesters are a dignified-looking sheep. They have a Roman nose and long, upright ears that give the impression that they are ready for anything, yet their personalities are docile and gentle. The fleece weighs about eight to twelve pounds with a long staple length of about six to ten inches, and radiant lustre. The wool has a micron range of 30–38.5, is tightly curled and incredibly hard-wearing. The breed is exclusively white. Handspinners enjoy working with Border Leicester wool for its easy handle. If you get a finer fleece, it can certainly be excellent for sweaters or socks, and other hard-wearing items.

There is no documented date of arrival for Border Leicesters in Canada, but it is generally accepted that they were imported from England in the mid-nineteenth century. The Border Leicester was one of the principal breeds used during the early days of sheep agriculture in Canada and was certainly utilized during settler migration across the Prairies. Settlers could rely on the Border Leicester breed because it provided clothing and food and was resilient in the sometimes-harsh environments that they experienced. The breed became less important as emphasis shifted to faster carcass growth and the industry shifted its focus from heritage breeds to the improved breeds.

I spoke with Tara about how she markets her wool and what her customers are looking for, though "spoke" is perhaps an understatement. Tara and I both enjoy the soap boxes we climb on when it comes to wool, and there is more than enough room for both of us up there! "There is so much space taken up in Canada by imported wool and yarns," she explained. "I would love it if more Canadians understood the incredible capacity of OUR animals to thrive in OUR environment and to make things that suit OUR homes and lives." Tara has focused on being transparent and authentic, and on building community with the customers that purchase her fibre. She has created a place that people are welcome to visit and meet the sheep and witness her land goals, but she also wanted accountability and something with teeth in it that would hold her to the highest standards of animal husbandry practices. Then she discovered the organization A Greener World and their animal welfare certification.

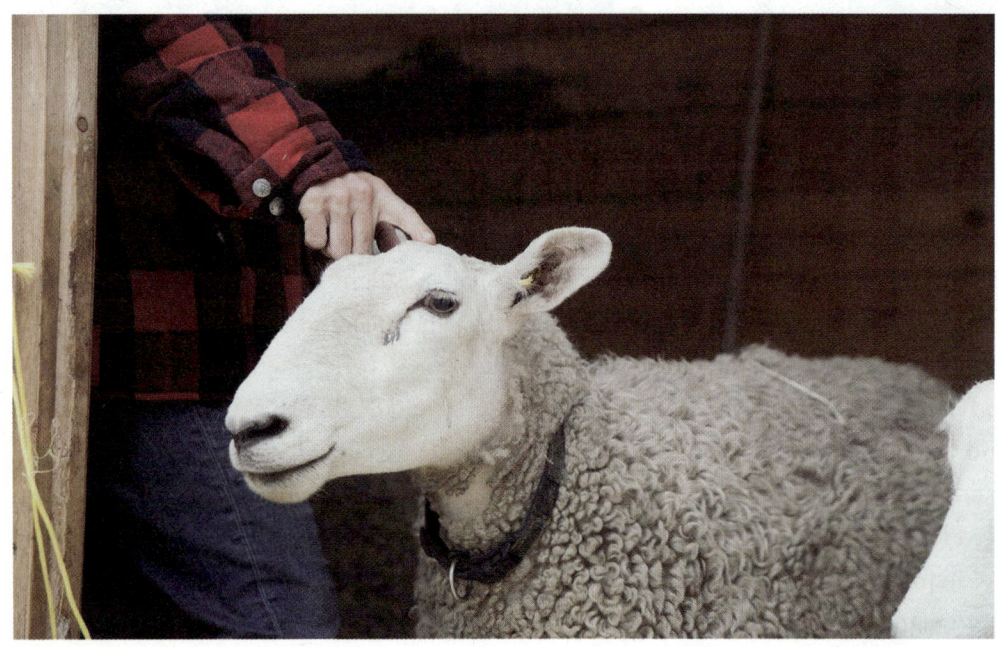

Tara filled out a fifty-page application, explaining every aspect of her sheep management protocols from what sort of water her sheep access, to shearing, hoof trimming, vaccinations, and even what quality of forages they eat. After she submitted the application, her farm was subjected to an in-person audit, and after some further questions and discussions she became animal-welfare approved. Being approved and having a clear starting point for transparency and accountability has been crucial for Tara, and she believes it also matters to customers. "Wool becomes more meaningful to people when it's not just a nameless commodity," she explained to me.

Tara wants to continue her work of land regeneration, animal welfare, community-building and wool production. She is working towards growing resilience on the land, which is both a challenge and a necessity after the last few years of drought and flooding. She is building a community of people who will come and go from the farm and work with both land and animals to understand all our places in this big system. And finally, she wants to see wool move beyond just craft, to contribute to a diverse, fibre-based economy.

Tara and I continued to talk about the wool industry: our hopes and frustrations—and strategy too. I always appreciate Tara's strategic approach to creating social change. She is a big-systems thinker, and if you want to know who the movers and shakers of the sheep and wool industry in the Prairies are, she is one of them.

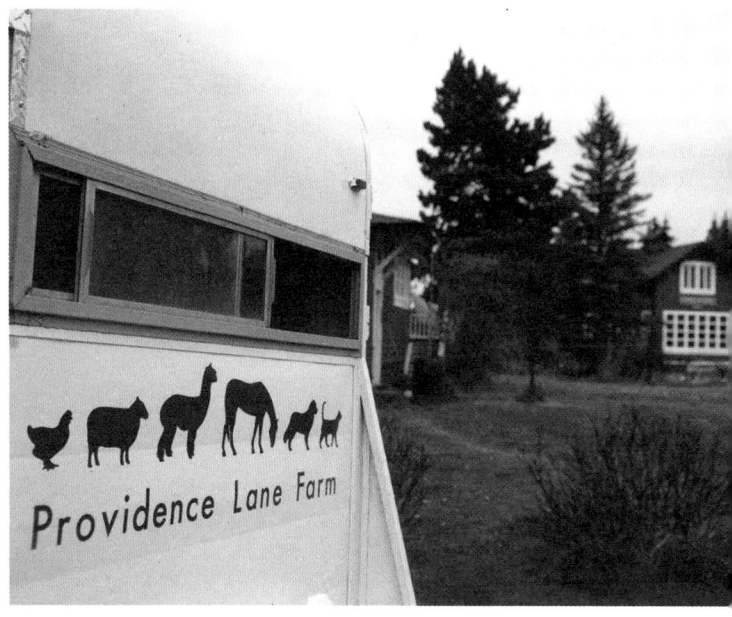

It was getting late, and I needed to get going (well, actually, I was hoping to finally see a glimpse of the mountains before the sun set). Every time I've been to Tara's farm it has been a rainy day and the mountains were obscured by cloud or fog. I pulled out of her yard and drove west towards the Rocky Mountains, up and down the rolling hills. I couldn't seem to escape the thick spring fog in the air and I never did get to see the mountains—maybe on the next visit. But I could imagine tall grass fescue prairies and roaming bison, and I was filled with hope and gratitude for the work of sheep farmers like Tara.

Saskatchewan
CORRIEDALE AND DOG TALE RANCH

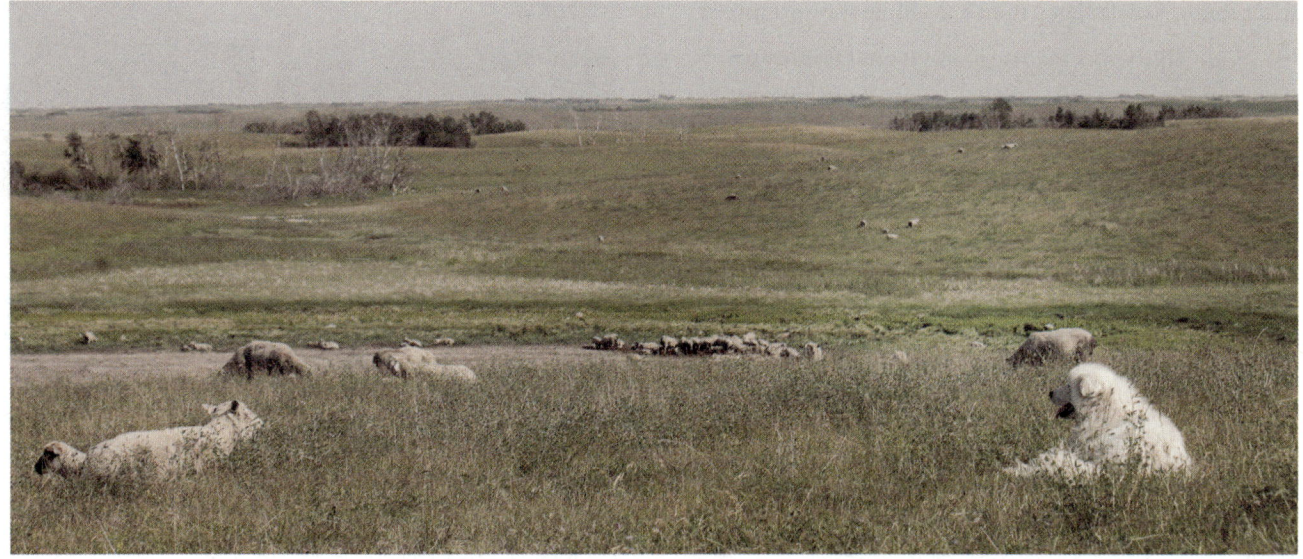

Livestock guardian dog watches over the large flock of Corriedale sheep at Dog Tale Ranch, Saskatchewan.

We visited Arlette Seib's farm in Watrous, Saskatchewan, on a sweltering July day. Everything about the landscape and the lonely single-lane highway screamed Saskatchewan prairie land. There were miles of wheat, barley, and canola fields under a sky that never seemed to end. The directions to her farm were, like most rural navigation, endearing and obscure: "At the Co-op Agro Centre, turn west and cross the railroad tracks. Immediately turn north and follow the curve back to the west again. Travel this grid road for twenty-four kilometres until you reach a *Yield* sign…" It reminded me of how fancy phones and built-in car GPS systems don't hold a candle to the internal compass that I've forgotten how to use.

When we finally pulled into Arlette's mile-long driveway, it was an obvious departure from the monoculture crop farmland that had been the backdrop for the rest of our road trip. This is a farm that has been cared for and stewarded with a passion for species diversity and animal and ecological health. Arlette started the tour of her farm with a walk to a stunning view at the top of a rolling hill that she uses for fall grazing. It was breathtaking. Vibrant and full of life, the collective hum of insects could be heard over the incessant chattering of birds. The field was a fragrant mix of clover, alfalfa, fescue,

Canadian thistle, and other grasses. The way Arlette spoke about the land made it clear that she genuinely cares about every species that calls it home.

The land didn't always look this wild. Arlette told the story of how, when she and her spouse, Allen, moved onto this 1600-acre conventional grain farm seventeen years earlier, it was a struggle to make the farm work. Arlette recalled of those first few years. "It's hard to believe that we were doing this for mother nature, 'cause it [conventional farming] was continually ripping into the soil; it was continually applying chemicals; it was continually taking something off the land, and we were struggling with 'does this even work?'"

They finally decided they weren't going to do it anymore. They turned the farm back to grassland and sold all the expensive farming equipment that was keeping them beholden to the banks. They developed a new plan and began working with Ducks Unlimited to develop conservation easements and restore the grassland to a diversified habitat for plants and animals.

Arlette didn't initially envision sheep as a way to restore health to this grassland; the sheep arrived with a different purpose. Arlette had a border collie that she loved working with and decided to get a few sheep for the dog to work. She built a "rickety little fence" around the yard and bought five sheep. Her flock grew from there.

The farm now has 380 breeding ewes, predominantly Corriedale and some Clun Forest. Corriedale sheep may seem, from afar, like any

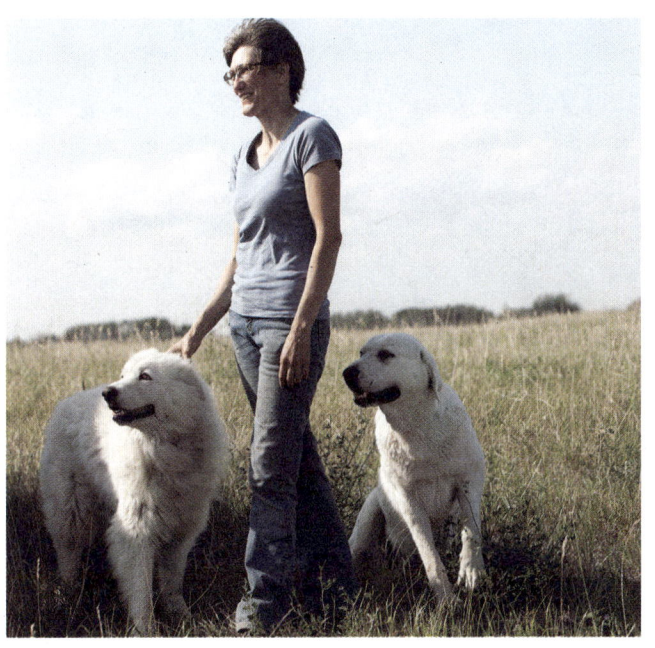

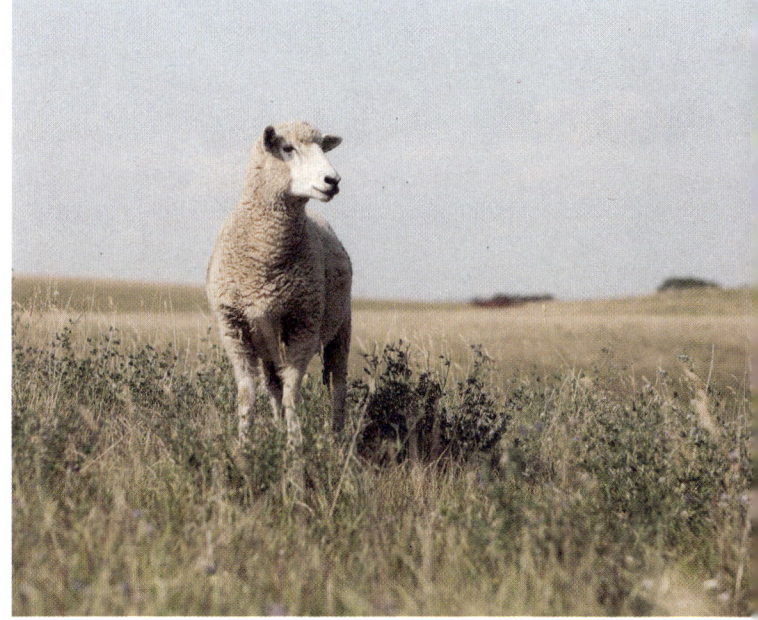

The Prairies 69

other flock grazing the vast ranges in the Canadian Prairies, but seen up close, their notable "top knot" fleece and gentle eyes set them apart from other fine wool breeds.

The Corriedale breed was developed in New Zealand in the 1880s as a dual-purpose breed. They were developed by breeding Merinos with Lincoln Longwool sheep. The goal was to develop a hardy animal that thrives in a range of conditions and provides excellent meat and wool. Corriedale sheep are a prominent breed in South America and can also be found in Australia, New Zealand, South Africa, Canada, and the U.S.

As we stopped and watched the ewes happily graze clover and alfalfa while their lambs ran or napped and occasionally called for their moms, Arlette explained that what makes her Corriedale sheep different from other breeds is their natural flocking inclination. Flocking is a survival instinct that tells animals they better stay together, or they will be in trouble. Arlette and her dogs move the sheep through the large eighty-acre grazing paddocks from May until October, and, like most true range breeds, the sheep thrive with minimal intervention.

As the name implies, range sheep are best suited for vast open ranges where they can spread out and

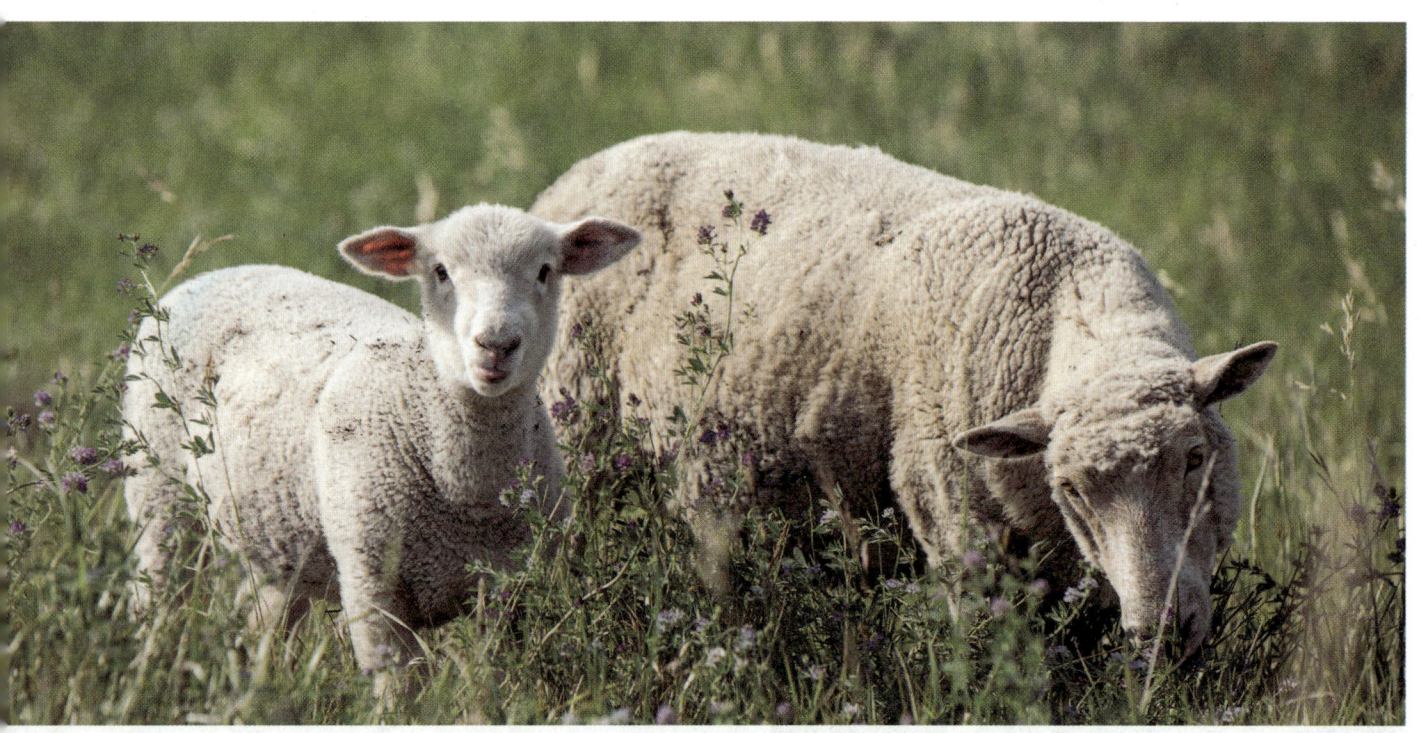

graze during the day and then come back together at night. Corriedales are a hardy breed and can thrive on a variety of forages, making them an excellent breed choice for the open prairies of Saskatchewan.

Range sheep, when managed well, can be integral to keeping grasslands healthy. They eat grass and encourage growth of certain species while inhibiting the growth of undesirable species. They leave behind manure fertilizer, and they reduce fire risk by controlling overgrown grasses and shrubs. Although not her original intention, Arlette views her Corriedale sheep as an integral part of land management and the ecological health and biodiversity of her farm.

It is clear that Arlette has a passion for the land and the animals, but her affection for wool took longer to develop. Arlette has been an artist for quite some time; drawing was her medium before she stumbled upon needle felting on the internet. She couldn't believe that the beautiful images she found were created with wool—something she had in abundance.

Corriedale wool is versatile and reliable. It is fine enough to wear next to the skin and has an elasticity and resilience that makes it perfect for harder wearing items likes socks, sweaters, and blankets. Corriedale wool is often naturally white but can also be grey, black, or brown. Corriedale wool can be found commercially as yarn or fibre for spinning and is often used as the fibre for both wet- and needle-felting projects.

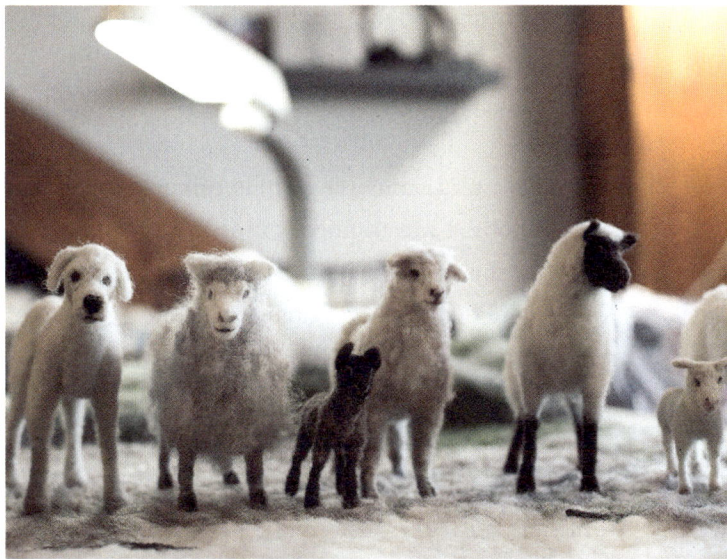

Arlette Seib's felted flock.

Arlette told me that one day, while she was out walking the range, she thought she would like to felt from her own flock of sheep. The flock was 500 head at the time and it seemed like a daunting task, but a year later she still couldn't shake the idea. She decided to just start with one sheep. She has since created a felted project—a community that reflects her own flock, with over fifty sheep and other assorted characters that make up her diverse farm, including guard dogs, a magpie, and an inquisitive little fox. As she worked on this project, she reflected that this art could be a tool to connect community to the source of their wool.

"What a way to promote wool—this is the community of wool that it's grown in. You can see it…this is the community your wool is grown in."

Manitoba
RIDEAU ARCOTT AND FERME FIOLA FARM

I met Christel Lanthier a year after my family moved to Manitoba. I was frantically in search of some straw for the three piglets I had just purchased. I still wasn't sure of what I was doing, but I was committed to learning by trying, and I was motivated by the impending delivery of the piglets. Then I saw a road sign advertising hay for sale.

I called the number on the sign, and Joey, Christel's husband, answered. I asked if I could pick up some hay. I can only imagine he rolled his eyes as I asked for "hay for bedding," but he was willing to educate me and told me to come pick some up.

I was delighted to find out that Joey's (and Christel's) farm was only half a kilometre from ours, and I was excited to talk to someone who could give me some insight into the history of the land base and some of its nuance and uses. We talked for about forty-five minutes at that first meeting: about the area, the soil, and about my plans to start farming sheep for wool. Joey suggested I contact his wife, as they were also considering getting some sheep.

Desperate for friends that lived within walking distance of my new, isolated, rural existence, I went home and looked her up on Facebook. After seeing

Hay & Straw

Yes, it's true, at this point in my farming journey I didn't know the difference between hay and straw. Don't worry if you aren't aware of the difference, and please don't judge if you are. Hay is food for ruminant animals and straw is bedding. Hay is harvested from the leaves, stalks, and flowers of grasses that are dried and cured with precision to capture the greatest amount of nutrients to adequately feed livestock in the winter. Straw is generally the stalks that are left behind after the seed heads of grains have been harvested; it provides dry, clean bedding for livestock.

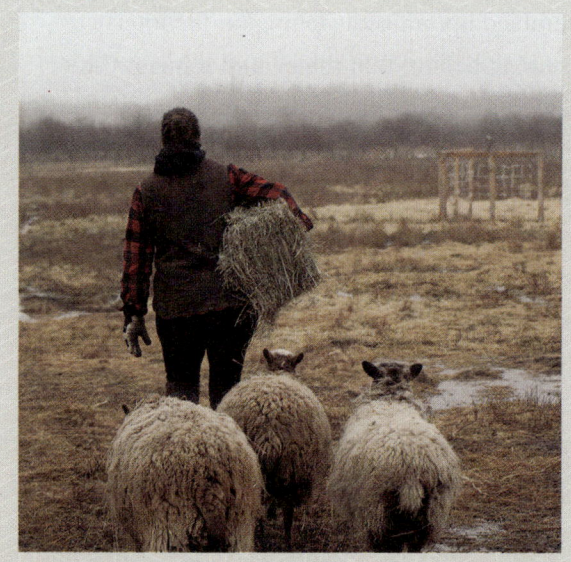

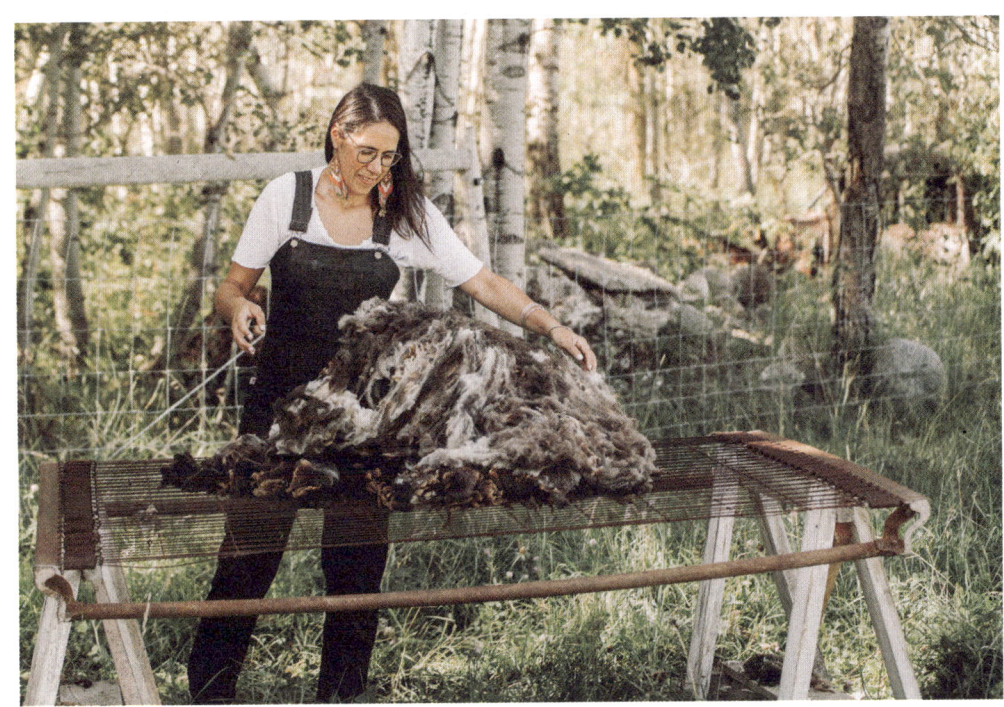

Christel Lanthier skirting wool at her farm in Eastern Manitoba.

that she was a baby-wearing, attachment parenting, left-leaning artist, I figured we could definitely be friends. I reached out, and within a few weeks we set up a time to get together and skirt some fleece. Little did I know that this first experience would lay the groundwork for many of our future ideas.

The thing is, neither of us had ever actually skirted a dirty sheep's fleece before. Skirting is the process of removing any undesirable wool or contamination from the fleece before having it processed. It sounds like a simple task, but if you have never done it, it is hard to determine if you are being too picky (yes, some people will pick out every single bit of hay or straw or dirt) or if you aren't being picky enough. Neither Christel nor I had ever done this before and neither of us really knew what we were looking for, but we jumped right in and started. I think our mutual desire to try something new, without fear of the unknown, made us fast friends—and pretty good at skirting fleeces. We still spend hours every spring and summer skirting fleeces together, but we are much faster now (although Christel is much more meticulous than I am). That first afternoon we discussed our individual plans for sheep and Christel shared with me the history of their farm.

Christel and her husband, Joey Fiola, along with their three girls, Olivia, Anne-Rose, and Lila, steward 120 acres of mixed hay, pasture, woods, and marshland that has been in Joey's family for

The Prairies 73

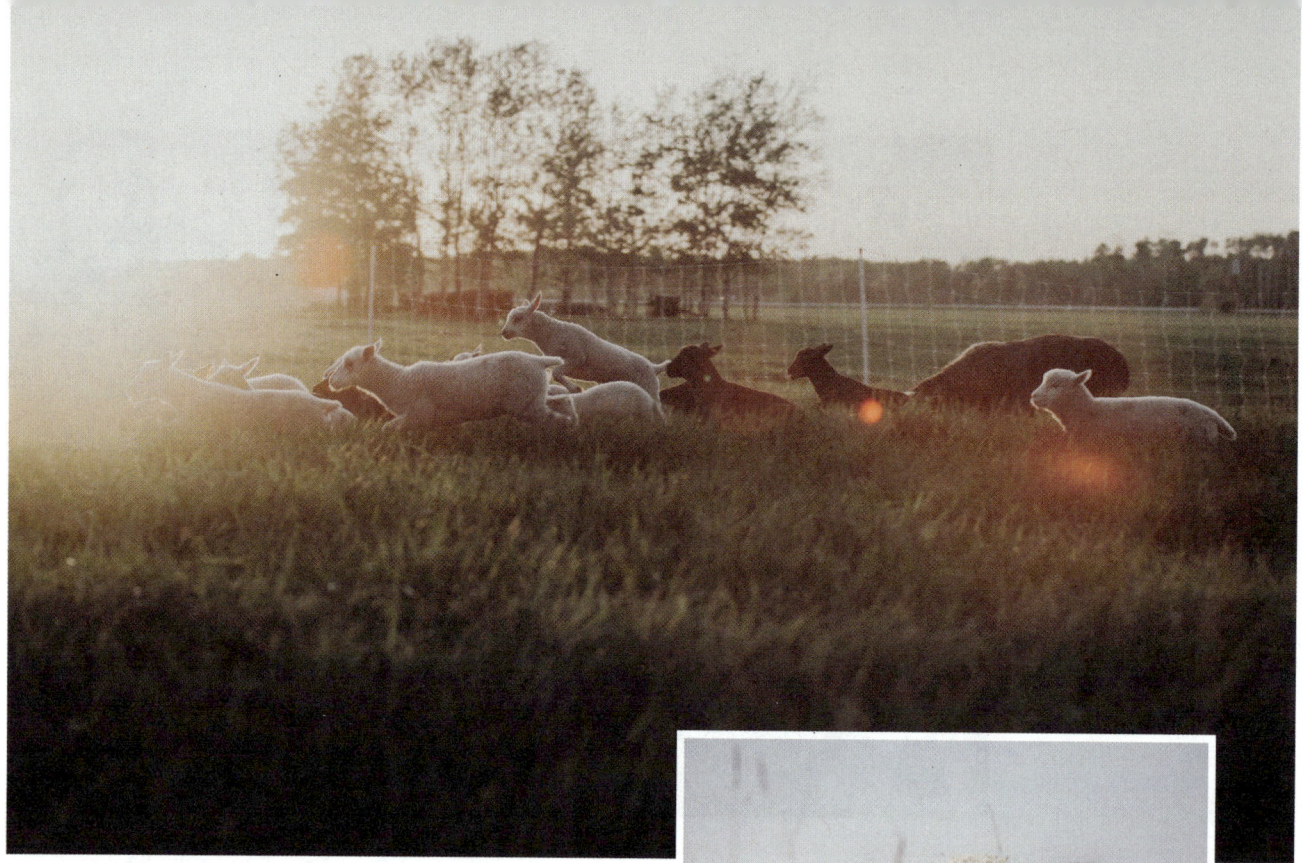

almost 100 years. Joey's great-grandparents, Noëlie and Ferdinand Fiola, along with their eighteen children, bought the homestead in 1922. They ran a subsistence farm which included several cows, chickens, rabbits, and a few sheep. Noëlie would use the wool from the sheep to hand-knit socks and other clothing for her children. The farm passed through the hands of various family members and operated as a dairy farm from 1956 to 1985, at which point it became a hay farm. In 2012 Christel and Joey purchased the farm and began growing hay and raising a few chickens.

    Christel fell in love with a farmer but didn't necessarily think she would be a farmer herself.

Previously, she had worked a variety of jobs, including barista, photographer, and for VIA Rail, and then she studied fine arts at the Alberta College of Art and Design. She was focusing on jewelry design, but then ended up studying photography, sculpture, fibre arts, and multi-media art. Initially, she was happy to move to the farm, start a family, and continue all her artistic pursuits. It wasn't until the idea of raising sheep—and producing fibre—came up that she became a farmer as well.

Christel was very clear on her goals for their flock. First and foremost, they wanted to add more fertilizer, in the form of manure, onto their hay land to help them with their sustainability goals. Joey has been making and selling hay on the farm since he was old enough to drive a tractor, and to avoid synthetic amendments to his hay land, the sheep made sense. Christel wanted a breed that could provide both meat and wool. They had a connection to a local farmer that produced excellent breeding stock with excellent carcass size and beautiful wool, and they decided to purchase their starter flock of Rideau Arcott.

Rideau Arcott is a Canadian-made sheep breed! Many of the sheep breeds in this book are from other parts of the world and have found a home in our various land bases, but the Government of Canada developed three breeds of sheep: Canadian Arcott, Rideau Arcott, and Outaouais Arcott. Arcott stands for Agricultural Research Centre of Ottawa. The Rideau was developed by crossbreeding Finnsheep, Suffolk, Shropshire, Dorset, and East Friesian breeds. It took the research centre about thirty years, between

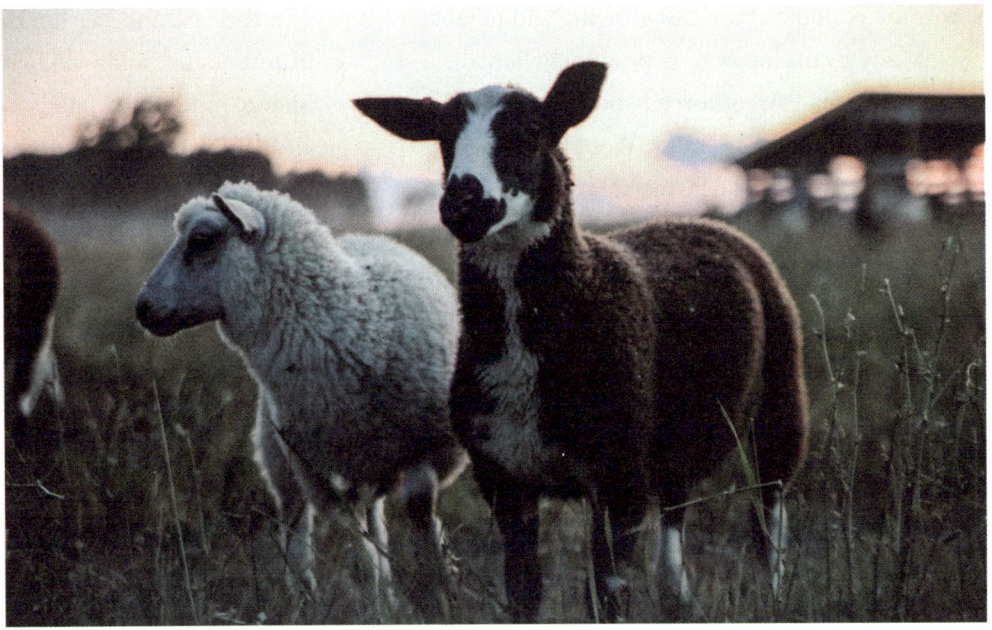

Rideau Arcott ewe at sunset in Eastern Manitoba.

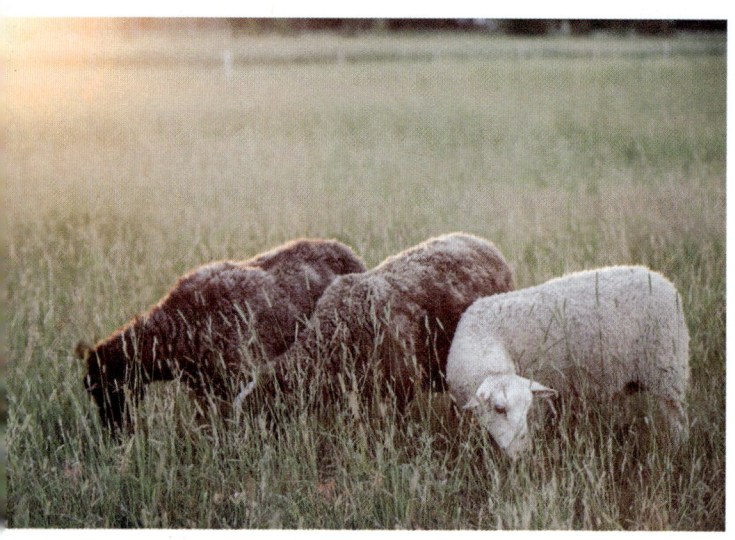

1958 and 1989, to fully develop the breed, as they were aiming for qualities of high fertility, good mothering, and excellent growth rates. Rideau Arcott is a popular breed in Manitoba and other provinces across the country as it is fast growing and reliable.

Many farms focused on producing lamb grow the Rideau Arcott breed and sell the wool to the Canadian Co-operative Wool Growers as a secondary goal. Some farmers, however, have worked hard to maintain Rideau flocks with excellent wool quality and to breed or crossbreed to increase wool fineness and colour. Rideau wool is already considered a variable wool; some are fine, long, and lustrous while others are more lofty and down. In this way, a keen eye for quality wool and a breeding program that focuses on the quality of wool is of great importance.

Christel is a multifaceted artist and has brought creativity and a holistic attitude into the development of her flock. "I am Franco-Manitoban, I am Métis, I am a mother and photographer and farmer. We are diverse beings and I want to live in a way that creates room for all of these things. This is how I feel about our sheep. They provide meat to nourish our bodies, they provide wool and sheepskins to clothe us, they provide manure to replenish the nutrients in our soil, I use their tallow to create balms. I use every part of the sheep, from nose to tail, with a spirit of gratitude and recognition of the circularity of our ecosystem."

Christel and Joey have truly adopted a holistic approach to their sheep production and farming. The wool is one very important part of the farm, but it is nestled among all the other aspects of raising sheep. Christel has developed a beautiful brand of single-source yarn for knitting and crochet that capitalizes on the unique characteristics of her Rideau, and her flock now includes Romney, Rambouillet, and California Variegated Mutant sheep. In fact, her labels include the name and a little information about the specific sheep that the yarn or fibre was sourced from. Her Rideau yarn has beautiful lustre and fineness, with a bit of bounce and resiliency.

The yarn and fibre is just one way that Christel utilizes the wool that her sheep produce. Pursuing her commitment to use every part of the animal—a way of honouring the animal's sacrifice to nourish our bodies—she is forging a new path of connection with her Métis heritage and her skills as a sheepskin tanner. Christel was introduced to hide tanning in 2012 through a Franco-Manitoban youth camp she was working for. She immediately felt connected to the practice but didn't dive deeper until she started raising her own sheep and wanted to be able to utilize everything from the animal. Christel is now an excellent tanner of sheepskins and other hides, and she teaches others in her Métis community about tanning. Christel can often be found framed by the epic Manitoban sunsets, scraping or softening a sheepskin. "The history of textiles and clothing on this land includes hides, skins, and furs. Working with wool as yarn is one expression of what sheep have to offer but honouring their death by utilizing their sheepskin as clothing is another expression."

The second time Christel and I ever hung out was while I chased my new-to-me llama through a swamp. The llama had been in my care for less than four hours before it cleared my four-foot fence like it was nothing and ran five miles away to a neighbouring farm. I was devastated and pretty convinced that I had failed at being a fibre farmer in the first five minutes. Christel showed up and helped me walk the llama back to our property, all while she had her ten-month-old baby strapped to her back. I knew then that she was a rock-solid friend. She encouraged me in that moment to keep going, and we've been encouraging each other in our own fibre and sheep aspirations ever since. I call her my farmwife or fibre-friend and I couldn't imagine making this book with anyone else. »

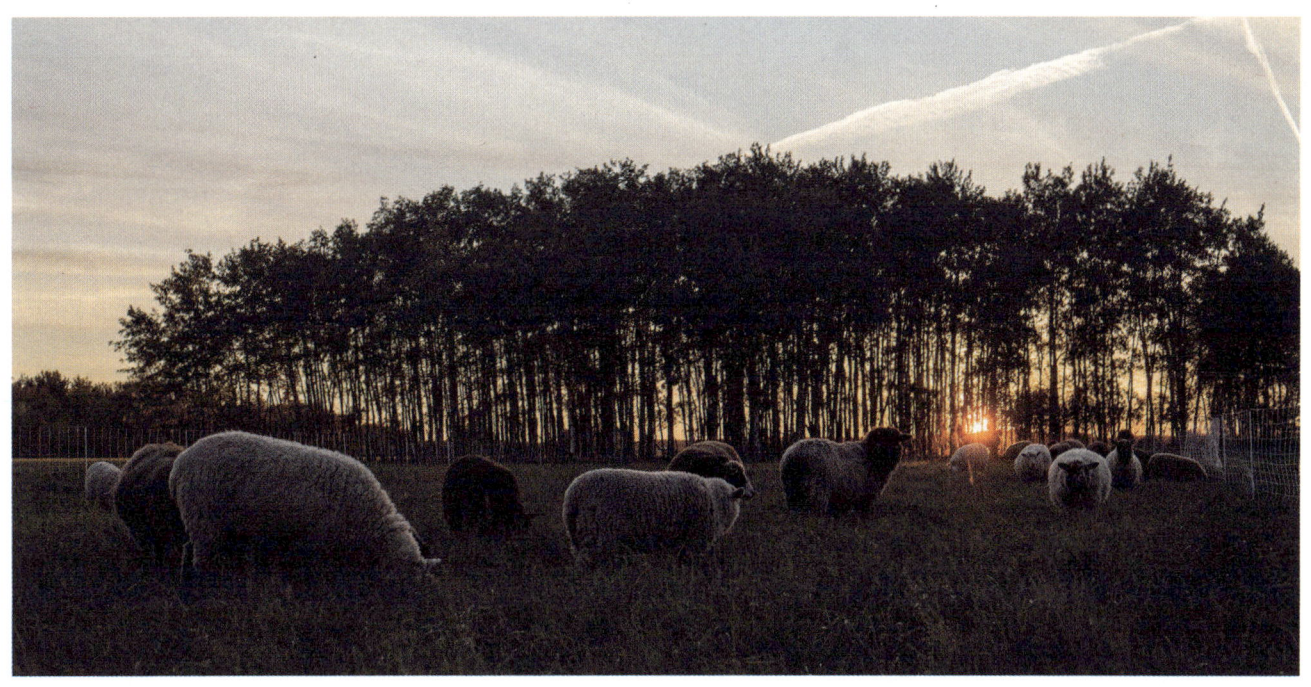

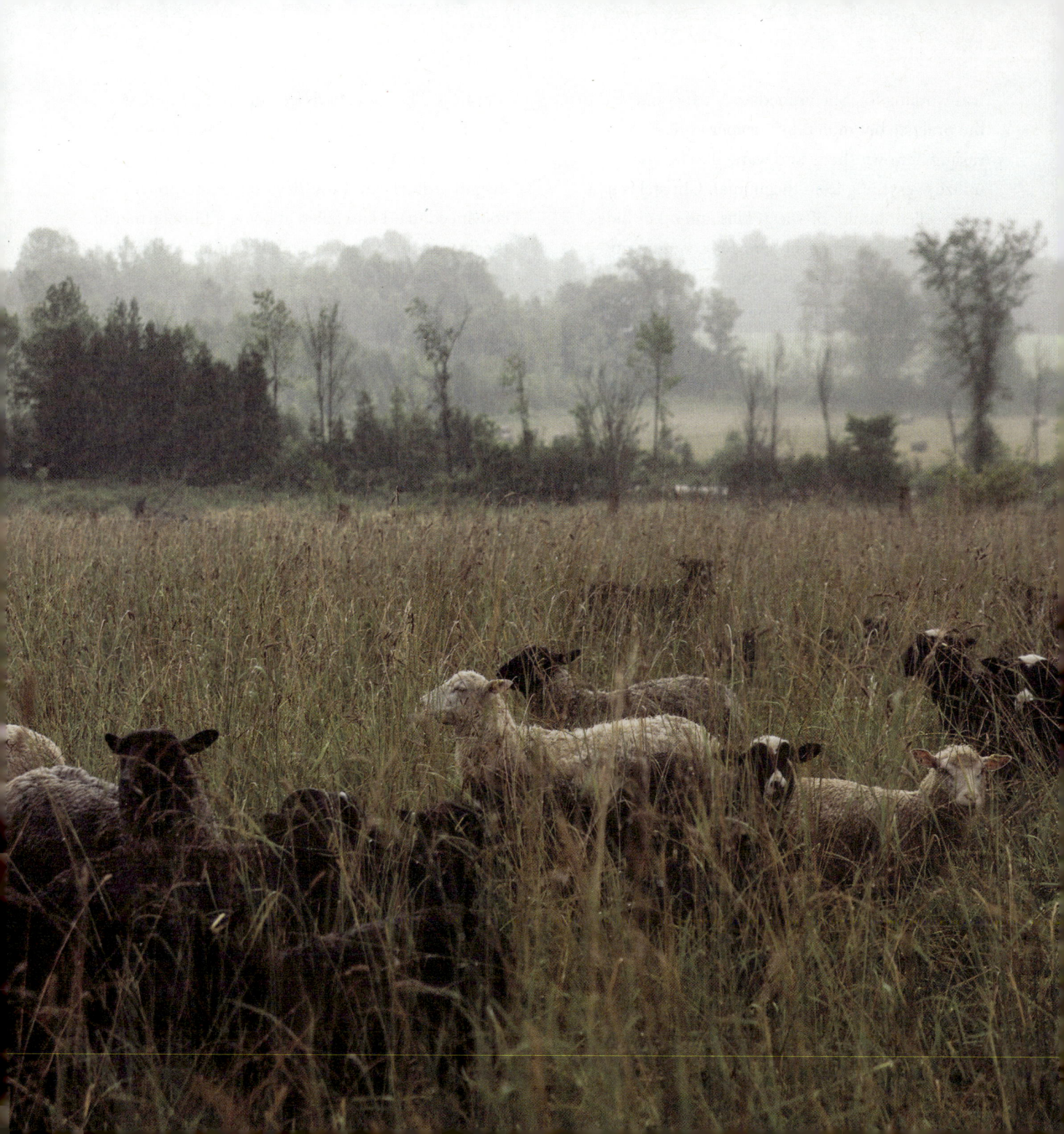

Ontario & Québec

Québec is where canada's story with sheep started, and Ontario is the largest sheep-producing province in Canada. There are a large number of intensive meat operations in Ontario, and also many fibre farmers raising a variety of sheep breeds. Ontario has a rich history of wool production and was the hub of most of Canada's textile production in the 1800s. I wish I could've dedicated more time to exploring some of the historical sites of wool manufacturing and production, but I was excited to continue visiting with farmers and learning their stories. The biggest challenge I faced was deciding which breeds to look at and what farms to visit.

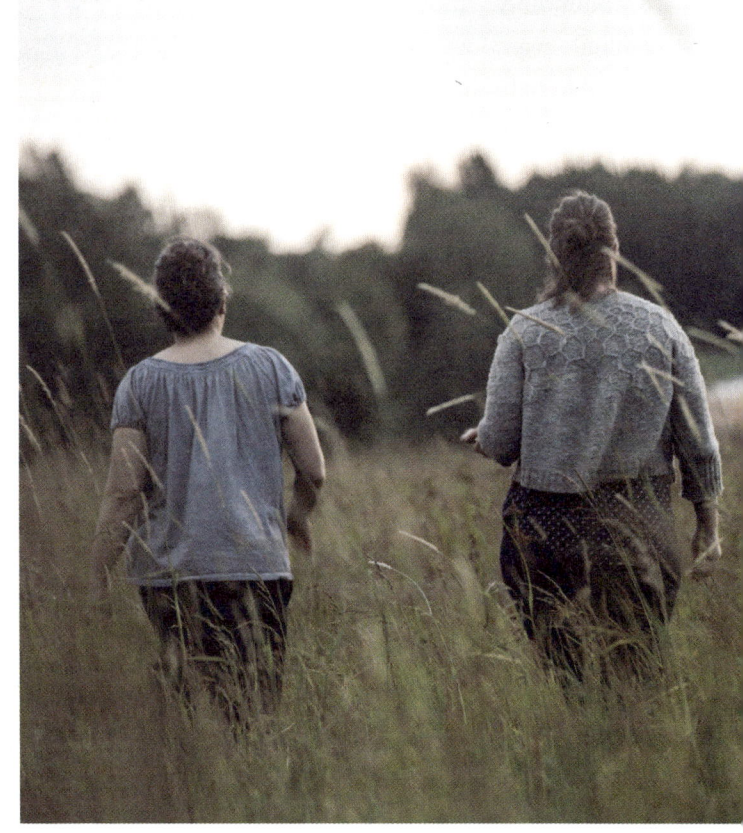

Opposite: Sheep grazing the tall summer grasses in Ontario.

Ontario
SHETLAND AND BLACK SHEEP FARM

It was dusk, warm, and wet in early July when you can feel the fertility of the soil and the air smells like growing plants. We found ourselves once again trying to outrun the setting sun as we drove through the winding roads of Grey County, northwest of Toronto. Maples and cedars and black spruce lined the highway as we drove, and Christel and I both remarked on how we would love to live in this community—though we did say that about every single region we explored during our travels. We had to fight the urge to pull over and take photos or at least a lingering look at all the old barns on many of the homesteads. We learned later that these beautiful old, stone-bottomed barns are called bank barns. Their name comes from being built into a north facing hillside, or bank, to allow for different elevations, good insulation, and ease of loading hay in and out. When we learned the history of these barns and why they were built this way, we realized why they don't exist in Manitoba: we don't have many banks or hills to build barns into!

We pulled into the driveway of Black Sheep Farm, framed by an overflowing canopy of lush green sugar and red maple trees and red pines.

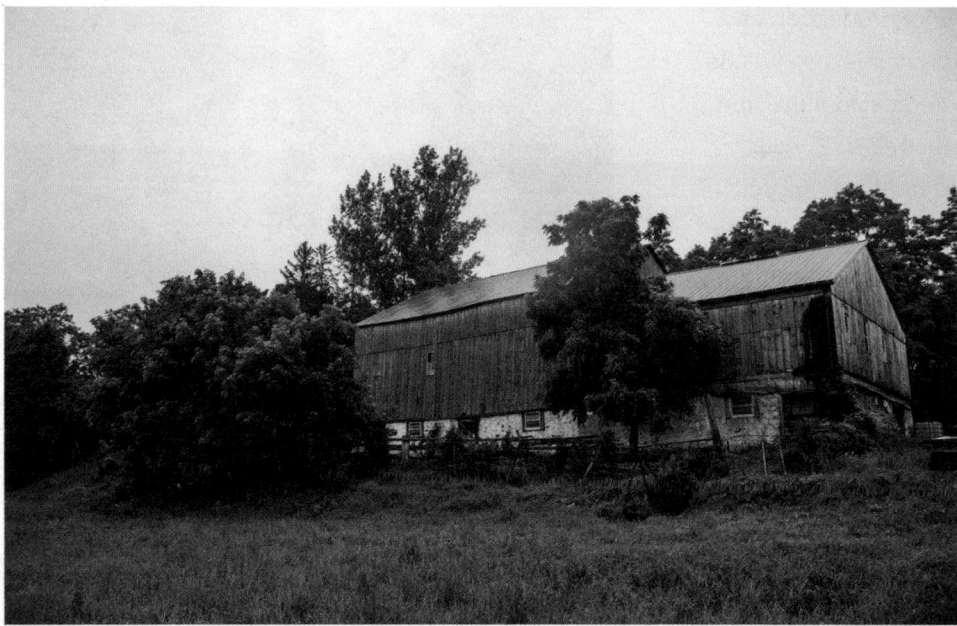

The old bank barn at Black Sheep Farm, Ontario.

Brenda Hsueh and her six-year-old daughter Emma were waiting for us at the door and we exchanged hellos and apologies for our late arrival. We quickly agreed that we could still get at least twenty minutes of pictures before the light would be gone, and we rushed to get boots on and camera gear ready. Skylar, Brenda's spouse, joined us, and we headed out to find the sheep.

Brenda and I had never met in person, and we didn't get into much small talk before I started rapid-fire questioning her about all the things they do on their farm. The first thing she pointed out was the brand-new hedgerow they planted with 200 poplars and willows. Hedgerows are generally a line of densely planted trees or shrubs to form a border. They help support wildlife, can be used to grow and harvest food, reduce the need for watering and help with water capture. Brenda explained to me they are at a high point for the headwaters of the North Saugeen River and Sauble River. Water hits the top of the ridge and just flows right down and across the land. Counter to conventional agricultural approaches that often look to drain excess water, Brenda is focusing on drawing down the water into the land. Using hedgerows, perennial grasses, no-till vegetable gardens, and managed grazing, she is working to stop the flow of water across the land and instead draw it down into the roots. "Whatever we do on this farm is to encourage more biodiversity and more water retention. Poplars and willows are sheep forage, but they also help with water." We found the sheep grazing in waist-high grasses.

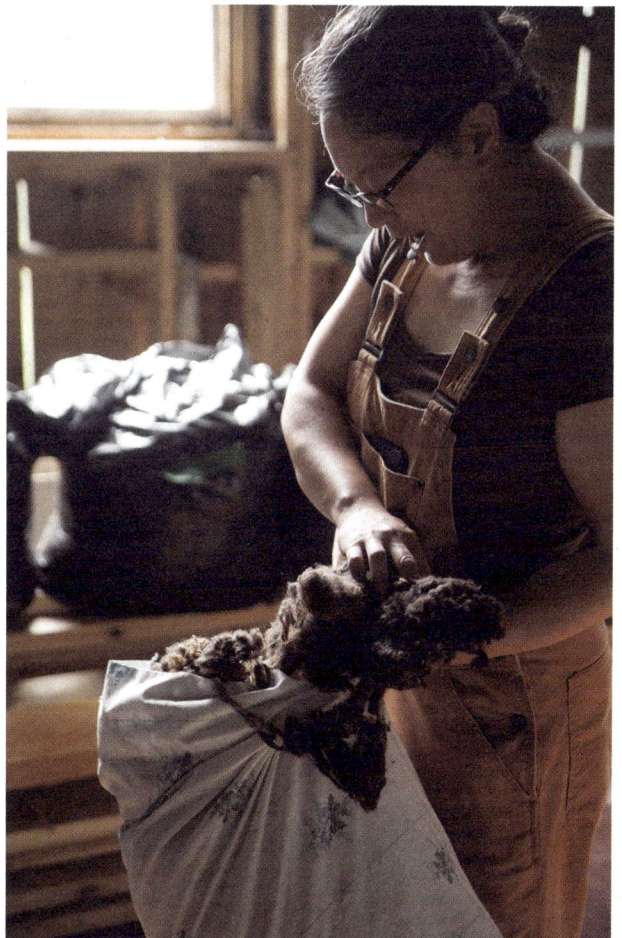

Brenda Hsueh showing off some Shetland wool, Ontario.

Despite it being a bit of a challenge for capturing clear photos of sheep, it was incredible to see the vibrant plant growth on the farm.

Brenda came to farming as an environmentalist, and she sees her flock of seventy ewes and their lambs as contributing to her goal of regeneration. "We practice intensive managed grazing. We want the sheep to put down their fertilizer [manure],

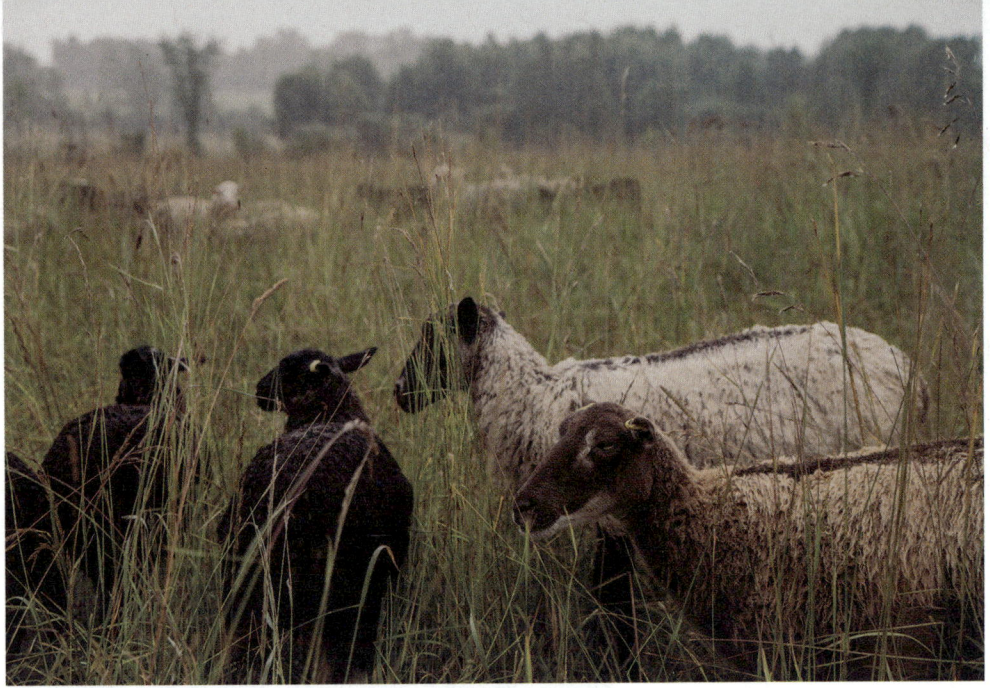

Shetland sheep grazing on a rainy summer day, Ontario.

wake up the soil with their animal movements, and keep the pasture plants as vegetative as possible." She raises a mixed flock of Shetlands, Gotland-cross and Romney-cross sheep. Beyond the land management goals with her sheep, she also sells lamb, wool, and sheepskins, and has run a market garden and community supported agriculture program (CSA) since she started farming in 2008.

After graduating from university, Brenda found herself working in finance in Toronto. She had a good life with a good income, and she enjoyed volunteering and having an active life engaging in the arts and culture of Toronto. But in 2007–2008 during the financial crisis, she realized she "...just didn't really like [the] morally bankrupt industry anymore," and she began planning her exit. She was looking at jobs related to food security and at non-governmental organizations, when she met Wayne Roberts, founder of the Toronto Food Policy Council. He pointed her to the Everdale Environmental Learning Centre, and she fell in love with the centre, which was kind of like adult summer camp. "I came into farming because I wanted to be somewhere that was at the intersection of environmental, food and social justice."

Brenda then started the process of looking for a farm, and in 2008 she found her current home: 40 acres, including a bank barn that was built in 1886. It was her dream come true. She started with a 1–2-acre market garden and CSA and focused on growing nutrient-dense, no-till vegetables. Brenda always had a few sheep on the farm, but it wasn't until 2018, when her daughter was born, that the sheep became a more integral part of the farm.

They have since sold lamb, and in the last few years have been focusing on marketing wool products.

In the beginning, she didn't have enough wool to sell, so she had it processed and then used it herself or gave it to family and friends. But the last few years have seen growth in the farm, and she developed some strategic partnerships to sell her wool. Conveniently located down the road was Emily Foden of Viola Yarns, who was more than happy to work with and market Brenda's wool.

At this point during our visit the sky had grown too dark for pictures, and we agreed that if we wanted to take more, we'd need to come back in the morning. We headed over to Emily's home and dye studio for the night, but not before more discussion of the sheep breeds, natural dyeing, and my favourite topic: Shetland sheep. Even though the Shetland breed has over thirty unique marking patterns and colour variations, I often find similar ewes in every Shetland flock I come across. Even with Brenda's Shetland crosses I saw similarities to my flock in the distinct markings and range of colour.

Shetland sheep originate from their namesake, the Shetland Islands, off the north coast of Scotland, where they have been evolving as a breed for over 1,000 years. There is a widespread debate and much disagreement on many aspects of the breed, how it was formed and influenced, and what is the breed standard for wool. Single-coated, double-coated, or somewhere in between; fine and soft, or coarse and scratchy—all of these are true of Shetland wool, and I often encourage people to get their hands on

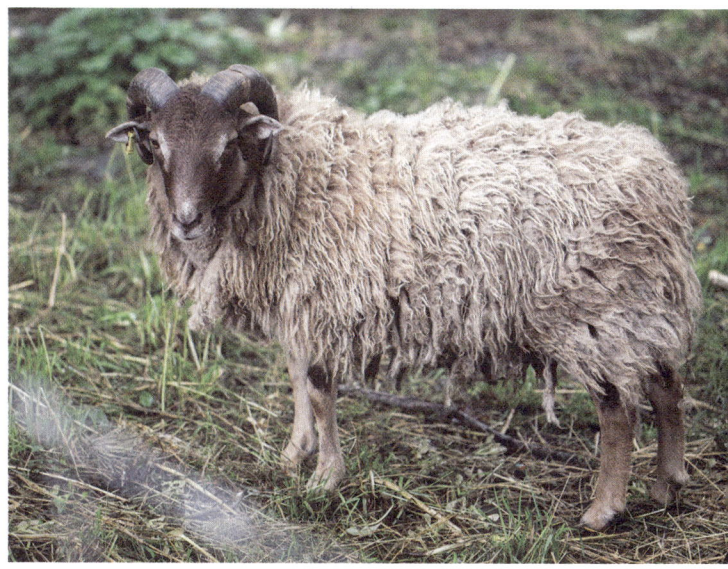

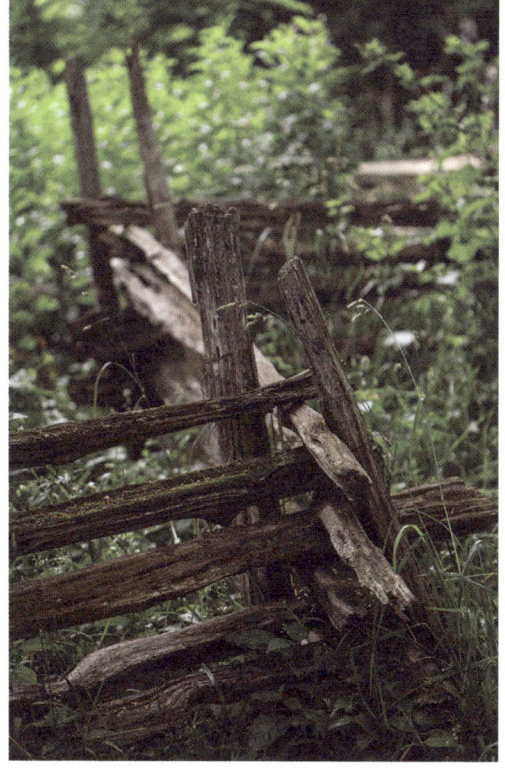

as much Shetland wool as they can so they can fully embrace all the variation this breed has to offer. The breed has eleven distinct colours, which is perhaps why so many are drawn to it. The natural shades offer an incredible palette for Fair Isle or colour-patterned knitwear. Shetland wool can be used for next-to-the-skin clothing, or rough and tumble outerwear. The sheep produce only two to five pounds of wool a year, with a staple length than can vary from 2 to 9 inches and a range of 20–50 microns.

In the 1980s, Shetland sheep were considered a threatened breed and were put on many rare-breed conservation lists with the hope that the breed would be saved. In 1980, Colonel G.D. Dailley, a man committed to the preservation of endangered species, was the first person to import Shetland sheep from the Shetland Islands to North America. He brought thirty-two Shetland sheep, twenty-eight pregnant ewes and four rams to Springfield Farm in Ontario, where he and his wife, Virginia, owned 125 acres. This flock was the foundation of all Shetland sheep in North America and continues to be a thriving operation for the breed.

We talked wool late into the night with Emily and Brenda; it made me wish that, geographically, we were not so far away from all the new fibre friends we met during the writing of this book. Brenda shared her challenges with marketing wool: the need for more infrastructure and greater awareness of her fibre and breeds. She has a deep understanding of her land management goals and how to raise healthy, happy sheep. Now she is focusing on creating a quality fibre product and expanding her markets.

Christel and I drove back to Brenda's farm the next morning and walked out to find the sheep under a blanket of moody fog. The skies opened up with rain and we got absolutely drenched, while the sheep continued to slowly and methodically work through the new pasture that Skylar had just let them into. I asked Brenda what made her Shetland sheep well

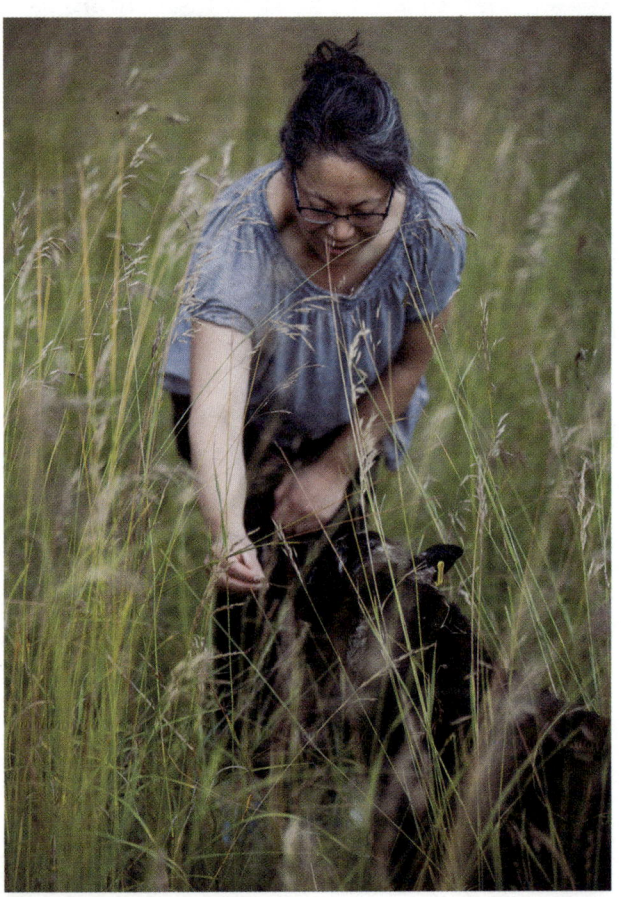

Brenda Hsueh and one of her Shetland ewes in the tall summer pasture.

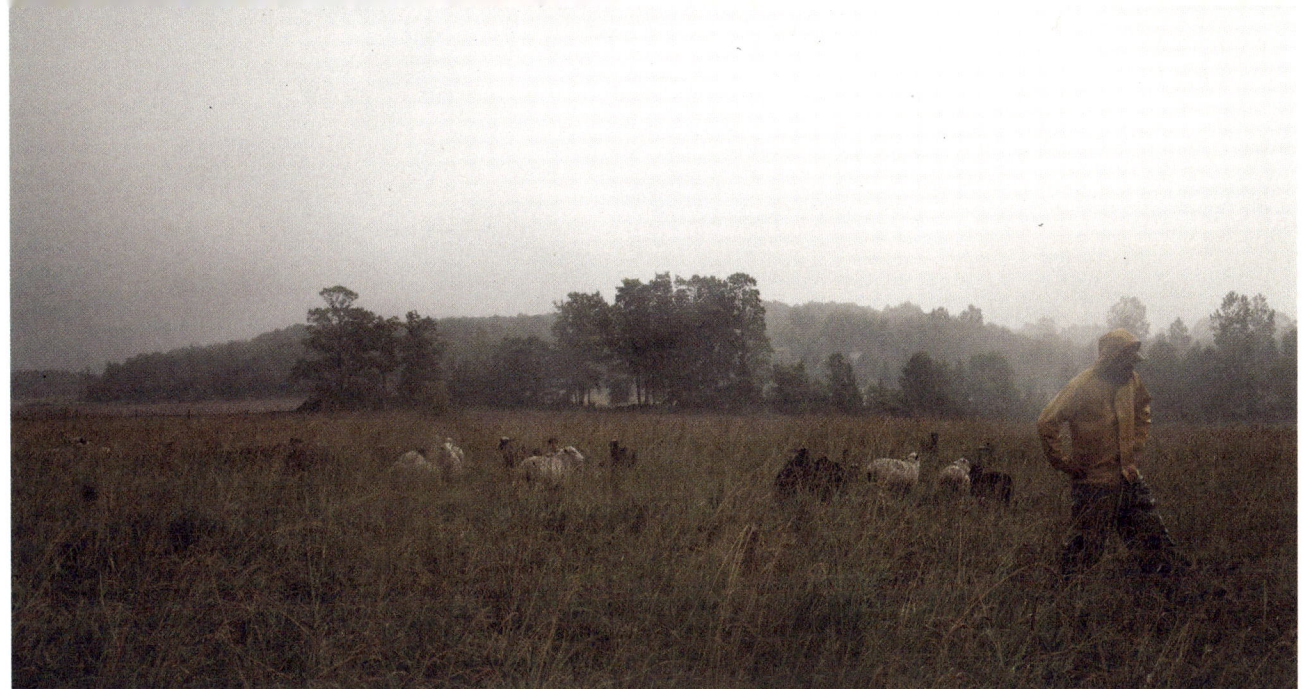

suited to this land base and she said, "They are best suited, or adaptable, to my land base because they are born here. If you want animals that thrive on your land base you birth them here. So, it doesn't really matter what breed you start with—you find the sheep with the characteristics you want and breed up for the traits you want as each generation that is born are the best ones born for your land." This reinforced the impression I got when talking to Brenda earlier: that she is absolutely committed to regenerating the forty acres that she stewards. And she is doing that through a process of quiet observation and flexible decision-making to adapt and plan for a dynamic farming system that prioritizes soil, animal, and land health.

After drying ourselves off from the rain, we looked at some of Brenda's beautiful yarn. The colour and handle of her Shetland wool is stunning, and I am eager to see how she grows this side of her business. The last thing I asked Brenda was how she named her farm. She explained that many years ago, she travelled to England in the springtime, and during a tour of some local sheep farms she saw one white and one black lamb, and the tour guide explained that the black lamb would be culled very soon because they don't use black wool. She stated that she was going to come back to Ontario and take everyone's to-be-culled black sheep and make suiting material so fancy that even Harry Rosen would use it! So, when she started her vegetable farm, she called it Black Sheep Farm. And here she is, fourteen years later, building a thriving, integrated farm with a flock of sheep and their beautiful fibre. I'm not sure if the folks at Harry Rosen have gotten the message yet, but I'm confident they will.

Ontario
COOPWORTH AND WOOLLEY'S LAMB

Christel and I were on our second coffee of the morning as we drove towards Norfolk County along the north shore of Lake Erie in Ontario. This region is sometimes called the "garden of Ontario," as it is home to the largest growers of asparagus, peppers, pumpkins, squash, zucchini, tart cherries, and ginseng. It is also the number one grower of cabbage, rye, and strawberries in Ontario. We were on a circuitous route through smaller highways and back roads, past ginseng fields covered in massive black shade tarps, and huge tobacco plants. It was clear that this region was rich with agriculture, but very few sheep or other livestock could be seen, and I was slightly worried we had taken a wrong turn—that there were no large sheep operations in this community. As I carried on following the GPS

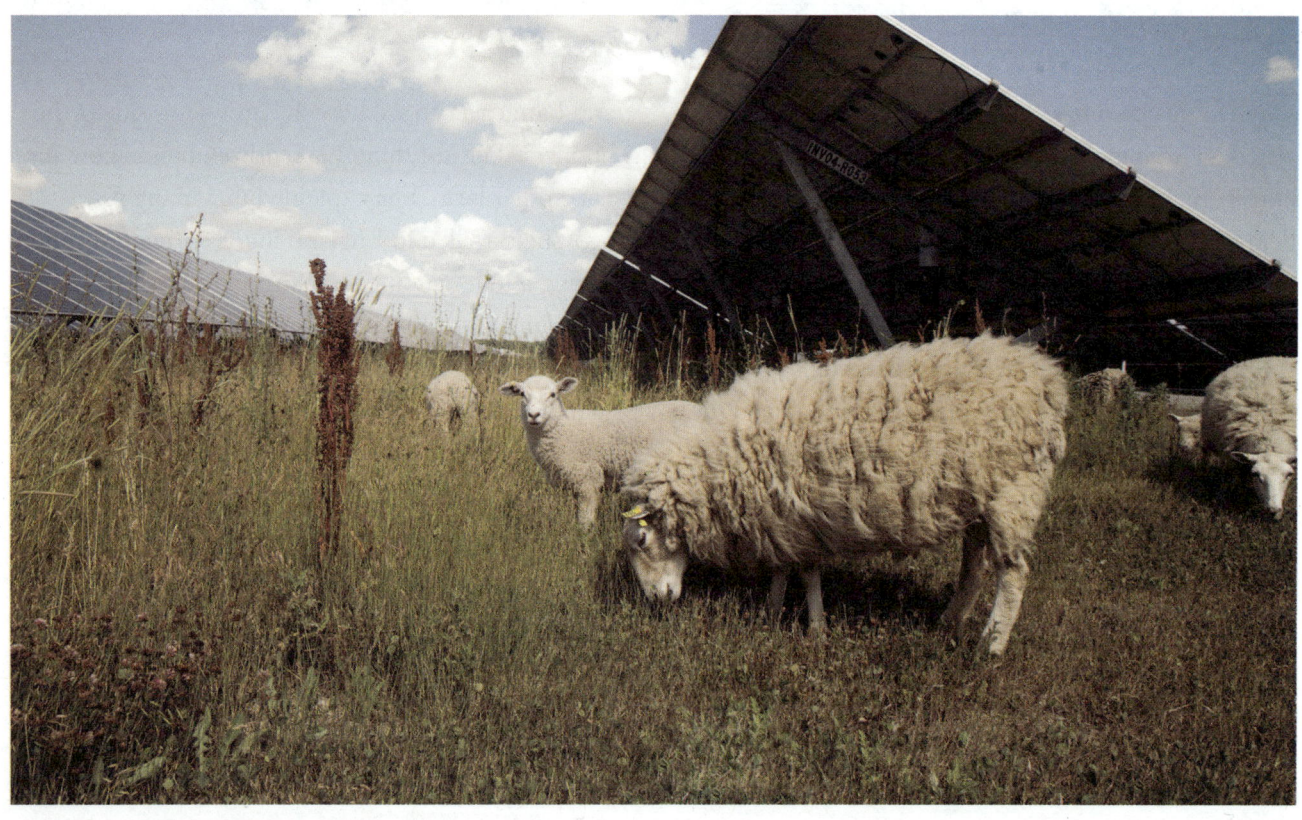

directions, doubt lingered in the back of my mind. This doubt grew as we pulled into the long driveway lined with hundreds of sweet cherry trees and I thought to myself, "This cannot be a sheep farm."

I was not prepared for the size and scope of the farm when we pulled up to a very large building that looked like housing for staff; more than the occasional neighbourhood helper that we usually use on our farms, but rather buildings big enough to accommodate dozens of full-time farm staff. We saw two other large buildings in the background and a dedicated building just for administration and offices. I paused for a moment as I stepped out of the car and realized this was unlike any of the operations I had been to thus far. I felt a bit intimidated. Carrie came out of the office and immediately put me at ease, suggesting we hop in her jeep and drive to the sheep who were at a contract grazing site at a nearby solar farm.

I first came across Carrie's Instagram account (@carriewoolley1) while looking for examples of silvopasture in Canada. The pictures of her Coopworth sheep caught my eye; they're not a very common breed in Canada, so I started following her and reached out when I knew we would be travelling to Ontario.

One goal for this book is to highlight the different strategies and methods for land and sheep management. Every farmer has their own unique approach to animal husbandry, land management, wool harvesting, and marketing. Carrie Woolley—yes that is her actual surname—manages her sheep

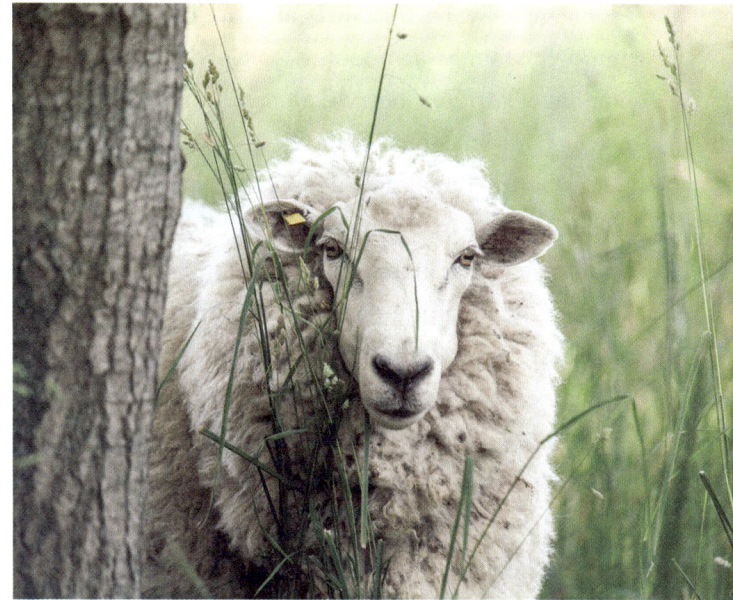
Coopworth ram at Woolley's Lamb.

in a silvopasture operation. Silvopasture integrates trees, woodlots, orchards, and vineyards with managed grazing in a mutually beneficial way. When we think of sheep grazing, we usually picture open grasslands, rolling hills, and lush green paddocks—not dense forest. But silvopasture is a system of farming that works for both the sheep and the forest, or, in Carrie's case, the orchards.

As we drove to the solar farm, Carrie shared her story of becoming a sheep farmer. Brett Schuyler, Carrie's husband, is the eighth generation in his family to farm in this region. Brett's father, Marshall, and his brother, Drew, took their average-sized family farm and grew it into a large agriculture operation by growing apple and sour cherry orchards and integrating large-scale vegetable production with some grain, corn, and soybeans. Not only did they grow the family farm, but they helped establish and manage Norfolk Cherry Company (a local processing facility) and the local Fruit Growers Association.

Carrie joined the farming operations in 2010, when she was first dating Brett and finishing up her master's degree in animal science at the University of Guelph. She didn't intend on raising sheep, but a friend suggested to her that sheep could graze the family's orchards, and despite her initial skepticism about the idea, she began to think it might actually work. As a test, she and Brett decided to rent some local sheep before investing in a flock of their own. When they brought the idea to Carrie's soon-to-be father-in-law, he insisted on two rules:

The sheep can't be eating the trees.
The sheep can't be running all over the roads.

With those guidelines in mind, they started integrating sheep into the orchards. They learned how to set up and utilize temporary electric fencing and how to care for the sheep. After that first test run went well, Carrie was ready to figure out what was next for the sheep. In 2012 they bought their first sheep, twelve North Country Cheviot and five Shetlands. It was a bit discouraging that first season, because she didn't have enough experience working with sheep, and she lost some during lambing, but she persevered and started researching and connecting with other producers in Ontario.

Sweet cherry orchard that the flock of Coopworth sheep will graze in the fall.

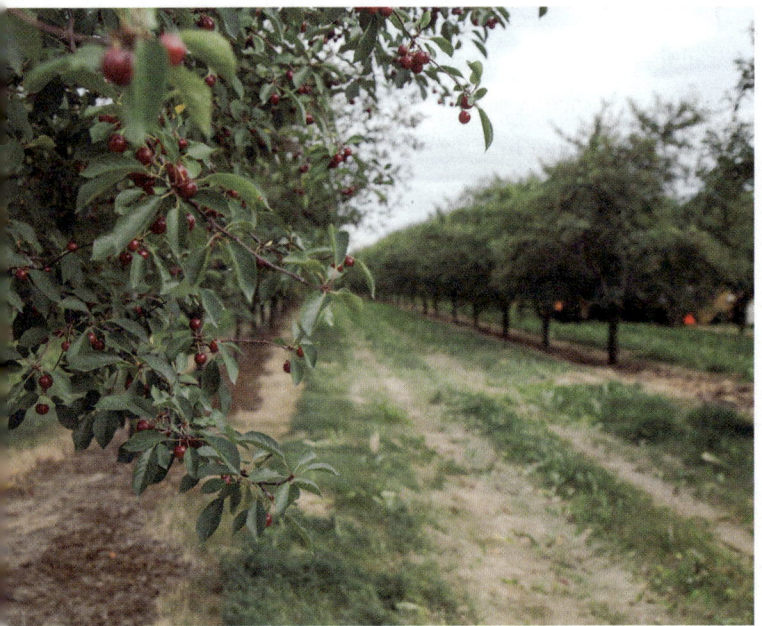
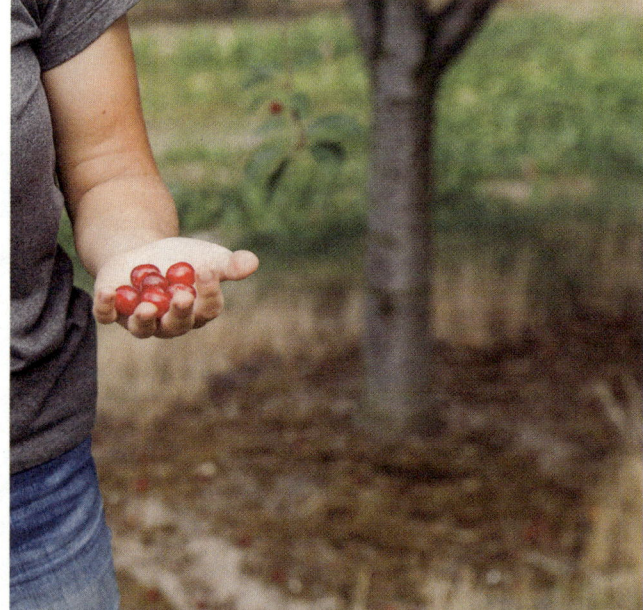

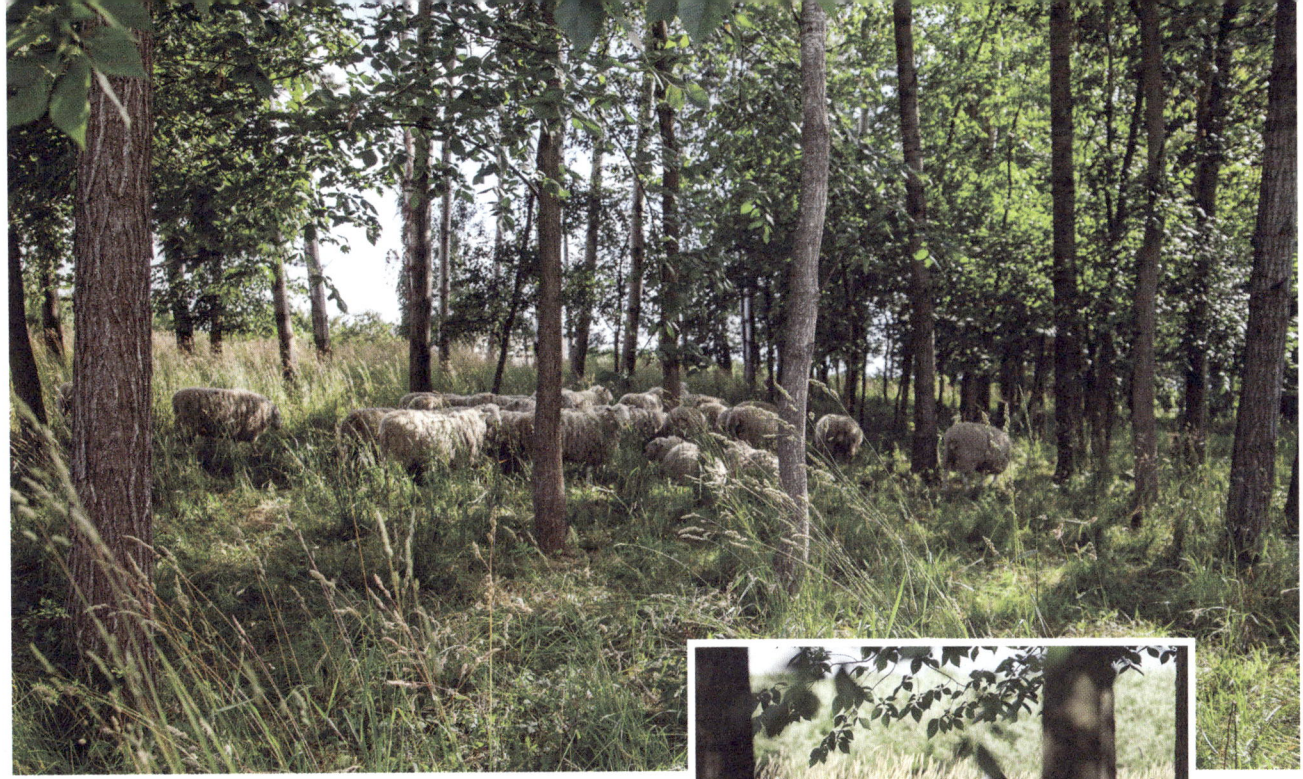

Using silvopasture techniques to manage the woodlot, Ontario.

Carrie knew she wanted to find a breed of sheep that could be raised outdoors year-round and was an easy-care, hardy breed that could lamb out on pasture. Shortly thereafter she met Mark Ritchie and Cherry Allen (now deceased) from Amherst Island, and their flock of Coopworth sheep. Carrie purchased Coopworth crossbred sheep from Mark and Cherry and has since imported Coopworth genetics directly from New Zealand.

Carrie has spent a decade fine-tuning her silvopasture operation, raising two children, and figuring out the marketing of her grass-fed lamb and wool. They pasture the sheep on permanent pasture and graze them in the woodlots from May to July. Then, after the cherries have been harvested in August, the sheep graze the cherry orchards. The mature ewes move into the sweet corn crops in August to clean up the corn stover (the leftover stalks and leaves after harvest), and then they graze the apple orchards after harvest and well into November. She rotates the sheep through the fields, to graze whatever is left behind after the combines have harvested the ground crops, and they generally only start feeding hay or baleage in January.

Ontario & Québec

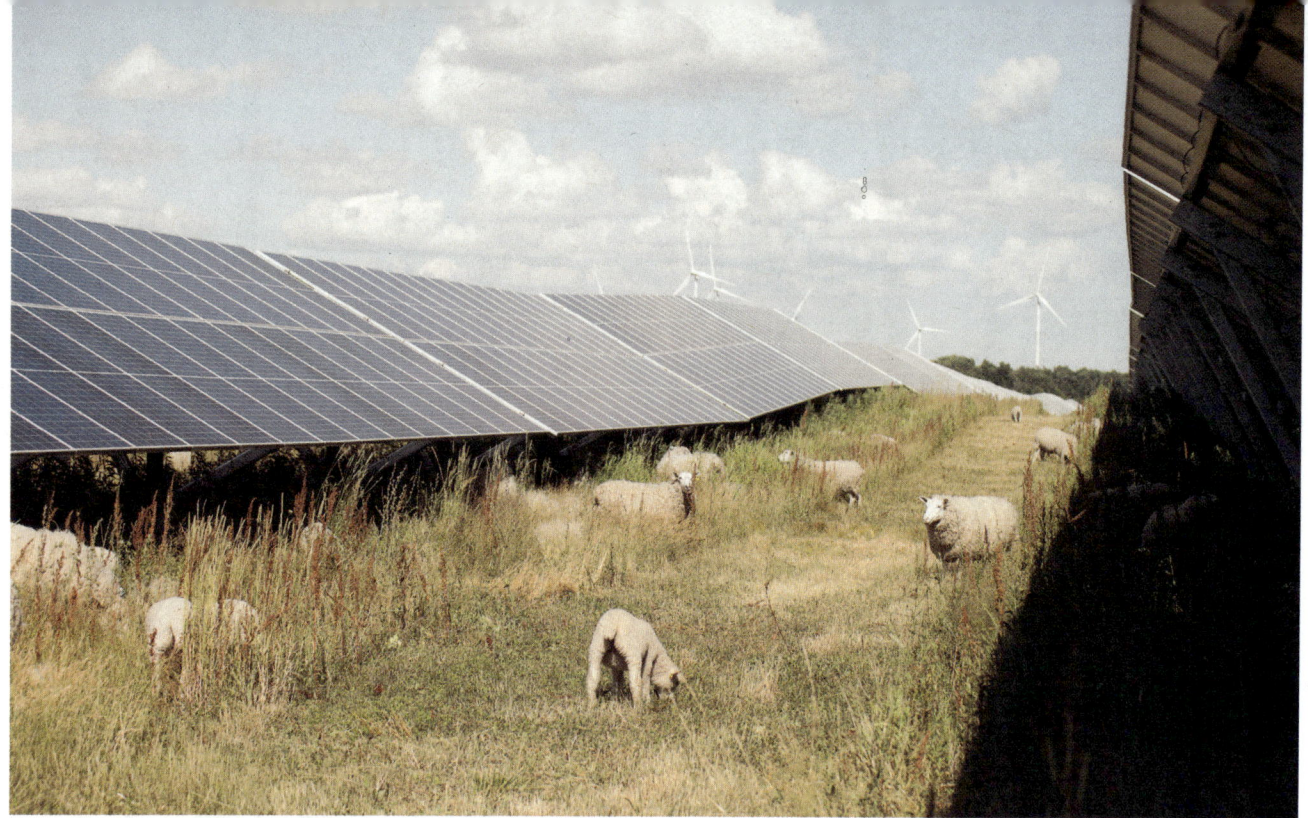
Sheep grazing the solar farm in Ontario.

Their management of the flock allows for the deposit of nutrients throughout their other crops and orchards. They have very few parasite or predation issues because the sheep are constantly being moved, and the farm has seen a large reduction in fossil fuel consumption because they no longer have to mow the grass between the orchard rows. "We have seen a huge change in how we manage the orchards," Carrie told me. "We are trying to increase forage growth. Whereas it used to be the opposite, you want slow or low growing grass (we used to keep the orchards golf green short) now there are waist-high 'weeds' in the orchard: weeds that feed the sheep." She is hesitant to say that grazing sheep in the orchard has increased orchard production, because there are so many other factors that affect yield, but now they also get a lamb crop off the orchard, so they have increased the production and profitability of the overall operation.

We didn't get to see sheep grazing the orchards because it was still too early in the season for them to be in there, but we did wander through one of the woodlots that her flock of more than forty rams were grazing. It was hot and dry with the afternoon sun directly above us, but the canopy of the forest kept us shaded and comfortable—and the sheep seemed to agree as they rested and ruminated on the variety of plant species that they have access to in the forest. The farm has 400 acres of woodlot that was not previously being utilized. Carrie decided to start integrating this forest for grazing and habitat for the sheep, despite some pushback from local conservationists who worried that it would ruin the woodlot. Historically, some farmers have over-grazed cows in forests and caused destruction through compacted ground and damaged trees, but a well-managed silvopasture benefits both the animals and the woodlots. Carrie pointed out how hardy her Coopworth sheep are and that easy-care and resilient traits were part of their decision to choose the breed.

The Coopworth breed was developed in New Zealand after World War II by a Lincoln College faculty member named Dr. Ian Coop. The goal was to develop a breed that would increase hardiness and lambing percentages while also maintaining wool quality. He started a rigorous crossbreeding program using Border Leicester and Romney sheep, and by 1963 the new breed had been developed and was named Coopworth after Dr. Coop. The goal was for the Coopworth breed to be a practical sheep rather than a pretty sheep. Unlike other breeds that are defined by their parentage, the Coopworth evaluation is more performance-based and focuses on fertility, fleece production and growth rate. Because of this there can be some variability in the wool, depending on which flock and what region the Coopworth comes from. Coopworth wool can range from 30 to 39 microns and has a staple length with a range of 5–8 inches. It is predominantly a white wool but can be naturally grey, and, in rare cases, brown. The wool has good lustre and will offer beautiful definition to structured garments.

Agriculture Canada was responsible for importing the first Coopworths to Canada in 1985, working with Jan and Trudy Van Stralen, founders of Louet North America[1]. They brought in twenty ewes and five rams and the breed grew from there. Eventually, new genetics were imported to Canada via artificial insemination from purebred flocks in New Zealand. "I really like the Coopworth philosophy of strict culling and adherence to the

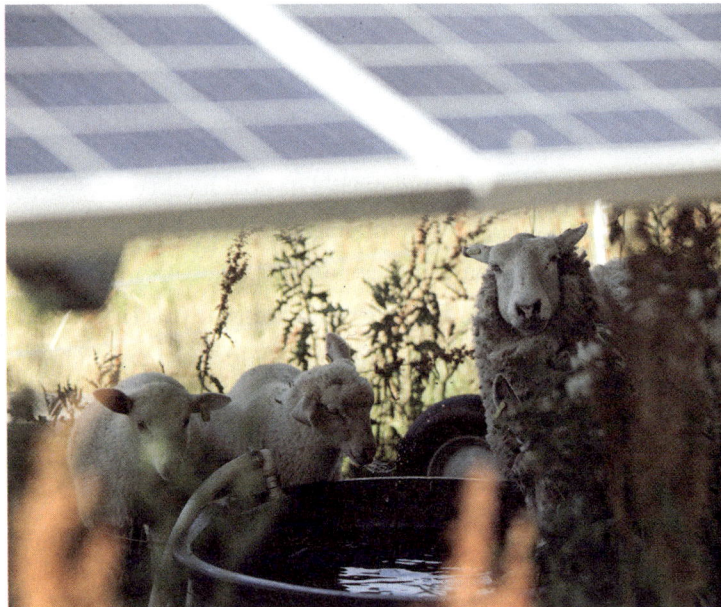

Coopworth ewe and lamb enjoying the shade under solar panels.

---

1 Obituary for Trudy van Stralen (Kropman): https://memorials.irvinefuneralhome.com/vanStralen-Trudy/2173920/obituary.php

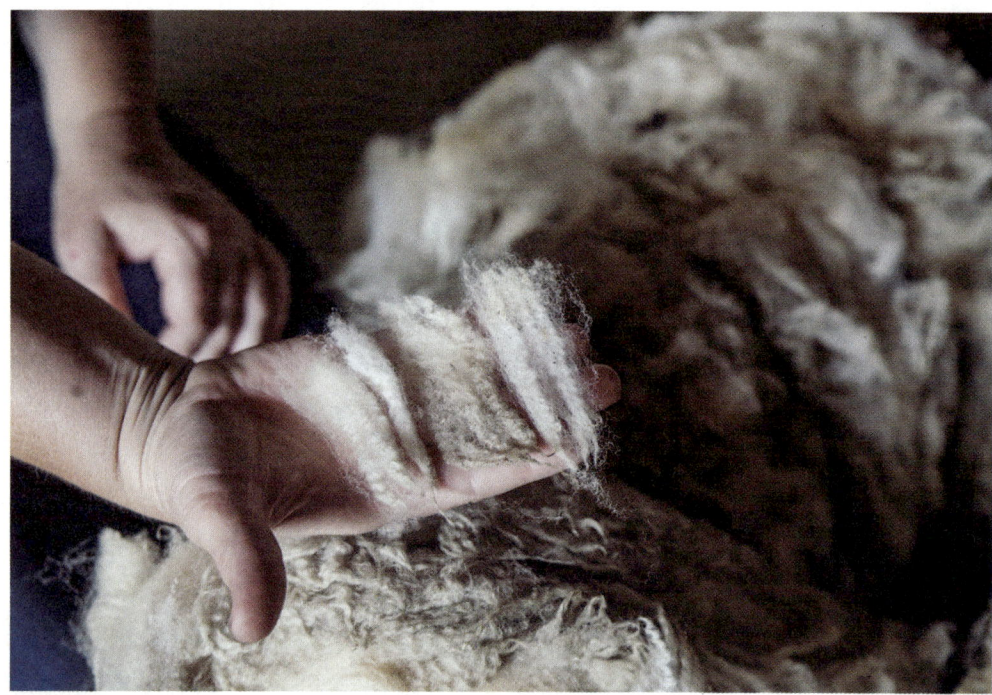

A few locks of Coopworth wool from Woolley's Lamb.

breed," Carrie told me. "The goal has been easy-care sheep, low maintenance, twins on pasture, and a focus on parasite resistance."

Easy-care would be an accurate description of Carrie's Coopworth sheep, and this quality has allowed her to move and graze over 2,000 sheep in a constantly changing landscape, including the new solar grazing operation that we toured. The local solar operation reached out to Carrie to see if they could use sheep to clear out the plants under the solar panels, in areas that they can't reach with mowers. Carrie was interested and open to seeing if the idea could work, and she took 500 ewes and their lambs there to graze. It turned out to be a win–win situation: the sheep get great forage, and the solar farm can have the grass cleared out without having to use fossil fuels and mowers that don't fit under the panels. A ewe with her two lambs hurried past us to the next bank of panels and started munching away on the mix of weeds and grasses in the shade of the large solar panels. Thinking beyond their incredible ability to add fertilizer and manage grass throughout the larger orchard and crop farming, I asked Carrie how she markets and manages the wool and meat.

She established Woolley's Lamb for her grass-fed lamb and has used many marketing strategies including wholesaling to local restaurants and employing a third-party farm-to-table ordering site called Niku Farms. Carrie has sold much of her wool to Wellington Fibre Mill in Elora, Ontario, and some to the Canadian Co-operative Wool Growers. Carrie didn't ever want to be a salesperson, and her main focus is land management and animal health. She brought us to a building that contained a dozen large bags of wool (200 pounds in each), and I was eager to open up the bags and dig into the fibre. It was beautiful fibre with a consistent crimp and lustre, and when I gently pulled the fibres apart next to my ear, I could hear its soundness. My suspicion that her sheep were in excellent condition was confirmed—it is a beautiful wool.

I suggested to Carrie that this might be an opportunity for collaboration: She isn't focused on creating a value-added wool product, but she has an excess of beautiful fibre that could be utilized. If there was an opportunity to collaborate with an aspiring fibre artist who didn't otherwise have access to a flock of 2,000 sheep, the possibilities could be incredible. The Canadian wool industry will benefit greatly from increased collaboration between shepherds, artisans, and entrepreneurs. I looked back at my tiny rental car and put the idea of purchasing large bags of wool out of my mind…at least on this trip!

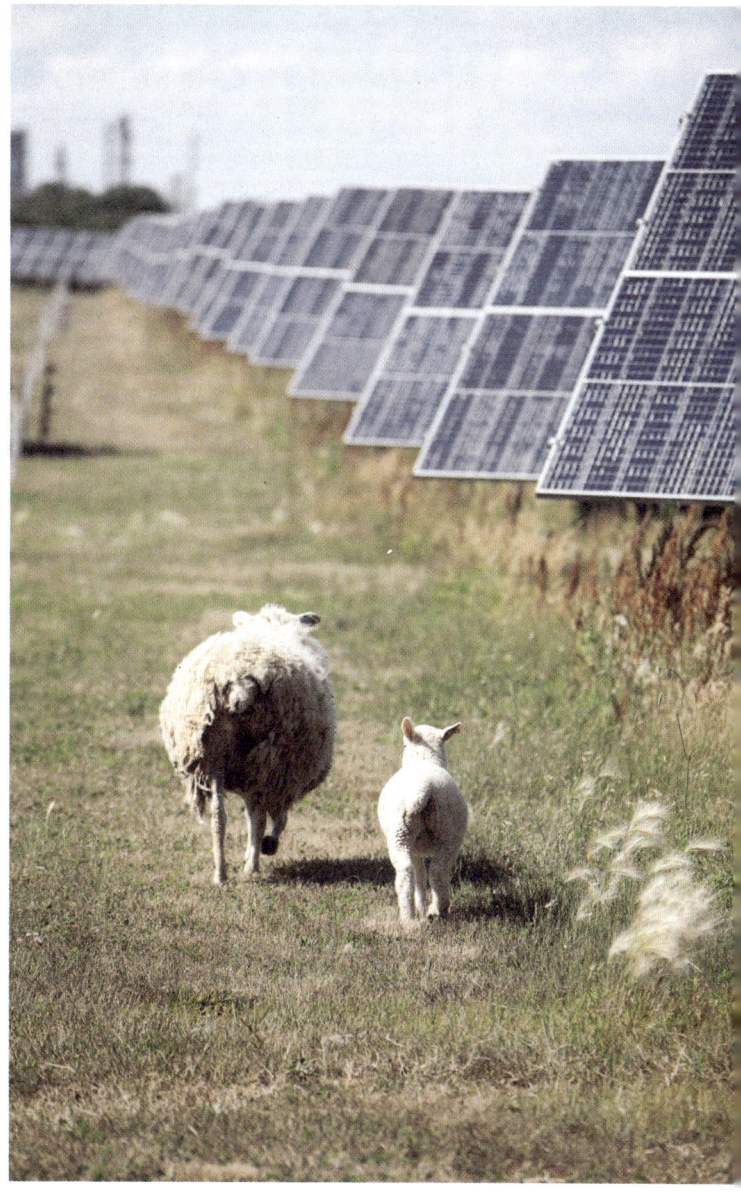

Québec
EAST FRIESIAN AND LES BREBIS DU BEAURIVAGE

I've made it my business to connect with as many fibre farmers across the country as I can. It's been easier in Western Canada, as I am geographically closer, and I've had more opportunities to meet farmers face to face. The further east we move, the more challenges I discovered—and Québec has certainly been my greatest challenge. Even though I studied French until grade twelve, my fluency lies more in understanding conjugation rules rather than in conversational French.

But one day, while scrolling through Instagram, I came across a sheep picture that blew my mind, and I knew I had to meet the person (@brebisdubeaurivage) behind the photo. The person is Audrey Boulet, owner and operator of Les Brebis du Beaurivage, where she raises East Friesian sheep in Levis, Québec.

The photo I'd seen was the backsides of twelve East Friesian sheep "all bagged up" (a farm term to describe udders that are very full of milk) and hooked up to a milking machine. I was aware that there are a few excellent milk sheep breeds out there, and I am a huge fan of sheep's milk cheese, but I didn't actually know any farmers with this sort of operation.

The sheep dairy industry in Canada is fairly new and is not as robust as the meat or even the fledgling wool industry. To have found a creative,

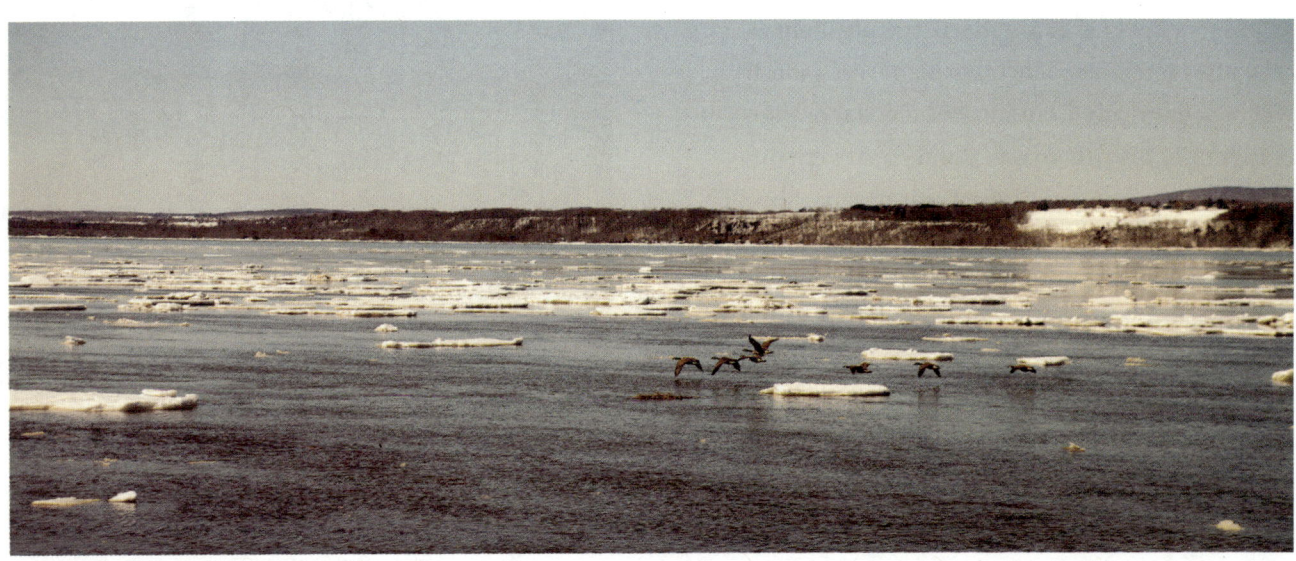

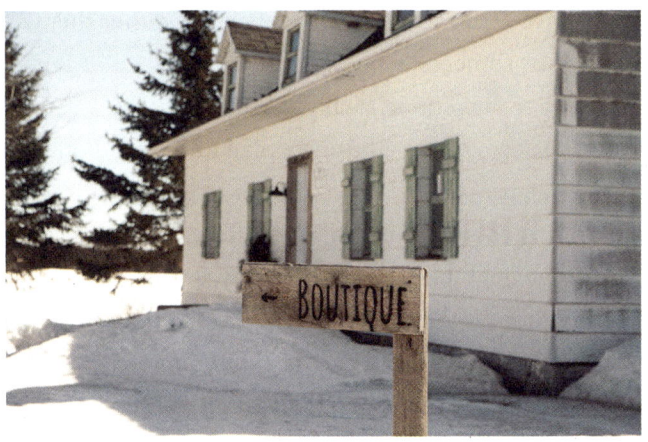 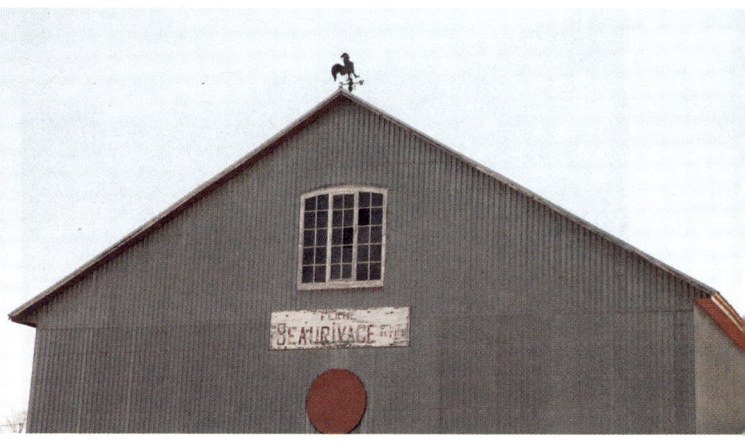

The boutique yarn shop at Les Brebis Du Beaurivage Farm.

entrepreneurial farmer who is focusing on sheep's milk and *also* doing a kick-ass job of marketing their wool and value-added wool products, I knew I had to meet her.

Christel and I, along with our favourite sidekick Nicole, piled into a car (thanks to Arianne for the excellent drive and tour), and headed out of Montreal along the south side of the St. Lawrence River, up towards the Chaudières-Appalaches region.

It was a beautiful day: the sun was warming the ground and reminding us that spring was around the corner. The St. Lawrence was speckled with huge chunks of melting ice and snow that were slowly drifting north towards the gulf, washing away the last of the winter snow and sludge and welcoming spring growth.

Loosely translated, the name of Audrey's farm means "Sheep of the Beautiful Riverside." And the description couldn't have been more literal as we drove along the St. Lawrence and imagined the beauty of a summer day in this region filled with orchards and vineyards, local cheese makers, cider houses, and artist studios. We drove down the lane and pulled up to her picturesque white farmhouse with green shuttered windows, which also serves as a small boutique store for her yarn, fibre, sheepskins, and other products. The house, which dates back to the early 1800s, is the ancestral home of Olivier Beaurivage, Audrey's spouse, and his family has managed the land and cared for animals there since the early 1900s. They raised cattle, chickens, pigs and all the other animals one would need to feed a family, and now its most recent iteration is a sheep dairy.

Audrey did not come from a farming or shepherding background, and wool wasn't even her initial motivation to get into raising sheep. She had been driving to Québec City twice a day and working as an industrial designer. She and Olivier

Ontario & Québec 95

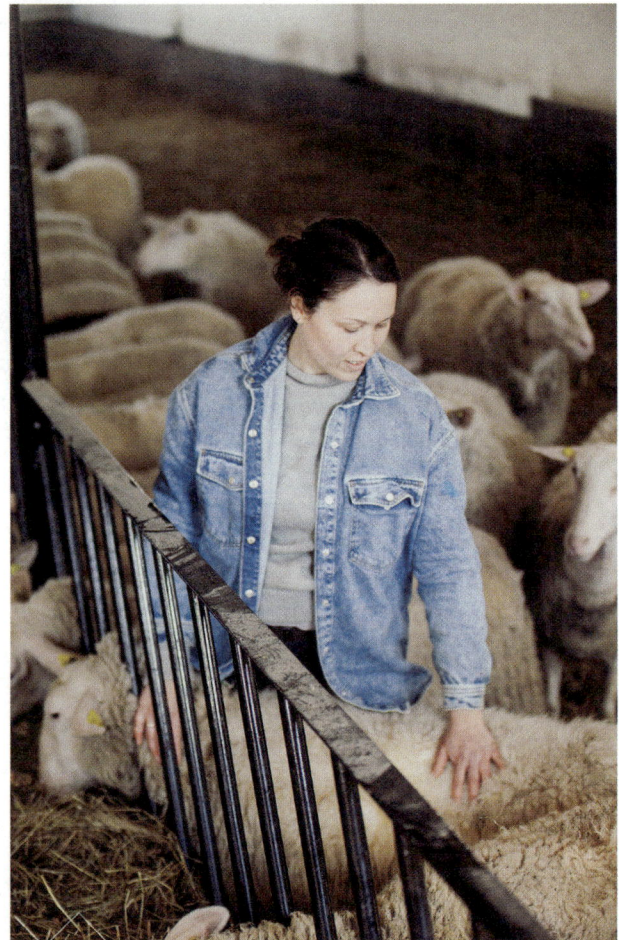

Audrey Boulet and her East Friesian sheep.

had great jobs and were very entrepreneurial, but when Audrey became pregnant with their first daughter they had a feeling that they wanted a different kind of life. Because Olivier's father had the farm property, they thought it would be a great place to start. So, in 2016 they moved to the farm and, "… just started with sheep right away. Crazy like that," Audrey told me with a giggle—not a nervous or dismissive giggle either, but rather the laugh of someone who had just taken a leap of faith and done something totally unexpected.

Audrey wrote a business plan and visited other sheep dairies. She decided that their plan for the farm would be to start with sixty East Friesian ewes, with the goal to make great quality sheep's milk. They did this for the first two years, until 2018, when they identified a demand for lamb meat and sheepskins. Audrey created an online shop to sell sheepskins, and she started getting requests from local yarn dyers in Québec for more yarn. In 2019 she decided to diversify her products and began selling yarn and fibre. She couldn't find a local mill in Québec, or a large enough one close by, to handle the size of her wool clip, so she sent her wool across the country to Alberta for processing by Custom Woolen Mills.

As Audrey shared her story of becoming a sheep farmer, and eventually a wool producer, it became clear that she is a woman with vision and serious marketing skills. Her background in industrial design taught her about diversification of products, and she had experience working with suppliers, planning transportation, and marketing, so developing a yarn business on top of the milk, meat, and sheepskins was a natural extension of her skills and interests. "I've been knitting since I was eight years old, and I love to draw. I'm a creator. But I didn't have the wool in mind because everyone said the wool wasn't worth anything and to just throw it away."

Despite the perspective among some other breeders that East Friesian wool is not high quality due to its high micron count (28–37 microns) and more rustic feel, Audrey has created a thriving business with her wool. She sells it in her on-farm boutique shop and her online store, and she works with local natural dyers to develop a line of beautiful tonal yarns. Her sheep are sheared twice a year and each ewe produces ten to twelve pounds of wool a year. She focuses on producing breed-specific yarn and, although they have occasionally introduced other milking breeds to her flock, she is focused on the highest quality East Friesian wool for her yarn and fibre. "Each breed has its own quality and characteristics, and we can't lose that," she says.

"It's not acceptable to me." Audrey has strategically marketed her wool as a quality product by working with designers and dyers and setting herself apart. She has added value to the resource that too many other farmers are trashing. This is the type of innovation and entrepreneurship that our industry needs, and that I hope this book will inspire.

The East Friesian breed is a German dairy sheep originating from the Friesland region that straddles the border between Germany and the

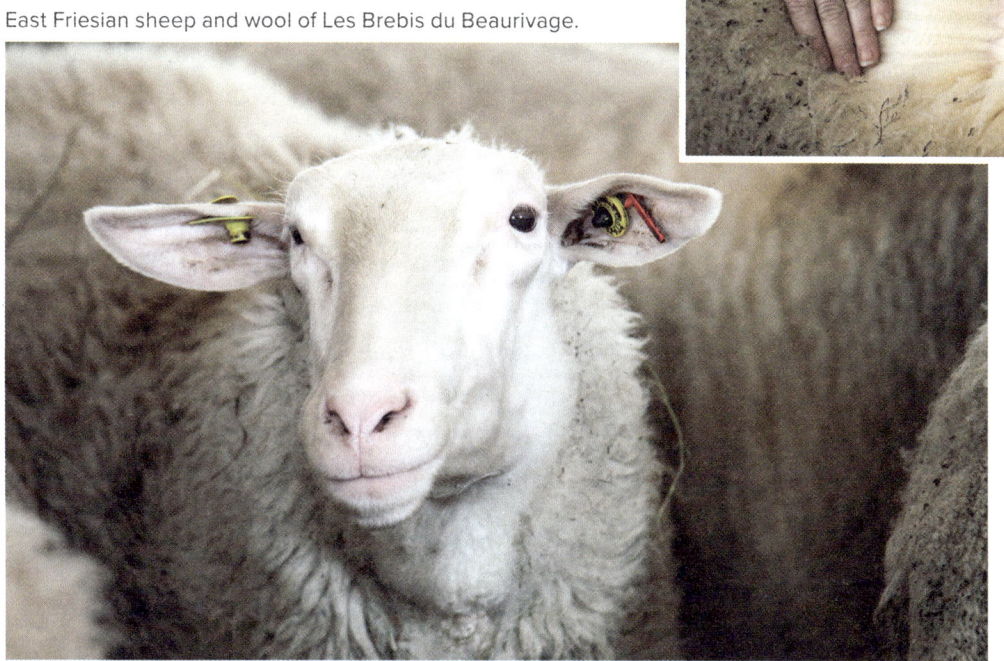

East Friesian sheep and wool of Les Brebis du Beaurivage.

Ontario & Québec 97

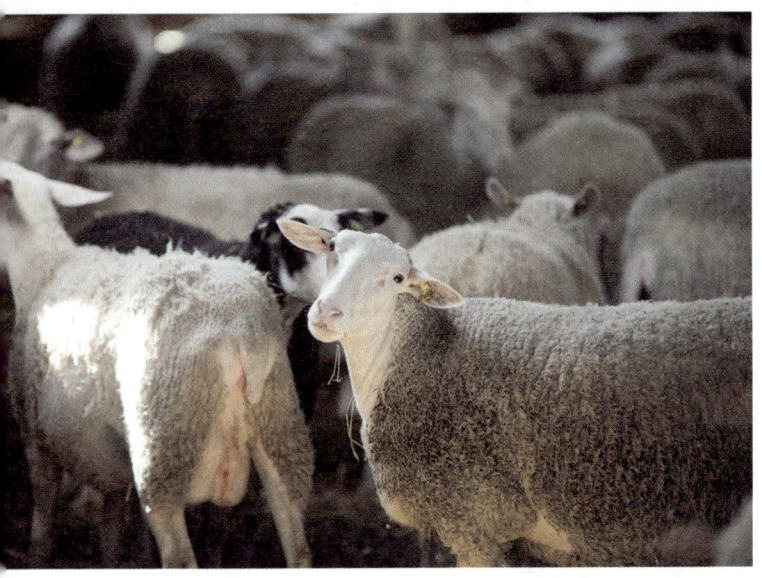
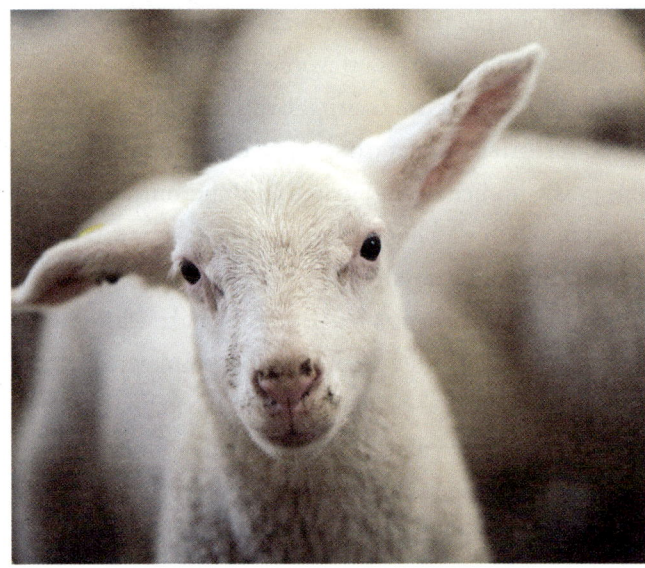

Netherlands. The breed had an interesting journey to Canadian farms. Chris Buschbeck and Axel Meister met while attending university in Germany and shortly afterwards, in the 1980s, they immigrated to Canada to begin a sheep farm, Wooldrift Farms, near Guelph, Ontario. They believed that Canadians were missing out on all the delicious sheep milk cheese that they had loved in Germany, but they couldn't find quality dairy sheep in North America. So, in 1994 they imported East Friesian embryos from Germany and implanted sixty-seven of them into Rideau Arcott ewes. Five months later, they had thirty-two purebred East Friesian sheep, and the breed began to thrive in Canada. It has since grown in popularity in both Canada and the U.S.

East Friesian sheep can be white or black, and they have very trusting attitudes; it is not a nervous breed, which makes it an excellent choice for a twice-daily milking operation. The wool can be variable, with a micron count between 28 and 37 microns, and it generally has a 3–6-inch staple length. In the beginning, Audrey was breeding for milk production, but now that the wool business is thriving, she focuses on both. "That's what I like about East Friesians," she explained. "We have the milk, the lamb, the wool. They have many qualities. They are very calm and docile, and I really like to work with them." Audrey's sheep produce two to three litres of sheep's milk a day for the first four months after lambing and then about one litre a day for the next four to six months. Audrey sends 30,000 kilograms of milk a year to local cheesemaker, Fromage Nouveau France.

After touring the barns, the milking parlour, and the nursery (where we were swarmed by so many adorable lambs that we didn't want to ever leave), we headed to the charming boutique shop, located in the front entrance of the house that they have been restoring to expose some of the original, 150-year-old beams and wood. In the shop, a hutch was full-to-overflowing with beautiful yarn and roving, and the cutest clothesline of socks hung on a wall above sheepskins and blankets and sweater samples made from Audrey's wool. I bought socks—because let's be honest, between the farming and the mill, I hardly ever make time for knitting anymore. I also bought some maple syrup that they tap from the trees on the ridge line above their home. None of us wanted to leave the boutique; it felt warm and inviting, and I think if there had been a couch I would've sat down and actually done some knitting. Audrey showed off the multiple samples she or others have knit out of her yarn, and I appreciated her candour about the quality of her wool. Her wool is beautiful for sweaters or mittens and will keep the wearer cozy and warm during cold Québec winters. She isn't trying to convince people who only knit with Merino that her wool is just as soft, but she knows it is something special with its own bounce and elasticity and warmth. When I asked Audrey what her goal is for the farm, she said it is simply to transform all her quality wool into a product that shows off the breed, first and foremost! 》

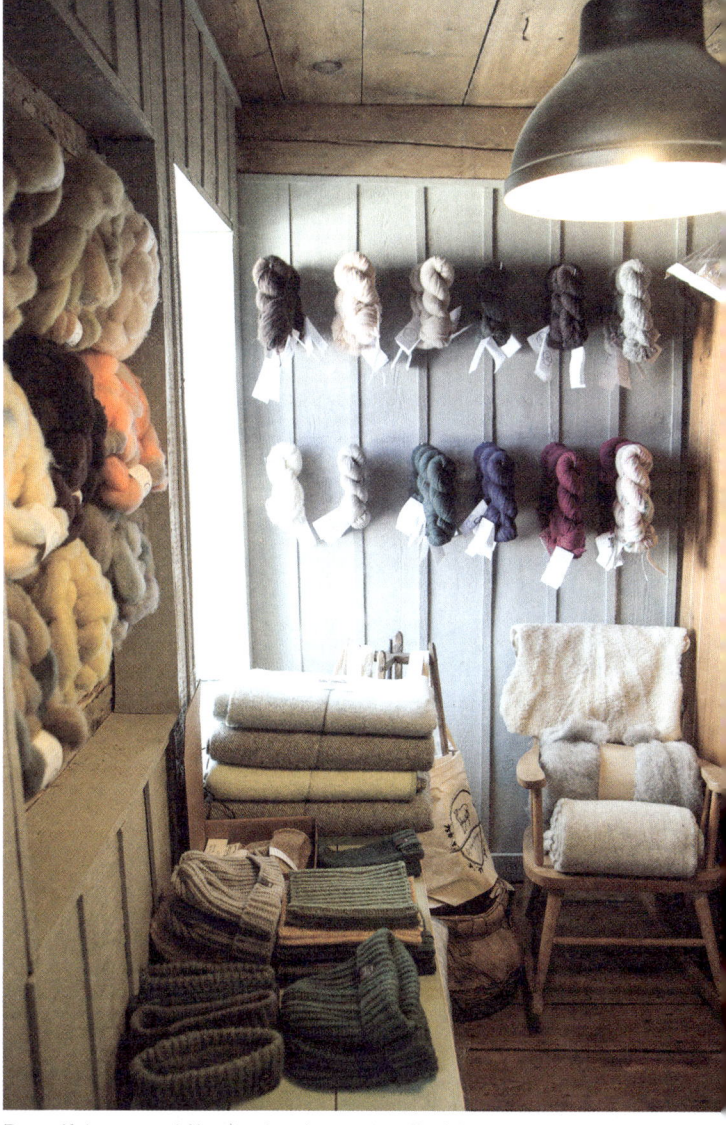

Beautiful yarn and fibre in the shop at Les Brebis du Beaurivage.

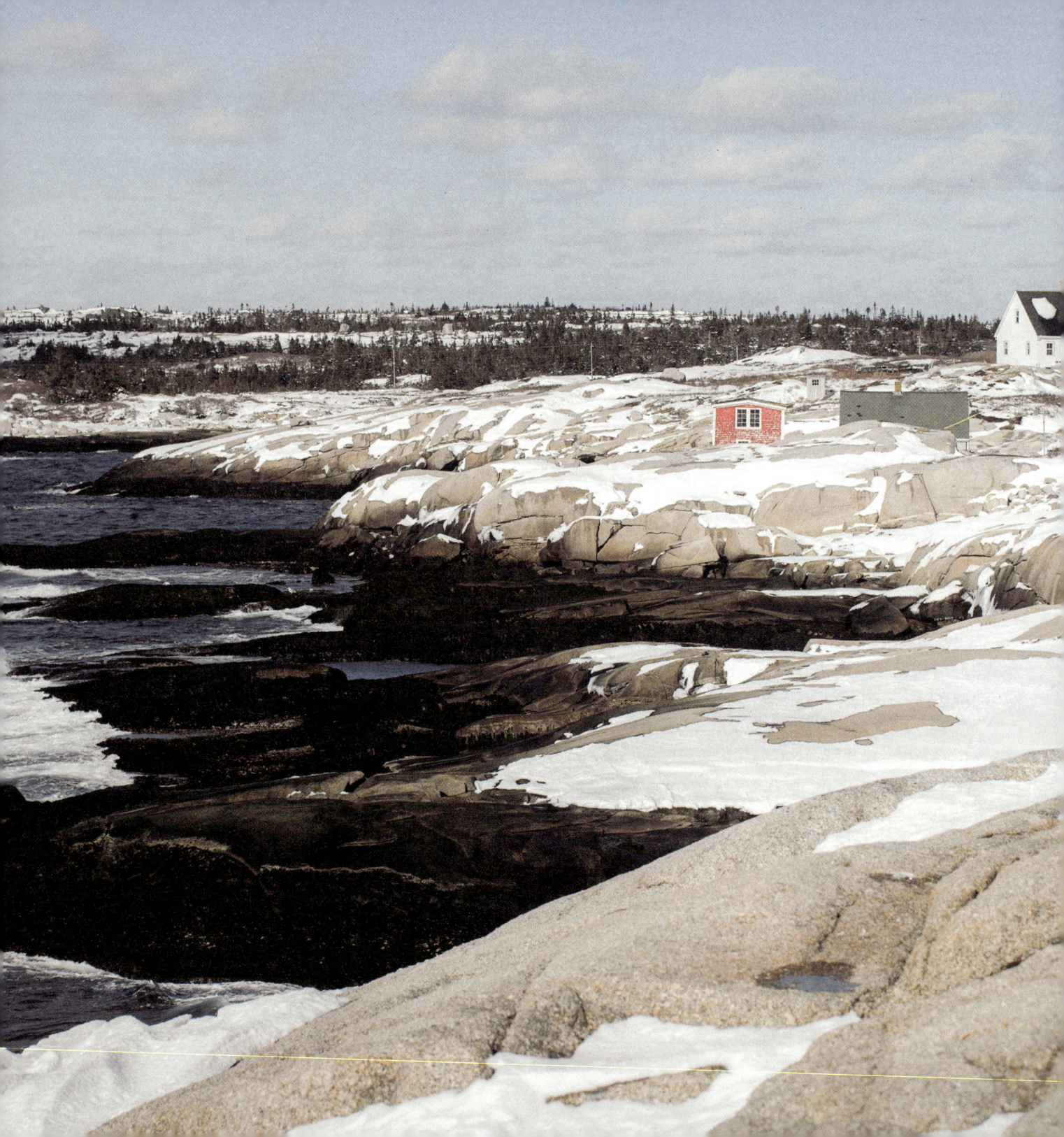

East Coast

I'VE FOUND MANY INFORMATION SOURCES claiming that sheep were first brought to New France in the 1660s, and I've also found references to sheep arriving in Port Mouton, Nova Scotia, as early as May, 1604. There is a long and rich history of fibre production in Atlantic Canada. Most Acadians wore clothes exclusively made of wool and linen that they grew and processed on their farms. It is not surprising that farmers in Canada's Atlantic Provinces are responsible for many of the breeds we have across Canada today and are home to some of the oldest wool-processing mills in the country.

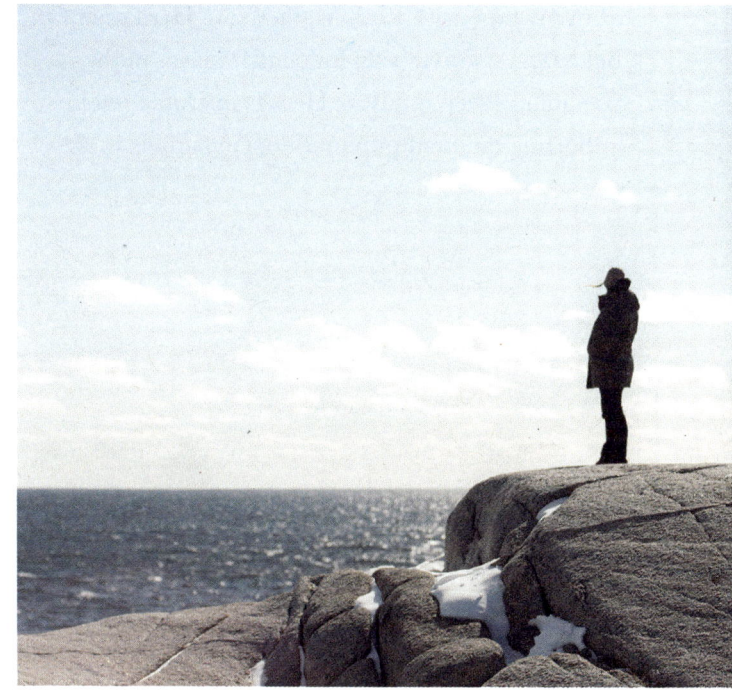

Anna staring out over the Atlantic Ocean at Peggy's Cove, Nova Scotia.

Nova Scotia
NORTH COUNTRY CHEVIOT AND WOOLIES OF UPPERBROOK FARM

As I've travelled across the country meeting with fibre farmers and hearing their stories of sheep and wool and land, I've noticed certain key themes emerging, each one illuminating different opportunities and challenges that exist in the Canadian wool industry and furthering my resolve to fight for growth in the industry.

Tradition and *legacy* are the themes that emerged from my time with Ruth Mathewson. Her father, Bill Mathewson, was an influential player in the Canadian sheep industry. He was instrumental in importing different purebred sheep, and his work impacted future farmers through his teaching and, after his passing, through a bursary fund for agriculture students, set up in his honour. Learning about Bill's story and how his daughter, Ruth, has continued his legacy and forged her own path with sheep and wool was truly an honour.

I met Ruth for the first time in 2017 at the Manitoba Fibre Festival, where we took a wool judging class together. I appreciated her candor about starting a wool mill, and I remember being impressed by her understanding of wool and the industry. It wasn't until she shared the story of

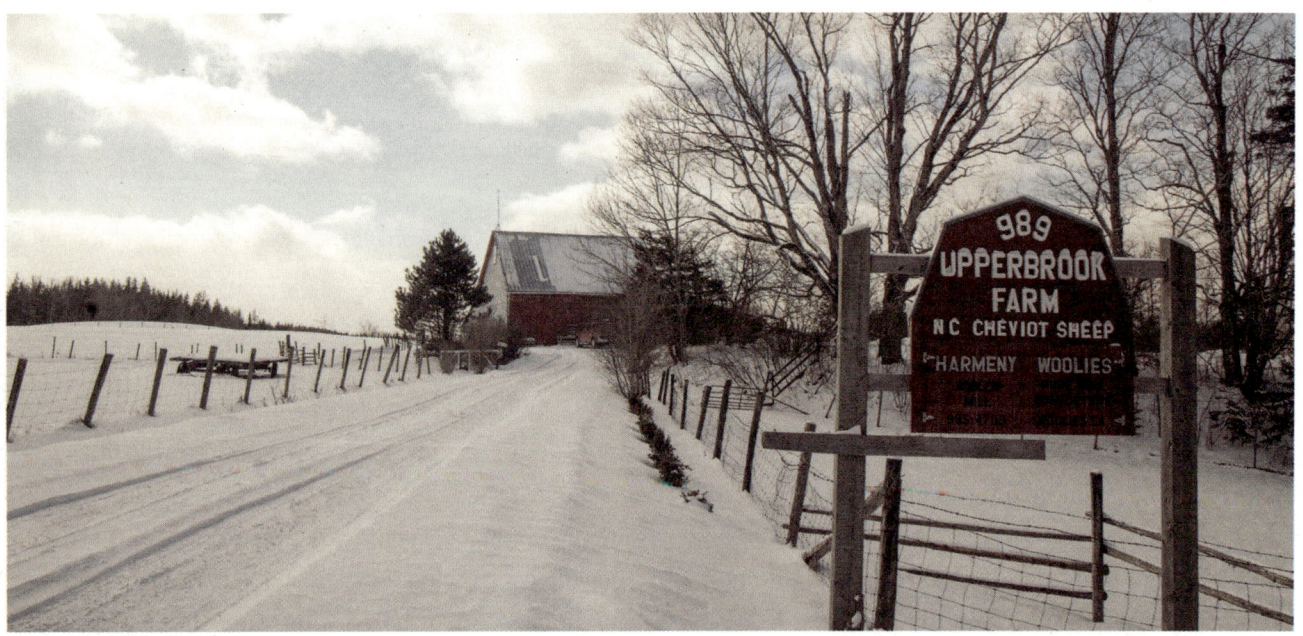

her farm that I understood where that depth of understanding comes from. Ruth—and Upperbrook Farm—have an incredible story that is inextricably linked to the North Country Cheviot breed.

Christel and I drove along the windy, snowy, single-lane highway through a canopy of trees and under a bluebird sky. We were thankful to have missed a snowstorm the day before, because in its wake we had a clear sky for taking photos, and a beautiful fresh snow backdrop for our drive. We pulled into the driveway, where a decades-old sign for Upperbrook Farm stood, proud and tall. Ruth's dog announced our arrival and, as we stepped from the vehicle, he let us know that he was protector of the sheep and the humans at this farm.

First, we stepped into the wool mill and yarn shop. It one of those classic farm scenes: a bright red building set against the clear blue sky, with white windows and doors, and snow on the roof. The cozy storefront welcomed us with the wood stove aroma and the low, sloped ceiling. The beams had been preserved from an old barn and had been full of square nails that they'd had to pull out by hand. A tedious job for sure, but the end result was a space that felt both rustic and homey—a place where one would want to pull up a chair and start knitting. The walls were lined with shelving that was bursting with fibre for felting, wool pillows and hand-tied duvets, tapestry weavings, handknit mittens (with the trigger finger—a nod to Newfoundland knitters). It was clear that every item in the shop was created with attention to detail, using local supplies and influences.

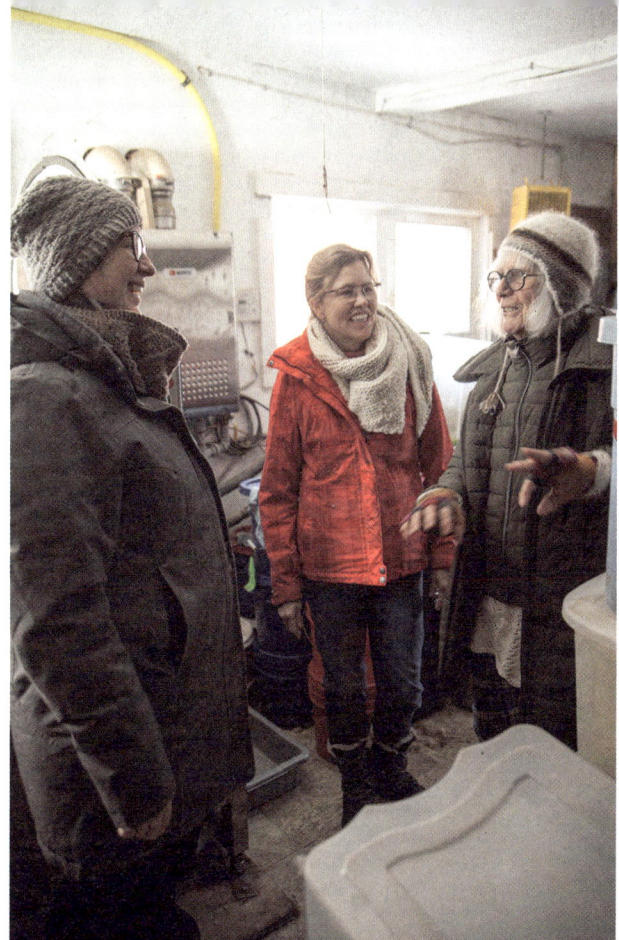

(L–R) Anna, Ruth Mathewson, and Delia Burge laughing at the challenges of small-scale wool processing in the Woolies mill.

Next, we toured the sixteen-by-twenty-foot mill that Ruth operates single-handedly. I was amazed at how effectively she uses her tiny space. We talked shop about her mill, about things that perhaps only other mill owners would find interesting, like how does your water heater set up work, how do you organize processing notes and fleeces, and how many pounds a day are you processing…and are you feeling overwhelmed like me? There is a certain type of camaraderie I shared with Ruth: When so few are

East Coast 103

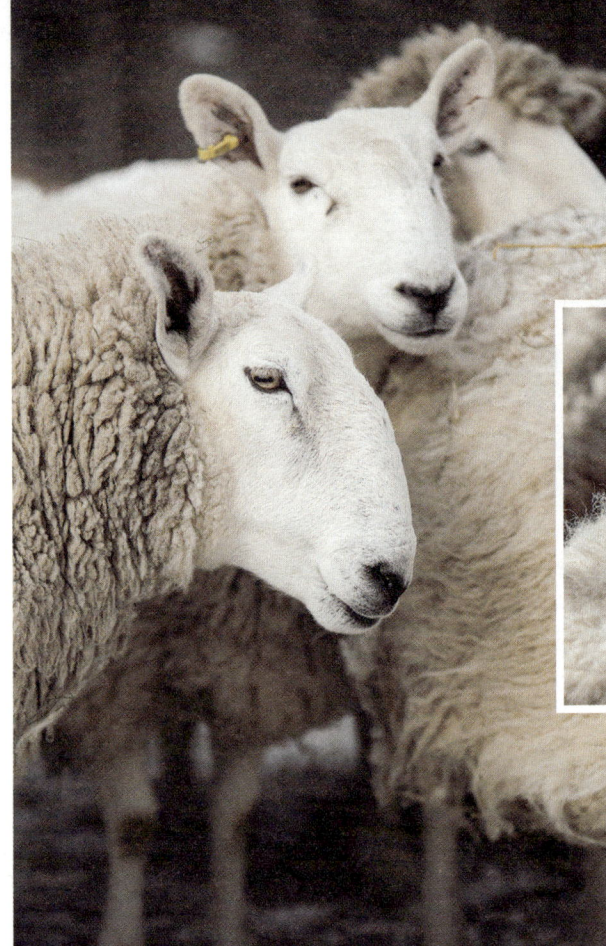

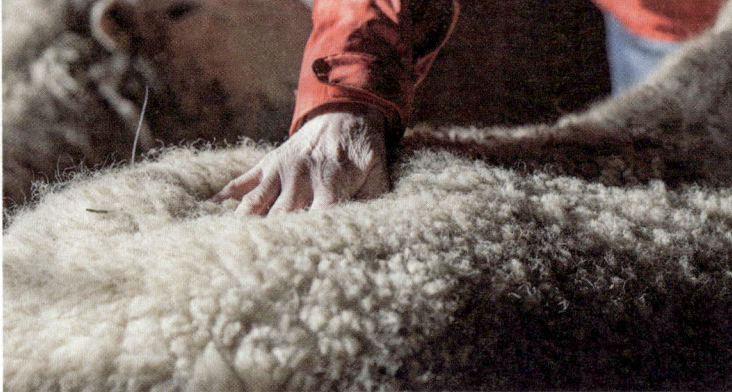

Ruth Mathewson demonstrating the loft of North Country Cheviot wool.

involved in an industry as challenging and as isolated as fibre processing millwork, it was comforting to share stories with her and know that I'm not alone. She then ushered us into her quaint little farmhouse for a beautiful spread of homemade muffins, cookies, fruit, and tea. (Did I mention how well Christel and I eat on these trips?) The hospitality of fibre farmers is truly unparalleled.

We were joined by Delia Burge, another Nova Scotia shepherd and fibre artist, and a dear friend to Ruth. Christel and I instantly felt that we were among kindred spirits and saw ourselves reflected in these women who care for their sheep, the land, and their friendship. We fell into the type of conversation you have with old friends as we heard their stories of shepherding and wool.

Delia shared her story of moving from the West Coast to a farm near Truro, Nova Scotia, in 1979. People laughed at her when she said she was going to raise sheep for wool, but she started with black face/grey face sheep, and then got a Romney ram, some Lincoln-cross, and some Finn-cross sheep. She now raises Wensleydale sheep, and, as far as I can tell, she is a stalwart presence in the Nova Scotia sheep and wool scene. Delia is well known for the wool she grows and sells as dyed locks, roving, felt, or handspun. Delia and Ruth shared the stories of their Friday afternoon get-togethers to knit and gossip and drink wine as Delia's rams wander around her yard, and we all shared a knowing laugh about the wine/knitting/farming moments. Delia has taught Ruth how to knit and spin, and they founded the website Local Fibre Love (localfibrelove.ca), a place to connect fibre farmers and consumers in Nova Scotia. After sharing our experiences with the various typical ram personalities and commiserating over the behaviour of some in particular—ahem, Shetland rams, we are looking at you—I asked Ruth to tell us her story of shepherding.

To get the full picture of Ruth's farming background, we have to go back a generation to Ruth's parents, Bill and Greta Mathewson.

Bill grew up on a hilly sheep farm in Scotland; he studied agriculture in the U.K. and then travelled to Trinidad and Tobago to study tropical agriculture. After completing his studies in 1949, he moved to Tanzania to work as an agricultural engineer. There he met Greta, a young, "action-oriented lady," according to Ruth. Greta was from Calgary but felt a calling to go to Africa to work as a nurse. At the age of twenty-three, she travelled by herself to New York, then by boat to Tanzania, where she ended up running a 500-bed leprosarium. Bill and Greta met during this time and decided to marry and start a family. They continued to work in Tanzania where they had Ruth's three older siblings, and then Ruth

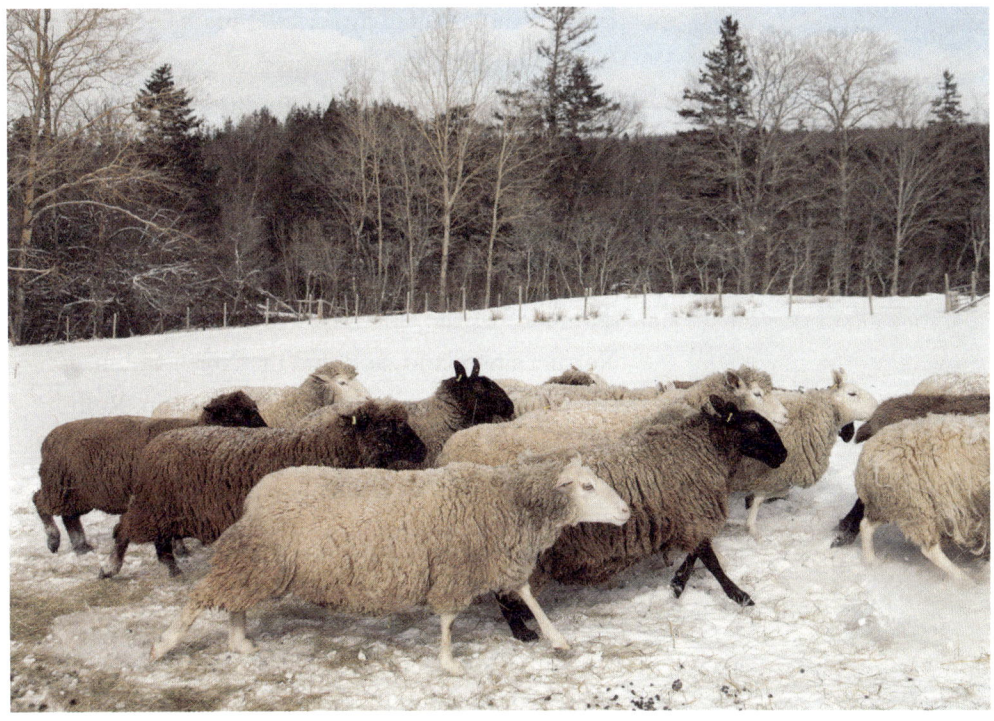

North Country Cheviot sheep in the wintertime at Upperbrook Farm.

came along after a trip home to Scotland. In 1965, as Tanzania was working to gain independence from British Rule, they moved back to Scotland.

They struggled to find work in Scotland, so, in 1968, Bill travelled to Canada to look for farm work in Calgary. During this trip he had an interview at the Dalhousie Agricultural College in Nova Scotia, and they offered him a job as a professor of sheep and beef husbandry. Greta travelled to Canada with Ruth, and her siblings, and they began farming. It seemed an obvious choice for Bill to import North Country Cheviot sheep, as they were native to the region of Scotland where he was from, and he had experience working with the breed.

The North Country Cheviot sheep originated in Northern Scotland around 1791, when Sir John Sinclair crossed Border Cheviots with Leicester bloodlines. They have been raised primarily for meat and for their hardiness in rough conditions. A small group of ten ewes and two rams were first introduced to Canada in 1944, to Macdonald College in Québec, and the resulting lambs caught the attention of the Canadian Department of Agriculture. In 1953, many more were imported to Canada, and the North Country Cheviot became a popular breed with Canadian sheep producers.

Bill was influential in bringing the breed to Eastern Canada. He imported a small flock of North Country Cheviot to his own farm, both to raise, and as an opportunity for his students at the Agricultural College to experience hands-on learning in sheep husbandry. It was during this time that Bill became a founding member of the Purebred Sheep Breeders Association of Nova Scotia. He recognized that much of the land base in Nova Scotia was like Northern Scotland, and that the North Country Cheviot could thrive on this rough terrain. Ruth still raises sheep from the lineage of that original flock that her father brought over.

In 1972, the family moved their farm to its current location near Truro, Nova Scotia, and added purebred Scottish Shorthorn cattle to their flock

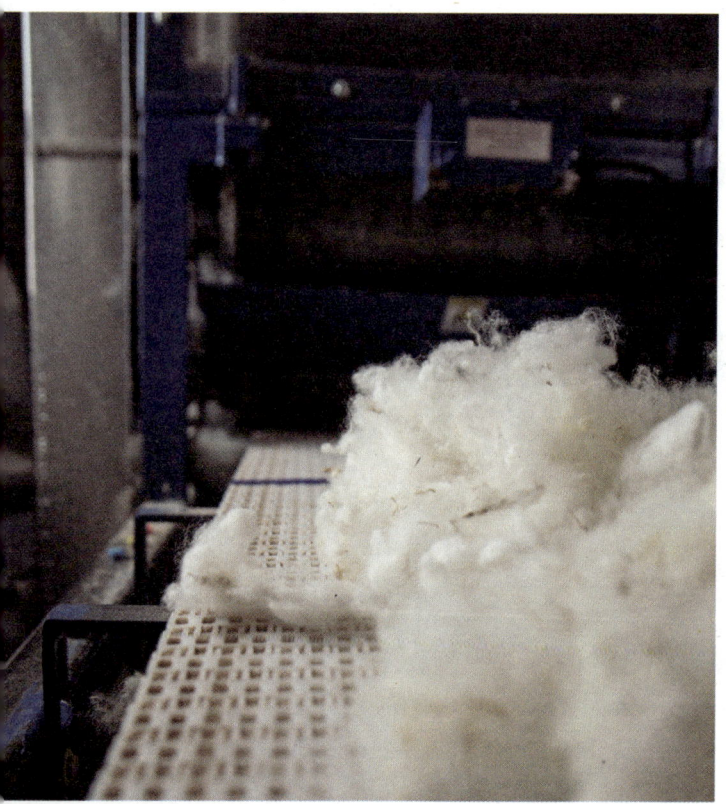

Wool carding at the Woolies mill.

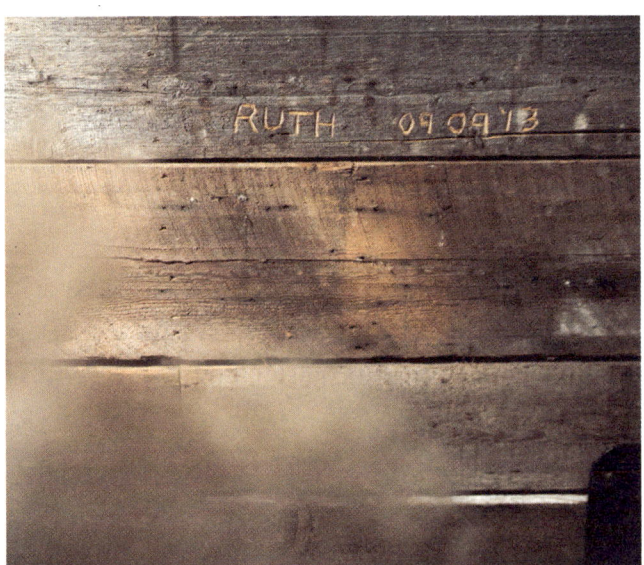 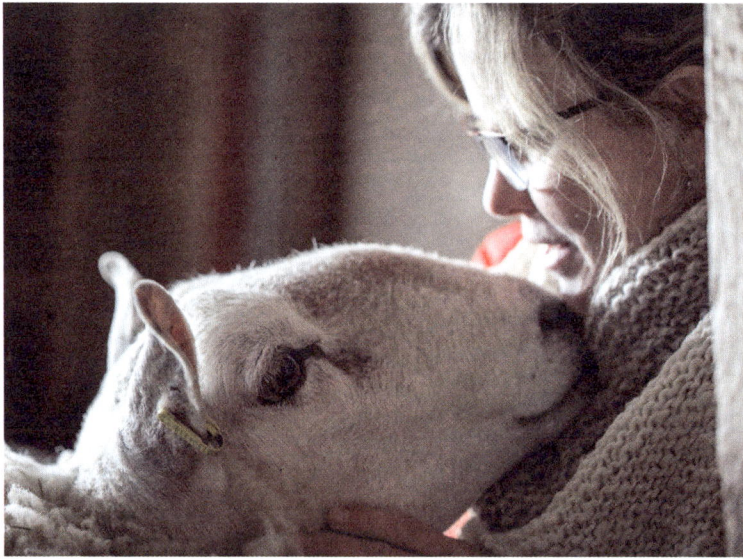

of purebred North Country Cheviot sheep. Ruth's introduction to wool came in the late 1960s when her mother started making wool comforters because no one wanted to use the North Country Cheviot wool for anything else. She would wash the wool by hand, outside in the summer and in a tub on the porch in the winter. Ruth remembers it smelling just awful, but it was something they all got used to. Greta had a picker and a hand carder, and the batts she prepared were twelve inches wide by eighteen inches long. She would use a hundred batts to make a comforter, using cheesecloth and running stitches that she sewed by hand. These comforters were well-known and they would be sent all over the region.

Ruth grew up around wool and sheep and learned so much from her parents during this time, but she didn't plan to take over the farm and wool business. After she graduated from high school in 1982, she went to university and earned a bachelor's degree in applied art. She spent time travelling in New Zealand and Australia, then returned to Canada, where she worked in Toronto, and then moved back to Halifax, Nova Scotia. It wasn't until her father died at the beginning of lambing season in 2008 that she returned to the farm to help her mother with the sheep and farm work, and she hasn't left since.

Despite growing up on the farm and helping her parents, Ruth wasn't prepared for running the farm herself, but her mother was an incredible resource and mentor. It was a steep learning curve, but you would never know this while watching Ruth effortlessly handle her sheep and run the farm and mill business with steadiness and grace.

Ruth still makes comforters and pillows out of their North Country Cheviot wool. It is a lot of work: Even though she has a commercial-size carder and picker, she still hand-ties every comforter that she creates. "North Country Cheviot wool is spongy like fresh bread, it springs right back, and you know it's not going to felt." North Country Cheviot sheep can produce six to ten pounds of wool a year, and the wool would likely be considered a more rustic fibre for next-to-the-skin items. It runs between 27 and 33 microns and the breed only produces white wool. Besides being a perfect choice for wool bedding like comforters and pillows, with its full-bodied bounce and resistance to felting, it would also make incredible outer layers like sweaters, socks, or blankets.

Ruth asserts that the North Country Cheviot are a perfect breed for their land base, well suited to take the rugged terrain with its sparse forage and convert it into food and thus wool. Raising fine wool sheep in a wet climate like hers would not provide the best environment for the sheep to thrive.

Ruth is hopeful for the future of wool in Canada, cautiously optimistic about what needs to be done, and who will heed the call to do this work. She is equally open to growth and new plans for her mill and wool business as she is confident in the strong legacy started for her by her parents, which she has been able to carry on.

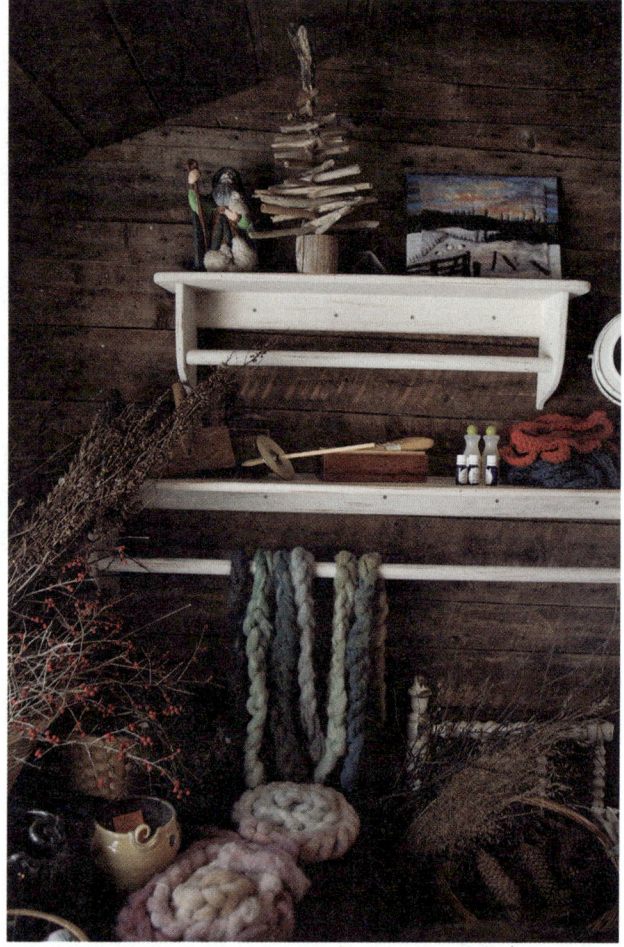

Beautiful fibre and yarn in the Woolies on-farm yarn shop.

Nova Scotia
LINCOLN LONGWOOL AND HIDDEN MEADOW FARM

In the years prior to writing this book, I've had the pleasure of meeting many of the fibre farmers I've profiled here, at fibre shows or other wool-focused events, but I had only ever admired Stacy Corkum from afar, scrolling through her dreamy feed on Instagram (@farm.meadow). From the beautiful pictures of her highland cattle and long-wool sheep, to her commitment to preserving heritage breeds, I was fascinated. I had to learn more about what motivated her to care for and preserve the Lincoln Longwool breed.

Christel and I set out for Stacy's farm in the Annapolis Valley of Nova Scotia, already a little bit behind schedule. Despite my careful planning—and even contingency plans—we still felt as though, throughout this adventure, we were always racing the light for perfect pictures. The Annapolis Valley is a stunning part of Canadian geography that, regardless of the time of year, is breathtaking. The region runs along the Bay of Fundy coastline and is known for its shifting landscape of rocky shores, marshes, beaches, and stunning tides. It has a distinctive micro-climate,

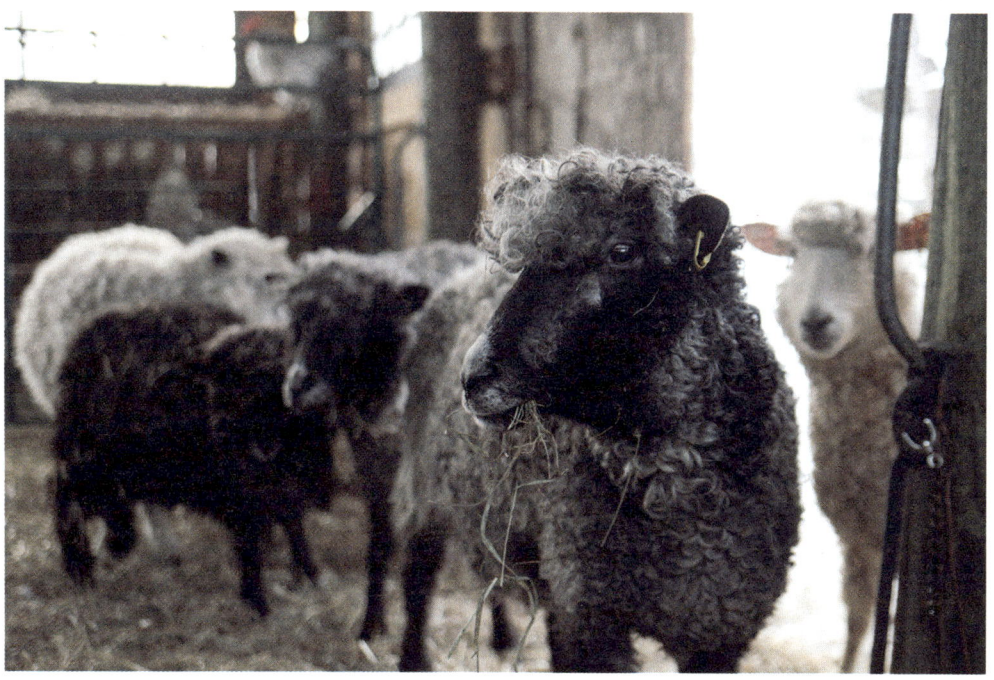

Lincoln Longwool sheep at Hidden Meadow Farm.

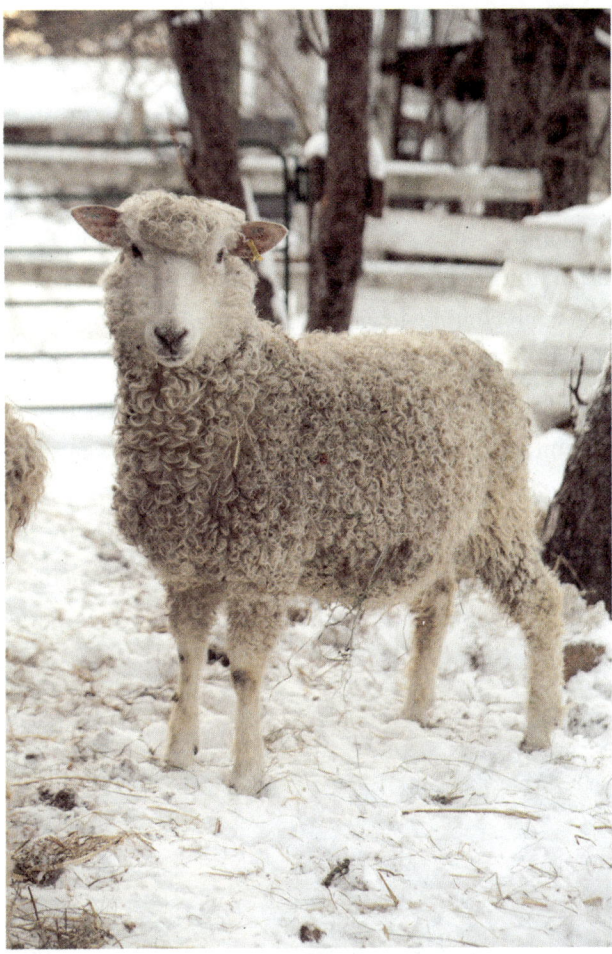

making it an important fruit-growing and wine-producing region. (Christel and I may have splurged on an extra-large bag of apples, even though it was March, and far too much wine and cider for what was most definitely a work trip.)

We overshot Stacy's driveway and had to turn around on a small, single-lane highway in the diminishing light, with thick, wet snow everywhere, and desperately hoping we wouldn't get the rental car stuck in the driveway of a stranger's property. Agriculture is different in the Annapolis Valley than it is in the vast prairies of Manitoba. In fact, most farmers we spoke with couldn't believe that we were going to drive between New Brunswick, Nova Scotia, and Prince Edward Island in the three days we spent in Atlantic Canada. They balked when I said I often do three hours of driving, at home in Manitoba, just to get to a neighbouring sheep farm to pick up wool. In the Maritimes, everything seems closer together, and I was surprised to find this 165-acre parcel of farmland sandwiched between other homes and farms.

Having avoided getting stuck in the snow, I pulled into the driveway, and Stacy and her ten-year-old daughter, Alexis, were waiting for us and ready to start the tour. The sound of the incessant rooster crowing was only slightly louder than the rapid shutter sound of Christel's camera, since we were once again rushing to outpace the impending sunset so we could get quality pictures of the sheep. Christel looked over at Stacy and asked, "Can I climb over these hay bales to get over the fence so I can get a photo of the sheep from this angle? I don't want to use the gate 'cause I don't want to freak them out." Part of what I love about working with Christel is her all-in commitment to my wild ideas. This sometimes means laying down on snowy-wet pasture for the perfect shot, or forgoing using the gate and instead climbing over hay bales—all for the sake of a better angle.

Stacy laughed and told her to go for it. Christel avoided the gate, but the sheep were alarmed anyway, and they ran to find safety and comfort from Stacy and Alexis. I was immediately enamoured by her Lincoln Longwool sheep, with their long locks of wool that obscured their vision and made them look slightly dorky.

Stacy Corkum's circuitous route to wool farming started when she was working as a cook in a small, homestyle restaurant and wanted to seek out the best ingredients to cook with. She spoke with other chefs and learned that it really came down to the breed selection of the plants and animals that she chose. She started researching breeds and, in 1998, started her farm, Hidden Meadow. She raised heritage turkeys, geese, pigs, ducks, highland cows, and then, finally, sheep. She now farms Highland cattle and Lincoln Longwool sheep.

This journey of seeking out, and then raising, the best breeds of animals and plants for food led Stacy into the world of livestock conservation, and ultimately to protecting and growing a flock of Lincoln Longwool Sheep.

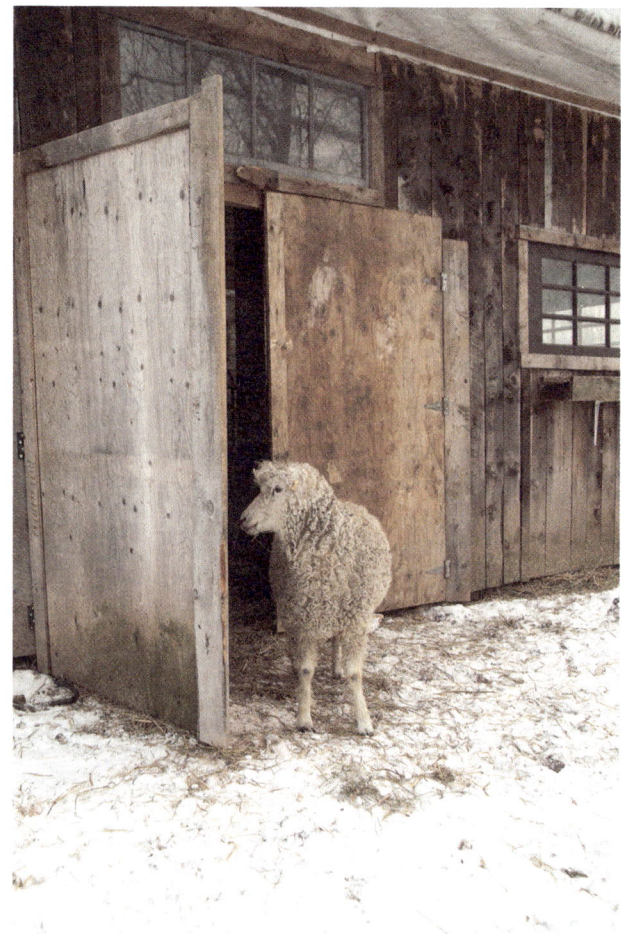

Lincoln Longwool sheep peeking out from the barn at Hidden Meadow Farm.

"Everything we have here on the farm is a rare or heritage breed," she told me. "We raise them solely for breeding purposes or wool. And you just fall in love with them so quickly as a breed—and the long wool, I love all long wools."

Stacy's commitment to, and passion for, preserving at-risk sheep and other animal breeds is inspiring, and her love and affection for her sheep is authentic. When I first started researching what breed of sheep I wanted to raise on my own farm, I had not ever considered that livestock or farm animals could be at risk of extinction, and I was not even aware that a movement to protect livestock breeds existed. Since that time, I have learned more

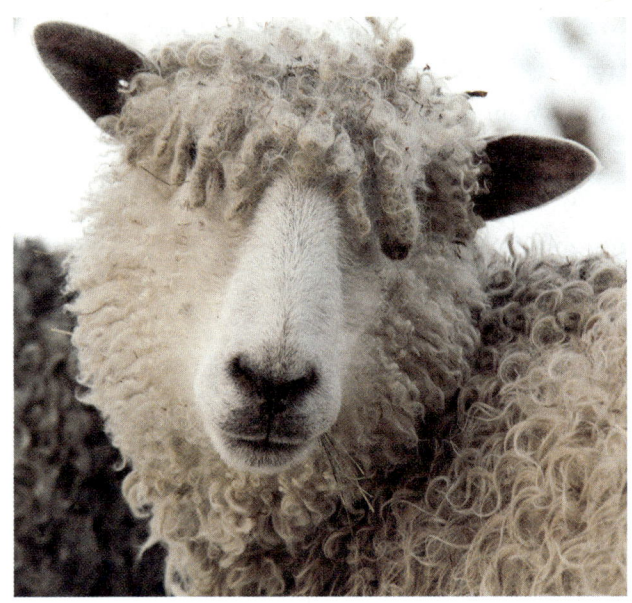

A Revolution in Sheep Breeding

Until the mid-eighteenth century, there wasn't much consideration given to sheep breeding programs. Rams and ewes were housed together, and breeding was totally random. It is hard to imagine such a haphazard strategy to breeding now. We have Robert Bakewell, an English agriculturalist from the mid-1700s, to thank for our improved breeding programs and the development of many sheep breeds.

Robert Bakewell was born in 1725 at Dishley, in Leicestershire, England, to a family of tenant farmers. He spent many years travelling and studying farming operations in England before taking over the family farm in 1755. He wanted to see if he could improve livestock for meat production and carcass quality. Through experimentation, he developed a breeding program that separated the rams and ewes from each other, and then only used rams and ewes with desirable traits for breeding. He also introduced the practice of culling animals with undesirable traits. This practice of selective breeding, in-breeding, and culling animals with undesirable traits revolutionized the way sheep, cattle, and horses were bred in England. He shifted the focus of breeding sheep exclusively for wool to include breeding for larger carcass size, as well. His most important contribution, when considering the impact on wool breeds, was the development of about the many breeds that are at risk of extinction and the fantastic organizations and individuals committed to their survival and revival.

Stacy stroked the chin of her Lincoln ram Harry, as she told us the startling facts around the survival of this breed in Canada. Stacy has the only registered flock of Lincoln Longwool sheep outside of Ontario. She believes there are most likely some across the country that are not registered, but fewer than a hundred are actually registered; it is a breed that needs serious help and conservation.

The term "registered" means a sheep's lineage within the breed can be proven (from registered parents and grandparents) and it contains the breed the Leicester Longwool sheep: the foundation of so many other breeds.

Bakewell founded the Dishley Society in 1783 to assist livestock breeders in their endeavours, and his work and research influenced Darwin's theory of natural selection. When I came across the story of Robert Bakewell and his work's impact on sheep breeding, I was amazed by how one person could play such a huge role in changing an industry.

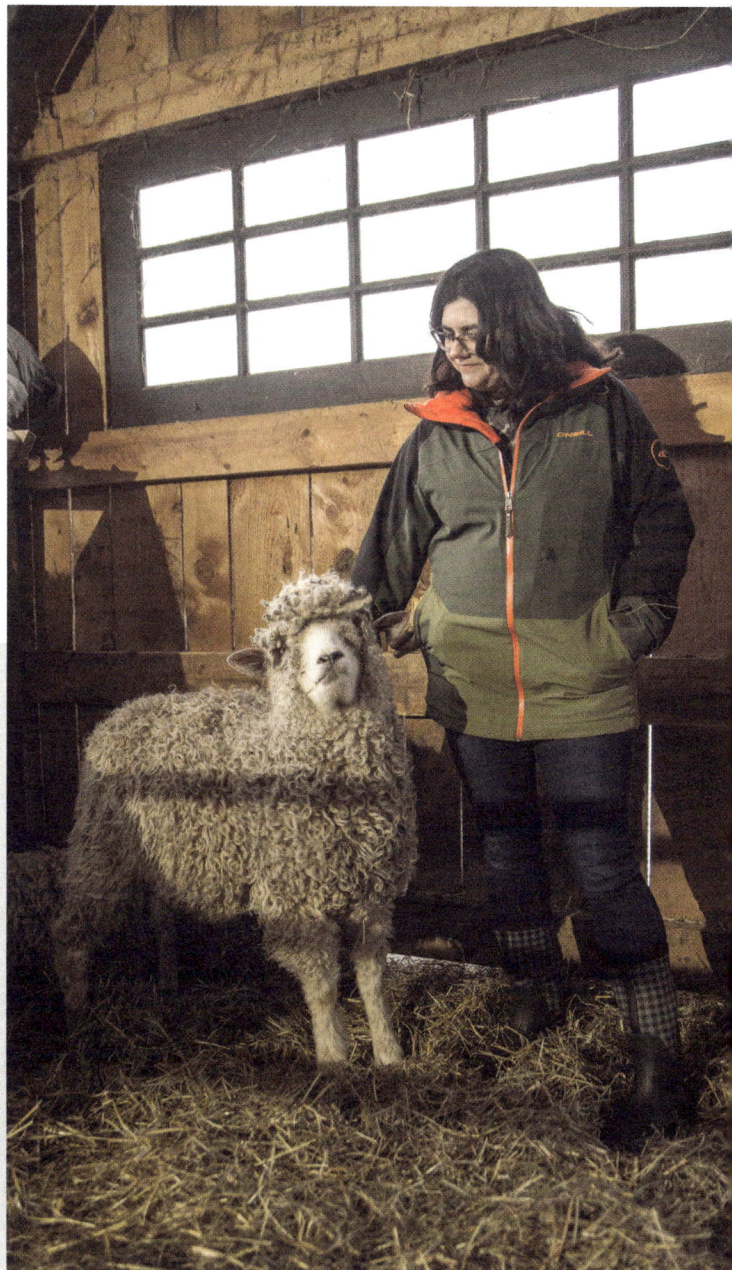

Stacy Corkum and her Lincoln Longwool sheep.

East Coast 113

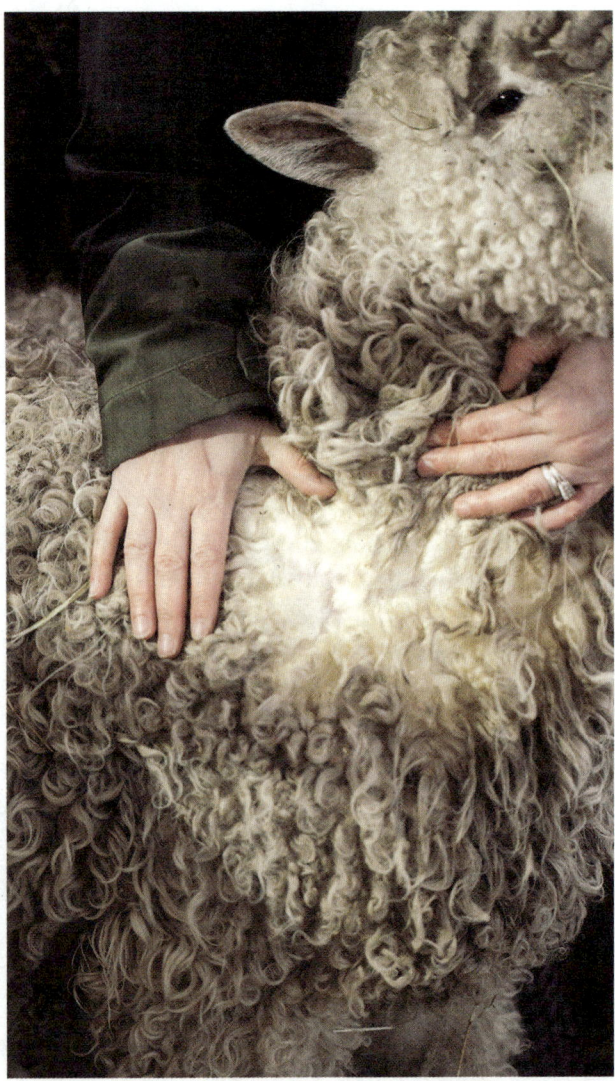

Beautiful long locks of the Lincoln Longwool sheep.

standards for wool, size, colour and genetic makeup. Stacy believes that preserving at-risk breeds and building up dwindling breed stock is crucial not only for the longevity of those specific genetics, but for vibrancy in our fibre arts practice. "Each sheep breed has different wool, with a different feel or quality, and we need to maintain that diversity. When we only work with Merino, we don't experience that wide variety of wool that is out there."

The Lincoln Longwool has one of the oldest stories of the domesticated sheep breeds. It is a large and important dual-purpose breed from Lincolnshire, England, developed during the Middle Ages at a time when wool was an integral part of trade. Robert Bakewell used the Lincoln rams in his revolutionary breeding programs in the late sixteenth century and returned to Lincolnshire with improved rams, contributing to the official designation of the Lincoln Longwool breed in 1796. The Lincolns are certainly the largest sheep among the British breeds, and likely the largest breed in the world, but they are also very docile animals. They have long, dense, lustrous fibre with a micron count between 33.5 and 41 microns and a staple length of seven to fifteen inches. The wool can be white, black, brown, or many beautiful shades of grey. It is a very lanolin-rich wool, and fleeces generally weigh between ten and sixteen pounds. Because of its length and resilience, Lincoln wool is a very hard-wearing fibre, and it will perform well in those items that are subject to more wear and tear, like rugs, furniture, and some garments.

Lincoln Longwool sheep were imported to Canada in the late 1800s and have been integral in the development of many other popular breeds that we know and love today, such as Corriedale, Columbia, and Targhee. Many of the farmers raising Lincoln Longwools recognize the importance of the breed and of preserving its genetics. Stacy chose to raise this breed because of how urgently it needs to be preserved. She has the background and knowledge of how to preserve breeds because of her work with Rare Breeds Canada and her experience farming rare breeds for more than two decades.

Stacy started out with Cotswolds (another endangered long-wool breed), and worked for years to help preserve that breed, but took a small break from raising sheep to have her daughter, Alexis. Later, she decided to acquire sheep again so her daughter could also be a part of the process. She has a small flock of registered Lincoln ewes and rams that she grazes on six of the 165 acres of her farm. She hopes to grow her flock to forty sheep and is working to establish a gene bank in Atlantic Canada to make registered sheep breed genetics available to other farmers for artificial insemination at a lower cost than the options that are currently available.

One of the greatest challenges Stacy faces with Lincoln wool is the processing. Because of the long staple length, there are very few mills that can process the wool; most mills' equipment is designed for use with shorter staples. Stacy showed me a pair

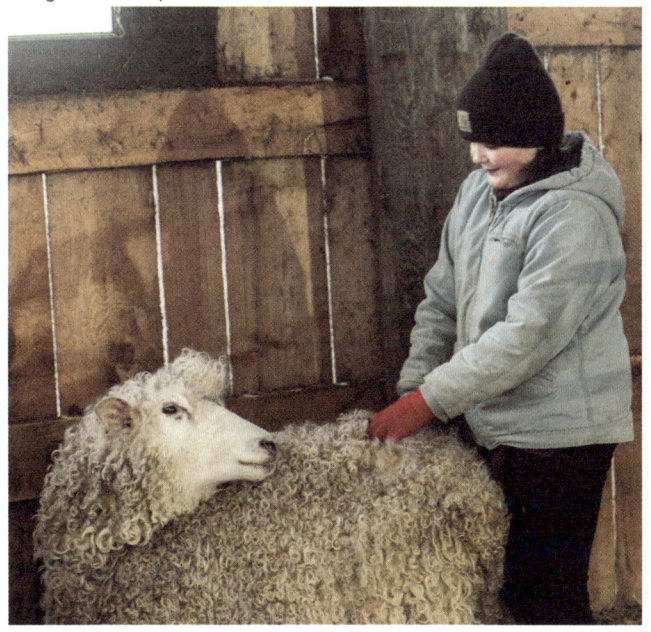

Alexis Corkum showing off one of her favourite Lincoln Longwool sheep.

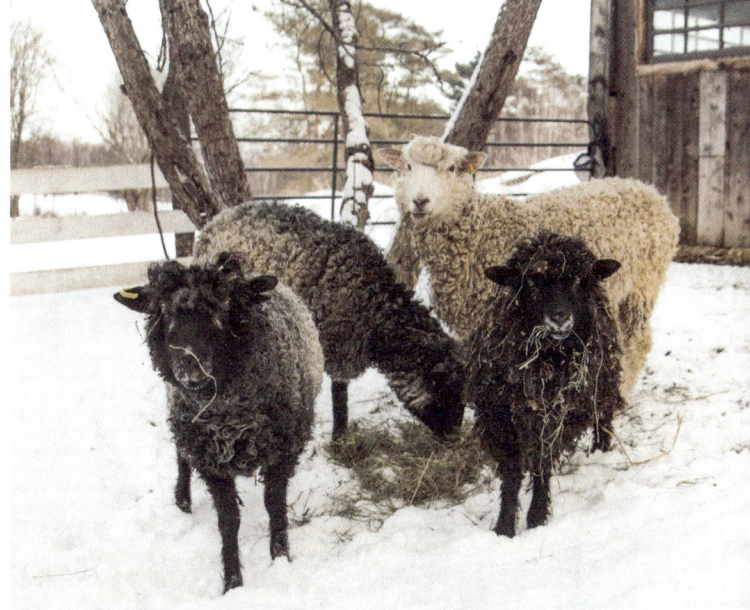

of socks made from some of her handspun Lincoln wool; they felt incredible, and even with the setting sun and diminishing light I could tell how lustrous the wool was. Stacy sees great potential for Lincoln wool in the development of products like horse saddle blankets and halters, because of its strength and resilience. But more than anything she wants to see more farms raising Lincoln sheep and preserving the breed. "For me, it's never been about anything more than preservation of the breed. I have been successfully breeding sheep for wool and breeding stock alone—and not meat sales—for fifteen years, and people should know there is a business in sheep without the meat side of things." Stacy is focusing her energy on building up and preserving these valuable and important sheep genetics, while seeking out other options for processing her wool and getting it into the hands of fibre artists. "I hope fibre artists will reach out to the breeder and buy wool and make a demand for these important at-risk breeds," she concluded.

As we drove away from Stacy's farm, I started considering the added challenge of processing long wool. We don't have enough processing infrastructure in Canada for our existing wool clip, let alone the specialized equipment for processing

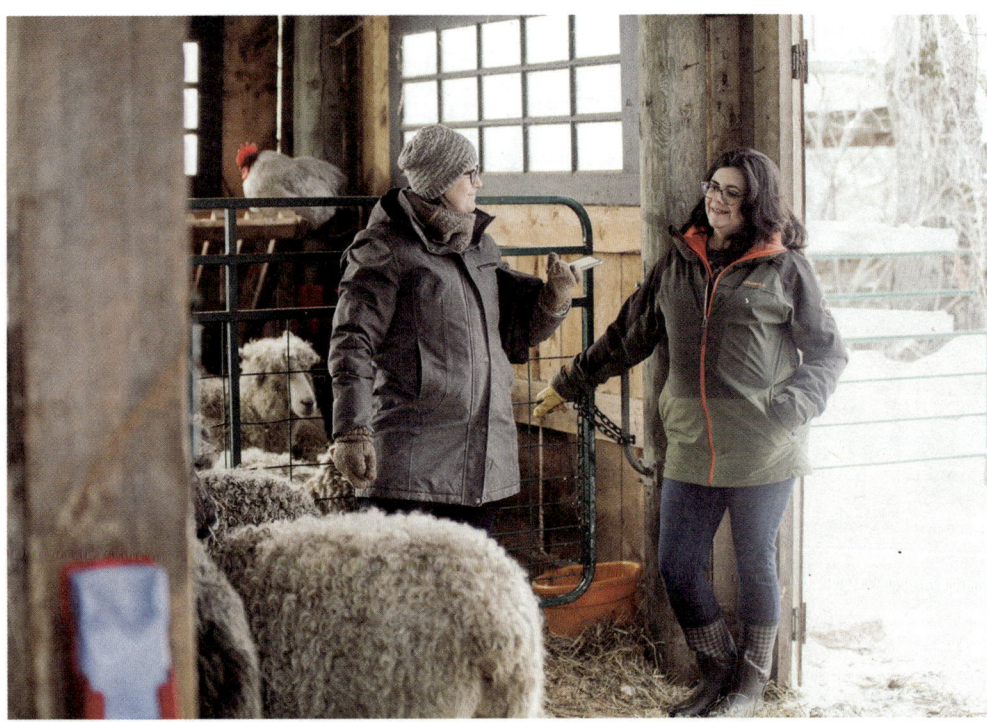

Anna discussing the value of sheep genetics with Stacy Corkum.

longwools. I felt inspired by the way Stacy used the food industry as a comparison for wool: When chefs seek out the best quality breeds for their restaurants, it drives demand and protection for those breeds, and it supports the small farms that grow or raise them. If we, as consumers, continue to support the farms raising longwool heritage breeds, we can directly impact their proliferation in our country and create a demand for the type of processing required for longwool.

As Christel and I went over our notes and photos from the day at a local cider house in Kentville that specializes in ciders made from Annapolis Valley apples, this notion was further reinforced. Our industry could take a page out of the small-scale breweries and cider house manuals: We can be nimble and innovative and respond to the needs of small-scale farmers raising heritage breed animals with beautiful longwool, and we can see our businesses and industry thrive, with strong connections from farm to processor to consumer.

Perhaps with this vision for the future is how this book is meant to end. »

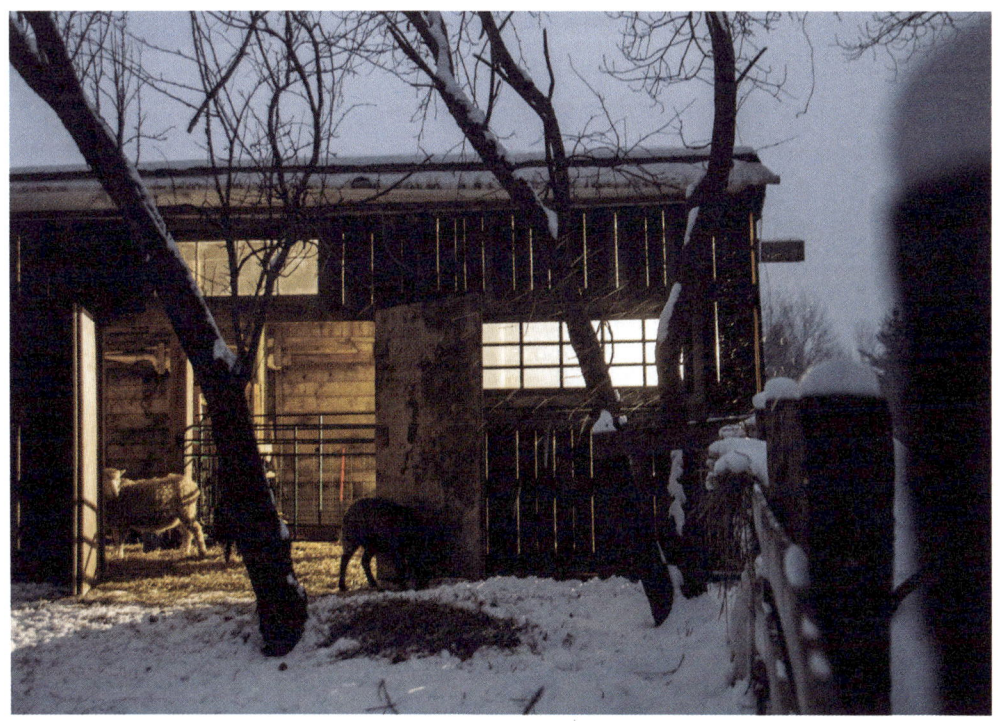

Where do we go from here?

How do I write the conclusion to a book that I feel is really just the beginning? The beginning of renewed interest in heritage and purebred sheep in Canada. The beginning, for some of you, of a journey into local, breed-specific yarn and fibre. The beginning of a new era for Canadian sheep and wool. Perhaps this book represents a bridge from the place where we have been stuck for the last few decades to where we will end up in the near future.

The COVID-19 pandemic revealed the fragility of many of our supply chains; the wool and textile industries were no exception. At the time that I am writing this, in late 2022, the Canadian Co-operative Wool Growers (the national organization that buys wool in bulk from farmers and sells it on the international market) has still not recovered from the shutdown of many wool processing mills globally due to the pandemic. Because of this supply chain disruption, hundreds of Canadian sheep farmers have not been able to sell their wool to the cooperative, so even more of this valuable resource is sitting in barns, sheds, or trash piles across Canada.

I hate to think about that wool going to waste, but at the same time I see this as a wake-up call to examine our highly centralized wool supply chain and seek out better solutions as we move forward. I think sheep farmers are working so damn hard already, they cannot be the ones to shift the rudder on this ship. Fibre artists, indie dyers, pattern designers, climate change activists, local yarn store owners and entrepreneurs must be a part of changing our globalized wool system to one of regional, resilient fibre economies.

That is a lot of buzzwords in one sentence, but what does this actually look like? Well, imagine if each of our regions in Canada had a centralized hub for scouring (the washing of wool). This process is the greatest bottleneck for mills, and it is also resource- and time-intensive. Once a scouring mill is set up, then existing small and medium mills can increase their production, because they will have access to more scoured fleece. New, innovative businesses could emerge, like wool carding for insulation, because the scouring is no longer a process they have to be responsible for; a scouring hub will have solved the bottleneck problem. So now we could have mills processing more yarn, which means they could supply local indie dyers with more consistent product for their businesses. Dyers could dye the yarn and then wholesale it to their favourite local yarn store (LYS), which in turn could get the yarn into the hands of knitters, crocheters, spinners and weavers. Now, LYSs could have twenty to forty percent of their stock as Canadian-grown and -milled yarn, instead of the maybe two to five percent which is the current average for most LYSs. The next step would be pattern designers being able to feature Canadian wool in their designs and generating even more demand for that wool.

Before we know it, Canadian-grown and -manufactured wool would not be such a new or rare item—it would be everywhere, creating security and sustainability for farmers and mill operators, protecting heritage and at-risk breeds of sheep, supporting local manufacturing, and creating jobs, especially in rural communities. Robust regional wool supply chains would decrease Canada's greenhouse gas emissions and carbon footprint, and through land management on regenerative sheep farms we would be sequestering more carbon than we release.

Wow—look at that—we have just created a vibrant, local textile economy that benefits the land!

This book is a call to action to seek out local fibre wherever you live. Get to know your local fibre farmers and see what they're doing on their farms to build community, transparency, and environmental regeneration. Commit to buying more local yarn and fibre, because every purchase makes an enormous difference to the farmers who grow it. Add your voice to the growing chorus of support for sheep farmers and local wool, and let's build a better, healthier path forward.

I know we can do it. I know we must do it. Together. 》

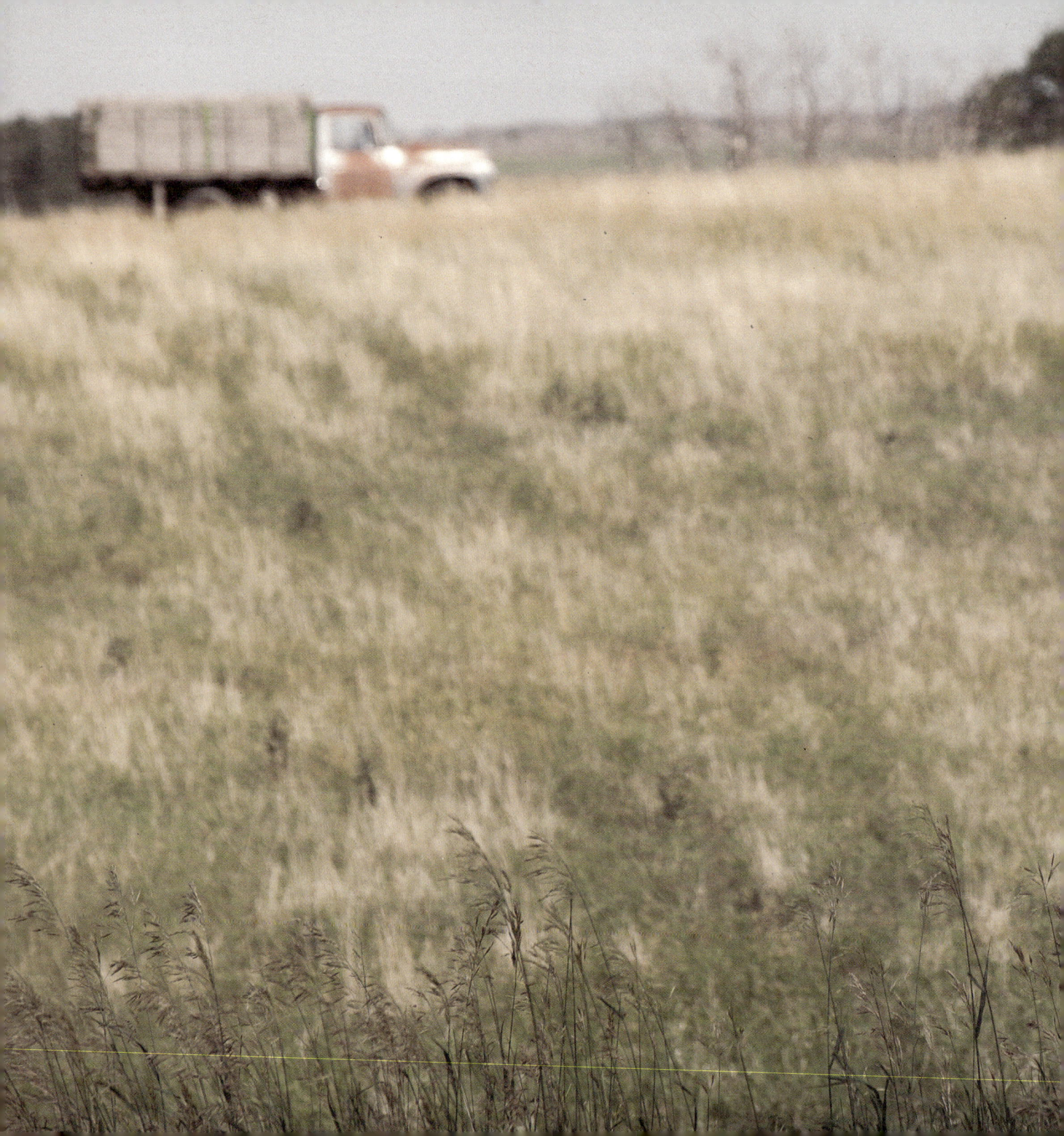

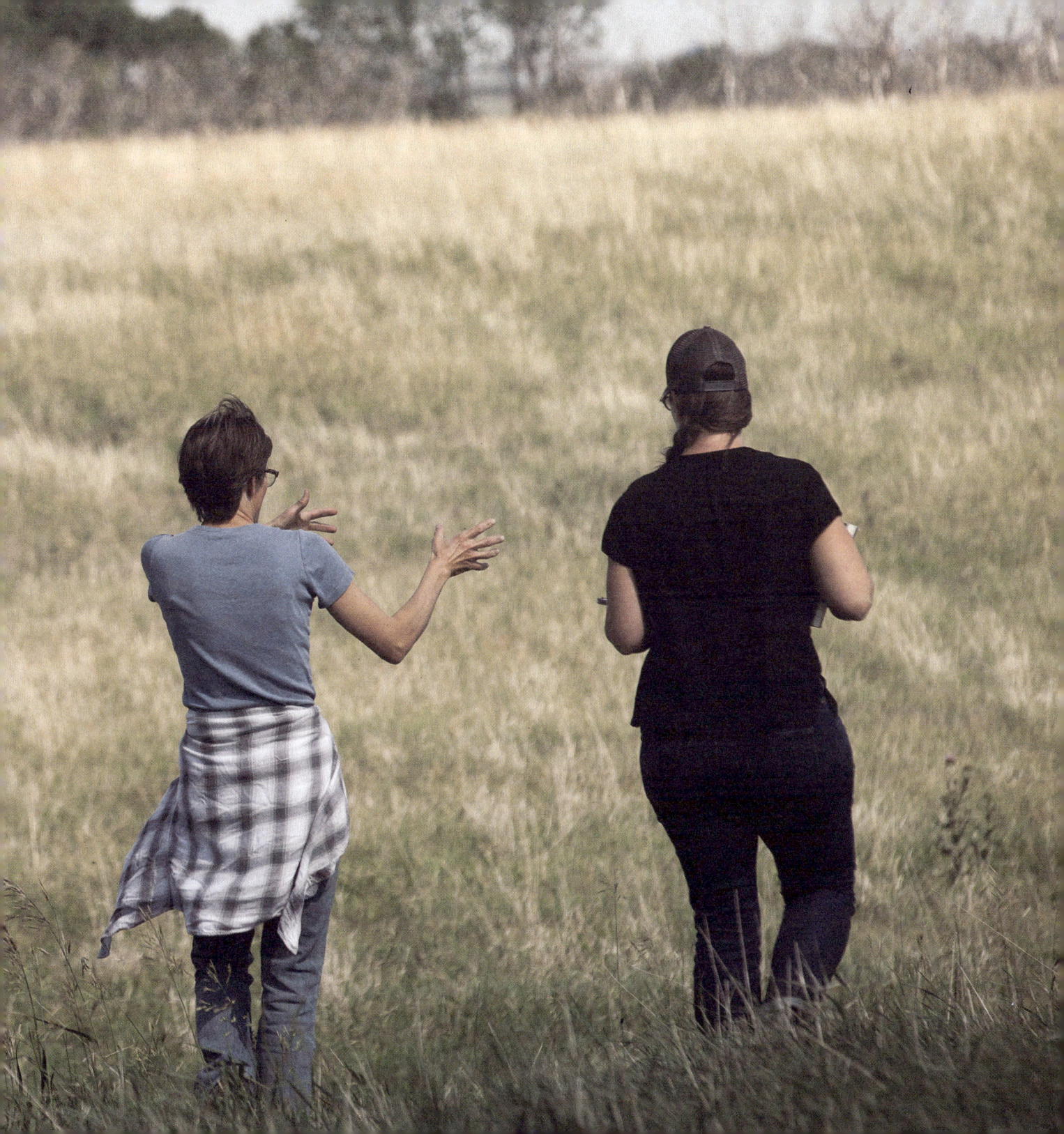

References & Resources

Robson, Deborah, and Carol Ekarius. *The Fleece & Fiber Sourcebook.* North Adams, USA: Storey Publishing, 2011.

Fournier, Nola, and Jane Fournier. *In Sheep's Clothing: A Handspinner's Guide to Wool.* Loveland, CO: Interweave Press, 1995.

Smith, Beth. *The Spinner's Book of Fleece.* North Adams, MA: Storey Publishing, 2014.

McCullough, A.B. "The Primary Textile Industry in Canada History and Heritage." Ministry of the Environment, 1992.

Burgess, Rebecca. *Fibershed: Growing a Movement of Farmers, Fashion Activists, and Makers for a New Textile Economy.* White River Junction: Chelsea Green Publishing, 2019.

McIntyre, Alastair. "Sheep Husbandry in Canada." 2021. https://electriccanadian.com/transport/agriculture/sheep.htm.

Dominion of Canada, Department of Agriculture. "Sheep Husbandry in Canada." Published by authority of the Hon. JAMES G. GARDINER, Minister of Agriculture. Ottawa, Canada, May, 1937. https://publications.gc.ca/collections/collection_2016/aac-aafc/agrhist/A12-8-30-1937-eng.pdf.

INTRODUCTION

Plumptre, Bora, Eli Angen, and Dianne Zimmerman. "The State of Freight: Understanding greenhouse gas emissions from goods movement in Canada." The Pembina Foundation, 2017.

SHEEP BREEDS AND WHY THEY MATTER

Hunter, Anna. "Wool in Canada Survey Results." Long Way Homestead, 2021. https://www.longwayhomestead.com/survey-resultus.

"What are Heritage Breeds?" Livestock Conservancy, accessed 2022, https://livestockconservancy.org/heritage-breeds/.

SHEEP AND THE LAND

Castonguay, Francois. "Sheep Farming." *The Canadian Encyclopedia*, 2013 https://www.thecanadianencyclopedia.ca/en/article/sheep-farming.

Biggar, E.B. *Canada's Wool and Woolens.* Toronto: Biggar-Wilson LTD, 1908.

"Number of sheep and lambs on farms (x 1,000)," Statistics Canada, Table 32-10-0129-01, https://www150.statcan.gc.ca/t1/tbl1/en/tv.action?pid=3210012901.

"Why Soil?" Regeneration Canada, 2022, https://regenerationcanada.org/en/why-soil/.

Toensmeier, Eric. *The Carbon Farming Solution.* White River Junction: Chelsea Green Publishing, 2016.

WEST COAST

Robson, Deborah, and Carol Ekarius. *The Fleece & Fiber Sourcebook.* North Adams, USA: Storey Publishing, 2011.

"Origin," Navajo-Churro Sheep Association, accessed 2022, http://www.navajo-churrosheep.com/sheep-origin.html.

"BFLs in North America," Bluefaced Leicester Union of North America, accessed 2022. https://bflsheep.com/bfls-in-north-america/.

THE PRAIRIES

Ward, Marcy. "Sheep Breeds Best Suited for Arid Climates." College of Agricultural, Consumer, and Environmental Sciences, New Mexico State University, March 2017 https://pubs.nmsu.edu/_circulars/CR684/.

Metera, Ewa, Tomasz Sakowski, Krysztof Stoniewski, and Barbara Romanowicz. "Grazing as a tool to maintain biodiveristy of grassland – a review." Animal Science Papers and Reports vol 28. (2010) no. 4, 315-334 Institute of Genetics and Animal Breeding, Jastrzębiec, Poland.

Fahmy, M.H. "New Sheep Breeds in Canada," Agriculture Canada Publication. Lennoxville, Que., 1850, https://publications.gc.ca/collections/collection_2015/aac-aafc/A63-1850-1990-eng.pdf

"Breed Information," Canadian Sheep Breeders Association, accessed June 2022, https://sheepbreeders.ca/berrichon-canadian-arcott

ONTARIO & QUEBEC

Knibb, Helen, and Nicole Klenk. "The Ontario Wool Study: Phase 1 Assessing the Needs of Ontario Wool Producers and Processors - Interim Report," January 25, 2018, https://www.ontariosheep.org/uploads/userfiles/files/Ontario%20Wool%20Study%20Interim%20Report.pdf

Kyles, Shannon. "Types of Barns and Farm Buildings," Ontario Architecture, 2016, http://www.ontarioarchitecture.com/barn.htm

"About Shetlands," North American Shetland Sheep Breeders Association, Wamego, KS, 2022, http://www.shetland-sheep.org/about-shetlands/

Precious, Carole. "Chassagne's Shetland Sheep," 2022, https://www.chassagne.ca/index.php/the-croft-mainmenu-30/chassagnes-shetland-sheep-mainmenu-45

EAST COAST

"History," Lincoln Longwool Sheep Breeders Association, England, accessed May 2022, https://www.lincolnlongwools.co.uk/History/.

"Nova Scotia Fibre History," Sheep Producers Association of Nova Scotia, accessed May 2022, https://localfibrelove.ca/.

"Robert Bakewell," Iowa State University College of Agriculture and Life Sciences, accessed May 2022, https://www.ans.iastate.edu/about/history/people/robert-bakewell

Simmons, Paula and Carol Ekarius. *Storey's Guide to Raising Sheep, 5th Edition*. North Adams, MA: Storey Publishing, 2019.

FARMS FEATURED

Long Way Homestead, longwayhomestead.com

Fibre & Forge, fibreandforge.com

Lone Sequoia Ranch, etsy.com/ca/shop/Lonesequoiashop

Providence Lane Homestead, providencelanehomestead.com

Disdero Ranch, disderoranch.ca

Dog Tale Ranch, woolstoneprairie.com

Ferme Fiola Farm, fermefiolafarm.ca

Black Sheep Farm, justblacksheep.com

Woolleys Lamb, woolleyslamb.ca

Les Brebis du Beaurivage, lesbrebisdubeaurivage.com/fr

Woolies of Upperbrook Farm, woolies.ca

Hidden Meadow Farm, facebook.com/profile.php?id=100057241196795

Index

Note: **Bolded** page numbers indicate pages with photos.

Agricultural Research Centre of Ottawa, 75–76
Agriculture Canada (earlier Canadian Department of Agriculture), 91, 106
Alberta
    Bluefaced Leicester in, 47
    Navajo Churro in, 54
    Providence Lane Homestead, **62–67**
    wool mills in, **21,** 51, 59, 96
Alex (of Rosebud River Fibre Mill), 45–46
Allen (Arlette's spouse), 69
Allen, Cherry, 89
animal welfare, 66–67
Annapolis Valley, 109–10
Arizona, 57

Baaad Anna's Yarn Store, 15
Bakewell, Robert, 64, 112–13, 114
bank barns, **80**
Beaurivage, Olivier, 95–96
bedding, 72, 107, 108
    See also blankets
Belfast Mini Mills, 19
Black Sheep Farm, **78–85**
blankets
    from Corriedale wool, 71
    from Disdero Ranch wool, 51–52
    from Lincoln Longwool, 116
    from MacAusland's, 21
    Navajo, 57
    from North Country Cheviot wool, 108
Bluefaced Leicester (BFL), **43,** 44, **45–46,** 47
Bob (Tara's husband), 62, 63
Border Cheviot, 106
Border Leicester, **30,** 61, **63–66,** 91
Boulet, Audrey, 94–95, **96,** 97, 98
breeding programs, 112–13, 114
breeds
    Anna's research on, 19
    approach to, 22, 38
    arrival in 1600s to 1800s, 30–31, 101, 115
    Bluefaced Leicester, **43,** 44, **45–46,** 47
    Border Cheviot, 106
    Border Leicester, **30,** 61, **63–66,** 91
    California Variegated Mutant, 48, 49, 76
    Canadian Arcott, 75

    Cheviot, 30, 65
    Churro, 56–57
    Clun Forest, 69
    Coopworth, **38, 86–87, 89–93**
    Cotswold, 31, 64, 115
    diversity of wool, 27–28, 114
    East Friesian, **34,** 94, **96–98,** 99
    environmental conditions and, 39
    Gotland, **28,** 45, 47, 82
    Hampshire, 31
    Leicester, 31, 106
    Leicester Longwool, 112
    Lincoln Longwool, 70, **109–16**
    meat breeds, 33
    Navajo Churro, 53, **54–57,** 58, **59**
    Outaouais Arcott, 75
    Rambouillet, **26,** 76
    Rideau Arcott, **26,** 35, **74–77,** 98
    Southdown, 31
    Teeswater, 65
    Wensleydale, 104
    See also Corriedale; Merino; North Country Cheviot; Romney; Shetland
Briggs & Little, 21
Britain, 31
British Columbia, **42,** 43–59
    Disdero Ranch, **24, 48–52**
    Fibre & Forge Farm, **22, 40, 43–47**
    Lone Sequoia Ranch, **53–57,** 58, **59**
Brook, Margaret, 16
Burge, Delia, **103,** 104–5
Buschbeck, Chris, 98

California Variegated Mutant (CVM), 48, 49, 76
Canadian Arcott, 75
Canadian Co-operative Wool Growers (CCWG), 22, 26, 32–33, 76, 118
Canadian Department of Agriculture (later Agriculture Canada), 91, 106
Canadian Department of Militia and Defence, 20
carbon, 36, 37–38, 119
carbon cycle, **36**
carders and carding
    history of mills for, 20, 31
    Long Way Homestead, **18**

    Woolies mill, **106,** 107, 108
CBC, 41
CCF (Co-operative Commonwealth Federation), 62, 63
CCWG. *See* Canadian Co-operative Wool Growers
Cheviot, 30, 65
China, 22, 32
Chris (of Dakota Spinning Mill), 18
Churro, 56–57
climate and landscape
    Border Leicester and, 65, 66
    breeds suited to prairie, 39, 61, 66, 71
    heritage sheep and, 28
    Navajo Churro and, 55, 57, 58
    North Country Cheviot and, 106, 108
    Romney and, 39, 50
    See also environment; grasslands
climate change. *See* environment
clothing
    Bluefaced Leicester wool for, 44, 46
    Border Leicester wool for, 65
    circular model of, 36
    Coopworth wool for, 91
    Corriedale wool for, 71
    East Friesian wool for, 99
    farmers', 39, 44
    on Ferme Fiola Farm, 74, 76, 77
    Lincoln Longwool for, 114, 115–16
    North Country Cheviot wool for, 108
    Romney wool for, 50–51
    Shetland wool for, 84
clothing manufacturing, 20, 31, 32–33, 34
Clun Forest, 69
colonization, 30, 56, 57
colours
    Bluefaced Leicester, 45, 46
    Border Leicester, 65
    Coopworth, 91
    Corriedale, 71
    East Friesian, 99
    Lincoln Longwool, 114
    Navajo Churro, 57
    North Country Cheviot, 108
    Romney, 50, **51**
    Shetland, 83–84, 85

comforters, 107, 108
community supported agriculture programs (CSA), 82
community-building, 62–63, 67
conservation, 111–14, 115–16
   See also endangered species
conventional farming, 69
Coop, Ian, 91
Co-operative Commonwealth Federation (CCF), 62, 63
Coopworth, **38, 86–87, 89–93**
Corkum, Stacy, 109–12, **113,** 114, 115, **116**
Corriedale, **3, 27**
   Arlette Seib's, **22,** 61, **68–70,** 71
   on Disdero Ranch, **24,** 49
   wool and yarn from, **23, 39,** 71
Cotswold, 31, 64, 115
COVID-19 pandemic, 118
crimp, 29
crocheters. *See* fibre artists
crossbreeds
   at Black Sheep Farm, 82, 83
   Border Leicester, 64–65
   Coopworth, 89, 91
   Corriedale, 70
   at Fibre & Forge Farm, 44, 45, 47
   mules, 46
   Navajo Churro and, 56–57
   North Country Cheviot, 106
   Rideau Arcott, 75–76
Cully, George, 64–65
Cully, Matthew, 64–65
Custom Woolen Mills, **21,** 51, 59, 96
CVM (California Variegated Mutant), 48, 49, 76

Dailley, G.D., 84
Dailley, Virginia, 84
dairy, 94–95, 96, 97–98
Dakota Spinning Mill, 18
Dalhousie Agricultural College, 106
Darwin, Charles, 113
Dave's Mom (sheep), 44
devaluation of wool, 22, 32–33, 59
Dine' (Navajo) peoples, 56–58
Disdero Ranch, **24, 48–52**
diseases, 39, 50, 90
Dishley Society, 113
Dog Tale Ranch, **22, 68–71, 120–21**
dogs, **68–69,** 70
down wool, 27
Down wool (from Down sheep), 29
Ducks Unlimited, 69

East Coast. *See* Nova Scotia
East Friesian, **34,** 94, **96–98,** 99

ecosystems
   circularity of, 76
   Long Way Homestead, 17
   prairie, 61, 63–64, 67, 69
   sheep's benefits to, 35–38
endangered ecosystems, 63–64
endangered species
   at Hidden Meadow Farm, 112–14
   Lincoln Longwool, 115
   list of sheep breeds, 25
   Navajo Churro, 54–55, 58
   Shetland, 84
England, 112
English breeds
   Bluefaced Leicester, 46
   Border Leicester, 65
   common, 31
   Lincoln Longwool, 114
   Merino, 56
   Romney, 50
environment, 22–23, 35–38, 90, 92, 119
   See also climate and landscape; regenerative agriculture
Everdale Environmental Learning Centre, 82
extensive management, 37
Exotic Fibres, 51

facial features
   Bluefaced Leicester, **45,** 46
   Border Leicester, 65
   Corriedale, 70
   Lincoln Longwool, 111
   Romney, 49, **50**
Fair Isle, 84
farms, list of featured, **7**
   See also *names of individual farms*
feeding. *See* food and feeding
felting, **22, 71,** 108
fencing, 16, **17**
Ferme Fiola Farm, 72, **73–77**
fibre artists
   approach to, 35
   call to action for, 118, 119
   collaboration with farmers, 26, 93, 116
   knowledge of different breeds' wool, 25, 27–28
   wool desired by, 23
fibre festivals, 43, 51, 52, 102
Fibre & Forge Farm, **22, 40, 43–47**
fibre friends, 48, 51–52, 84, 104–5
fine wool, 27, 61, 108
Fiola, Ferdinand, 74
Fiola, Joey, 72, 73–75, 76
Fiola, Noëlie, 74
Fischer, Mona, 48, 51–52
fleece. *See* breeds; *names of individual farms*

Fleece & Fibre Sourcebook, 29
flocking, 70
Foden, Emily, 83, 84
food and feeding
   Anna's experience with, 17
   for Border Leicester sheep, 64
   for Corriedale, 71
   and devaluation of wool, 33
   grown in Norfolk County, 86
   hay for, 72
   market gardens, 82
   on Woolley's Lamb, 87–88, 89, **90,** 91, 92
   See also lamb meat
forests, 90–91
Fromage Nouveau France, 98
Fruit Growers Association, 88
furniture, 114

General Agreement on Tariffs and Trade (GATT), 20
genetics
   Coopworth, 89, 91
   diversity in, 27–28, 39
   farmers and, 25, 89, 114, 115–16
German breeds, 97–98
globalization, 23, 32, 33
Gotland, **28,** 45, 47, 82
grasslands
   at Dog Tale Ranch, 69, 71
   fine wool breeds and, 61
   sheep's benefit to, 37–38
   tall grass fescue, 63–64, 67
grazing. *See* food and feeding
Greener World, 66–67

Hampshire, 31
handspinning, 50
Harry (sheep), 113
hay, 33, 37, 72, 89
hedgerows, 81
Helen (sheep), 45
heritage breeds
   genetic diversity and, 27–28
   Lincoln Longwool, 109, 112
   long wool, 117
   Navajo Churro, 57
   Romney, 50
Hidden Meadow Farm, **109–17**
holistic farming, 76–77
housing, 37
Hsueh, Brenda, **79, 81,** 82–83, **84,** 85

imported textiles, 31, 33
indie dyers, 118–19
Indigenous Peoples, 56–58, 76–77

Instagram accounts, 54, 87, 94, 109
intensive management, 37, 81

Juniper (lamb), **63**

Klager, Tara, 61–62, **63,** 64, 66–67
Knit City Vancouver, 43
knitters. *See* fibre artists
knitting, 13, **19, 47,** 52, 99
   See also clothing; yarn and yarn stores

lamb meat
   from Black Sheep Farm, 82
   from Ferme Fiola Farm, 75, 76
   focus of Canadian sheep industry, 32–33
   from Les Brebis du Beaurivage, 96
   sheep farming without, 116
   from Woolley's Lamb, 92
land management, 71, 84
   See also regenerative agriculture; silvopasture
landscape. *See* climate and landscape
Lanthier, Christel
   as farmer, 61, 72, **73,** 74–75, 76–77
   as fibre friend, 51, 52, 72–73, 77, 104
   as photographer, 41, **42,** 110–11
large mills, **20–21,** 51, 59, 96
legacy, 102, 105–8
Leicester, 31, 106
Leicester Longwool, 112
Les Brebis du Beaurivage, 94, **95–99**
Lincoln Longwool, 70, **109–16**
Livestock Conservancy, 28, 54
llamas, 77
Local Fibre Love, 105
local yarn stores (LYS), 34, 118–19
Lone Sequoia Ranch, **53–57,** 58, **59**
Long Way Homestead, **12, 14–19,** 72
Long Way Homestead Field School, **19**
long wool
   of Bluefaced Leicester, 46
   crossbreeds and, 56
   defined, 29
   mills for processing, 115, 116–17
   qualities of, 27
   of Romney, 39
Louet North America, 91

MacAusland's Woollen Mills, **20–21**
Macdonald College, 106
Maksymiuk, Leanna, 53, **54–55,** 58–59
Manitoba, **10–11**
   bank barns and, 80
   distances in, 110
   Ferme Fiola Farm, 72, **73–77**
   Long Way Homestead, **12, 14–19, 72**

Manitoba Fibre Festival, 102
manufacturing. *See* wool mills
market gardens, 82
marketing
   Black Sheep Farm, 83, 84
   Disdero Ranch, 51
   Fibre & Forge Farm, 47
   Les Brebis du Beaurivage, 95, 96–97
   Providence Lane Homestead, 66
   Woolley's Lamb, 92–93
Mathewson, Bill, 102, 105–7, 108
Mathewson, Greta, 105–7, 108
Mathewson, Ruth, 102, **103–4,** 105–6, **107,** 108
McNeal, Lyle, 57–58
meat. *See* lamb meat
Meister, Axel, 98
Merino
   crossbreeds from, 56, 70
   vs. East Friesian, 99
   on Fibre & Forge Farm, 45
   prevalence in fibre arts, 23, 26, 114
Métis, 76–77
Mexico, 58
microns
   Border Leicester, 65
   Coopworth, 91
   defined, 29
   East Friesian, 97, 98
   Lincoln Longwool, 114
   North Country Cheviot, 108
   Shetland, 84
milk sheep, 94–95, 96, 97–98
mills. *See* wool mills
mini mills, 19, 21
Morris, Laurie, **48,** 49, 50, 51, **52**
mules, 46–47

National Policy, 20
Navajo Churro, 53, **54–57,** 58, **59**
Navajo (Dine') peoples, 56–58
Navajo Sheep Project, 57–58
Navajo-Churro Sheep Association (N-CSA), 58
Nettleton, L. Brian, 47
New Brunswick, 21
New France. *See* Québec
New Mexico, 57
New Zealand, 50, 70, 89, 91
Newfoundland and Labrador, 41
Nicole (Anna's friend), 43, 51, 95
Niku Farms, 93
Norfolk Cherry Company, 88
Norfolk County, 86
North Country Cheviot, **31**
   on Upperbrook Farm, 103, **104–5,** 106, **107,** 108

on Woolley's Lamb, 88
North Dakota, 18
North Saugeen River, 81
North Thompson River, 49
Northwest Territories, 41
Nova Scotia
   Hidden Meadow Farm, **109–17**
   Peggy's Cove, **100–101**
   sheep brought to, 30, 46–47, 101
   Upperbrook Farm, **102–8**
Nunavut, 41

Ontario
   Black Sheep Farm, **78–85**
   Bluefaced Leicester in, 47
   history of sheep in, 30
   Lincoln Longwool in, 113
   wool mills in, 31, 93
   Woolley's Lamb, **4–5, 37–38, 86–93**
orchards, 87, **88,** 89–90
Outaouais Arcott, 75

Palka, Luke, 14, **15,** 16–17, **18**
pattern designers, 118–19
Peggy's Cove, **100–101**
personalities
   Border Leicester, 65
   Coopworth, 91
   East Friesian, 98
   Lincoln Longwool, 114
   Romney, 49–50
   Shetland, 105
pillows, 108
Prairies, 39, **60,** 61
   See also *names of individual provinces*
preservation, 111–14, 115–16
   See also endangered species
Prince Edward Island, 19, **20–21**
processing wool. *See* wool mills
Providence Lane Homestead, **62–67**
Provincial Exhibition, 31
Purebred Sheep Breeders Association of Nova Scotia, 106

Québec
   Les Brebis du Beaurivage, 94, **95–99**
   sheep brought to, 30, 79, 101, 106
   wool mills in, 31

Rainbow Fiber Co-Op, 58
Rambouillet, **26,** 76
range sheep, 39, 70–71
rare breeds, 84, 111–12, 115
Rare Breeds Canada, 58, 115

regenerative agriculture, 37–38, 67, 81–82, 85, 119
    See also environment
Regina Manifesto, 63
registered sheep, 113
Remple, Beatriz, 43–45, **47**
Remple, Glen, 43, 44
research study, Anna's, 25–26
Rideau Arcott, **26, 35, 74–77,** 98
Ritchie, Mark, 89
Roberts, Wayne, 82
Romney
    on Black Sheep Farm, 82
    climate for, 39, 50
    crossbreeds from, 91
    on Disdero Ranch, **24, 48, 49–51**
    on Ferme Fiola Farm, 76
Romney Marsh, 50
Rosebud River Fibre Mill, 46
Rosvold, Stacey, 17
rugs, 114
ruminants, 35–36

Saskatchewan, **22,** 61, **68–71, 120–21**
Sauble River, 81
Schuyler, Brett, 87–88
Schuyler, Drew, 87–88
Schuyler, Marshall, 87–88
Scottish breeds, 106
scouring, 118–19
Seib, Arlette, **22,** 61, 68, **69,** 70, 71, **121**
settlers, 56–57, 66
sheep farming
    Anna's journey to, 13–19
    approach to, 13, 22, 23, 35, 38, 41–42, 87
    See also breeds; *names of individual farms*
sheep population, 31, 32
sheepskins, 76–77, 82, 95, 96
Shetland, **33**
    on Black Sheep Farm, **78, 81–85**
    on Fibre & Forge Farm, 44, 47
    on Long Way Homestead, **12, 16–17**
    personalities, 105
    on Woolley's Lamb, 88
Shetland Islands, 83, 84
Shieck, Nicole, 64
Shirley (sheep), 36
silvopasture
    benefits of, 91, 93
    defined, 87
    photos, **37–38, 89–90**
    rules for Woolley's Lamb, 88
    solar farm and, **90,** 92
Sinclair, John, 106
skirting, 18, **73**

Skylar (Brenda's spouse), 81, 84
small mills, 21, 118
social justice, 82
soil, 17, 37–38
    See also regenerative agriculture
solar farms, 87, **90,** 92
soundness, 29
Southdown, 31
spinners (artists). *See* fibre artists
spinners (machines), **18, 35**
spinning, 50, 71
Springfield Farm, 84
St. Lawrence River, **94**
staple length
    Border Leicester, 65
    Coopworth, 91
    defined, 29
    East Friesian, 98
    Lincoln Longwool, 114, 115
    Navajo Churro, **55**
    Shetland, 84
Statistics Canada, 26, 32
Stralen, Jan Van, 91
Stralen, Trudy Van, 91
straw, 72
supply chains, 118–19
synthetic fibres, 31, 32, 33

tall grass fescue, 63–64, 67
Tammy (person who taught Anna to knit), 13
tanning hides, 76–77
tariffs, 20
Teeswater, 65
textile agriculture, 32–33, 34–35
textile manufacturing, 20, 31–33, 79, 118
textiles, 36
    See also clothing
Toronto Food Policy Council, 82
trade, 20, 31, 33
tradition, 102, 105–8
traits. *See* personalities

Upperbrook Farm, **102–8**
U.S., 31, 47, 56–58, 98

Vancouver, 14–15
variable wool, 76
Viola Yarns, 83

Waste Not Wool, 58–59
water retention, 81
weavers. *See* fibre artists
Wellington Fibre Mill, 93
Wensleydale, 104
West Coast. *See* British Columbia

woodlots, 90–91
wool
    approach to, 22, 23
    devaluation of, 22, 32–33, 59
    photos, **23**
    study on farmers raising sheep for, 25–26
    uses, 27
    See also breeds; *names of individual farms*
wool buyers and sales. *See* Canadian Co-operative Wool Growers; marketing
wool industry
    in crisis, 22–23, 32–34
    farmers' vision and understanding of, 67, 102–3, 108
    future of, 117–19
wool mills
    Anna's, 18, **19**
    in Atlantic Canada, **20–21,** 101
    Custom Woolen Mills, **21,** 51, 59, 96
    future of, 118–19
    history in Canada, **20–21,** 31, 32–33
    processing long wool, 115, 116–17
    Wellington Fibre Mill, 93
    wool sales through, 26
    Woolies, 102, **103,** 104, **106–8**
Wooldrift Farms, 98
Woolies mill, 102, **103,** 104, **106–8**
Woolley, Carrie, **37,** 87–88, **89,** 90–93
Woolley's Lamb, **4–5, 37–38, 86–93**

yarn and yarn stores
    Anna's, 14–15
    breed-specific, 25
    Corriedale, **39,** 71
    from Ferme Fiola Farm, 76–77
    fibre festivals, 43, 51, 52, 102
    from Fibre & Forge Farm, **22,** 45–46, 47
    from large mills, **21**
    from Les Brebis du Beaurivage, **95,** 96–97, **99**
    local, 34, 118–19
    from Upperbrook Farm, 103, **108**
Yukon, 41